Anonymus

Agricultural statistics of Ireland 1890

Anonymus

Agricultural statistics of Ireland 1890

ISBN/EAN: 9783742810526

Manufactured in Europe, USA, Canada, Australia, Japa

Cover: Foto ©Suzi / pixelio.de

Manufactured and distributed by brebook publishing software
(www.brebook.com)

Anonymus

Agricultural statistics of Ireland 1890

THE

AGRICULTURAL STATIST

OF

IRELAND,

FOR THE YEAR

1890.

DIVISION OF LAND; ACREAGE UNDER CROPS; NUMBER AND SIZE OF HOLDINGS; NUMBER OF OCCUPIERS OF LAND; RATES OF PRODUCE; AVERAGE PRICES OF AGRICULTURAL PRODUCE; NOXIOUS INSECTS; NUMBER, AGES, &c., OF LIVE STOCK; ENTIRE HORSES; BULLS; DISEASES OF CATTLE; EXPORTS AND IMPORTS OF LIVE STOCK; HONEY PRODUCED; NUMBER OF SCUTCHING MILLS; SILOS AND ENSILAGE; FORESTRY OPERATIONS; AGRICULTURAL MACHINES; AGRICULTURAL SCHOOLS; WAGES OF AGRICULTURAL LABOURERS; LOANS FOR LABOURERS' DWELLINGS; OBSERVATIONS ON THE PRODUCE OF THE CROPS BY SUPERINTENDENTS OF ENUMERATION; THE WEATHER.

Presented to both Houses of Parliament by Command of Her Majesty.

DUBLIN:

PRINTED FOR HER MAJESTY'S STATIONERY OFFICE

BY

ALEXANDER THOM & CO. (LIMITED),

And to be purchased, either directly or through any Bookseller, from
Hodges, Figgis, and Co., 104, Grafton-street, Dublin; or
Eyre and Spottiswoode, East Harding-street, Fleet-street, E.C.; or
John Menzies and Co., 12, Hanover-street, Edinburgh, and 88 and 90, West Nile-street, Glasgow.

1891.

CONTENTS.

SUMMARY TABLES.

CONTENTS.

Live Stock:

APPENDIX.

AGRICULTURAL STATISTICS OF IRELAND,

FOR THE YEAR 1890.

TO HIS EXCELLENCY LAWRENCE, EARL OF ZETLAND,

&c., &c., &c.,

LORD LIEUTENANT-GENERAL AND GENERAL GOVERNOR OF IRELAND.

MAY IT PLEASE YOUR EXCELLENCY,

I have the honour to submit to your Excellency the following Report and detailed Tables concerning Agriculture in Ireland for the year 1890, which have been compiled and arranged in the same manner as those for the previous year.

A review of the detailed Tables confirms the observations I made when presenting the General Abstracts in August, 1890, and the Produce Returns in December last.

The following is an analysis of the information contained in the tables:—

DIVISION OF LAND, TILLAGE, &c.

The acreage under Crops, Grass, Fallow, Woods and Plantations, and Bog, Waste, Water, &c., in 1889 and 1890, was as follows:— Division of land, 1889 and 1890.

—	1889.	1890.	Increase or Decrease between 1889 and 1890.	
			Increase.	Decrease.
	Acres.	Acres.	Acres.	Acres.
Under Crops, including Meadow and Clover, . .	5,056,016	4,919,726	—	136,290
" Grass, or Pasture, ...	9,505,797	10,718,246	213,959	—
" Fallow, ...	12,450	14,595	2,146	—
" Woods and Plantations, ...	326,616	327,441	825	—
" Bog, Waste, Water, &c.,*	4,935,354	4,854,713	—	80,639
Total,†	20,323,753			

The area under Crops in 1890, compared with 1889 shows a net decrease of 136,290 acres—there being a decrease of 42,402 acres in tillage, of 55,464 acres in the area under hay on permanent pasture or grass not broken up in rotation, and of 38,424 acres under hay on clover, sainfoin, and grasses under rotation. There is an increase of 213,959 acres under Grass, of 2,146 acres of Fallow land, and of 825 acres under Woods and Plantations, while there is a decrease of 80,639 acres under Bog, Waste, Water, &c.

Of the 4,854,713 acres given as under "Bog, Waste, Water, &c.," in 1890, 1,784,676 acres were enumerated as "Bog and Marsh," 2,185,492 acres as "Barren Mountain Land," and 884,545 acres as "Water, Roads, Fences, &c." Compared with 1889 "Bog and Marsh" appears to have increased by 14,185 acres, while "Barren Mountain Land" decreased by 90,211 acres, and "Water, Roads, Fences, &c.," by 4,588 acres.

* Including [illegible] acres under water. † Exclusive of [illegible] acres under the larger rivers, lakes, and tideways.

The area and proportionate extent of each crop in 1889 and 1890, with the increase or decrease in the latter year, are given in the following Table (I.), from which it appears that, compared with 1889, there was last year a net decrease of 20,339 acres in cereals, as, while wheat increased by 2,596 acres, and beans and peas by 14 acres, oats decreased by 17,929 acres, barley by 3,725 acres, and bere and rye by 1,305 acres.

In green crops there was a net decrease of 5,287 acres, potatoes having decreased by 6,429 acres, turnips by 2,597 acres, and carrots, parsnips, and other green crops by 2,384 acres, while mangel wurzel and beet root increased by 2,436 acres, cabbage by 3,527 acres, and vetches and rape by 244 acres.

Flax shows a decrease of 16,756 acres, and meadow and clover a decrease of 93,888 acres.

In 1890, 30·8 acres in every 100 under crops were under cereals, 24·7 under green crops, 2·0 under flax, and 42·5 under meadow and clover.

Potatoes.—The tables relating to the potato crop point to several important conclusions. It will be observed (see Table 14, page 70) that of the 780,801 acres planted with potatoes, 78·6 per cent. belonged to one variety, namely, "Champions," showing no appreciable difference in the percentage of this variety as compared with the previous year. Of the total area under potatoes 7·6 per cent. was under Flounders, 3·4 per cent. under Skerry Blues, 2·1 per cent. under White Rocks, 1·8 per cent. under Magnum Bonums, 1·1 per cent. under Kemps, 1·0 per cent. under Scotch Downs, and 4·1 per cent. under all other varieties exclusive of Champions. It will be seen by a reference to Table 16 that not only was the Champion variety the one planted in greatest quantity, but that it was generally the most prolific in its yield.

Table 16 also points out the best potato-growing districts in Ireland, and the varieties which appear to thrive best in particular counties.

Of the total extent under crops in 1890, 83·2 per cent., or over four-fifths, were under three crops—oats (24·8), potatoes (15·9), and meadow and clover (42·5).

(Table I.)—The Acreage under Crops in 1889 and 1890, and the Increase or Decrease in the latter year:—

Crops.	1889.	1890.	1890. Increase.	1890. Decrease.	Crops.	1889.	1890.	1890. Increase.	1890. Decrease.
	Acres.	Acres.	Acres.	Acres.		Acres.	Acres.	Acres.	Acres.
Wheat,	88,745	91,341	2,596	—	Flax,	113,633	96,896	—	16,756
Oats,	1,238,957	1,221,013	—	17,929					
Barley,	183,783	180,058	—	3,725					
Bere and Rye,	14,837	14,858	—	1,305	Total under Tillage,	2,968,494	2,925,032	—	43,462
Beans and Pease,	[illegible]	4,370	14	—					
Total Extent under Cereal Crops,	1,635,073	1,614,734	—	20,339	Meadow and Clover:—				
Potatoes,	787,224	780,801	—	6,433	Clover, Sainfoin, and Grasses under Rotation,	670,247	631,818	—	38,431
Turnips,	291,912	289,395	—	2,497					
Mangel Wurzel and Beet Root,	41,021	43,457	2,436	—					
Cabbage,	42,437	45,964	3,527	—	Permanent Pasture or Grass not broken up in Rotation,	1,517,290	1,461,816	—	55,461
Vetches and Rape,	13,008	13,252	244	—					
Carrots, Parsnips, & other Green Crops,	35,106	32,672	—	2,434					
Total Extent under Green Crops,	1,219,749	1,211,402	—	3,287	Total Extent under Crops,	5,026,016	4,918,726	—	137,290

The Proportionate Area under each Crop in 1889 and 1890 :—

Crops.	Proportion per cent. 1889.	Proportion per cent. 1890.	Crops.	Proportion per cent. 1889.	Proportion per cent. 1890.
Wheat,	1·8	1·6	Cabbage,	0·6	0·5
Oats,	24·5	24·6	Vetches and Rape,	0·2	0·3
Barley,	3·7	3·7	Carrots, Parsnips, and other Green Crops,	0·7	0·7
Rye and Bere,	0·3	0·5			
Beans and Pease,	0·1	0·1	Total Green Crops,	24·5	24·7
Total Cereal Crops,	30·5	30·6			
			Flax,	2·3	2·0
Potatoes,	15·8	15·9	Meadow and Clover,	43·8	43·6
Turnips,	5·9	6·0			
Mangel Wurzel and Beet Root,	0·8	0·9	Total,	100·0	100·0

Tables showing the extent of land under crops in 1890 by Counties and Provinces, and by Poor Law Unions, and from 1881 to 1890 by Counties and Provinces, are given at pages 38, 42 and 80 respectively.

Grazing Land, 1889 and 1890.

The extent of land under grass in 1890 (*exclusive of that under meadow and clover*) was 10,318,236 acres, or 50·2 in every 100 of the entire country, against 9,998,307 acres or 49·2 per cent. in 1889. The relative proportions under grass in each Province were —in Munster 54·6 per cent. in 1890, and 53·3 per cent. in 1889; Leinster 54·9 per cent. in 1890, and 53·9 per cent. in 1889; Connaught 49·3 per cent. in 1890, and 48·4 per cent. in 1889; and Ulster 42·0 per cent. in 1890, and 40·9 per cent. in 1889.

There appears to have been an increase of pasture land in 1890 in Leinster of 1·0 per cent. of the total area of the province, in Munster of 1·3 per cent., in Connaught of 0·9 per cent., and in Ulster of 1·1 per cent.

Grazing Land in 1890.

Of the counties—Limerick, Meath, and Westmeath had each above 60 acres in every 100 of their entire area under grass in 1890: Clare, Fermanagh, Kildare, Kilkenny, Leitrim, Roscommon, and Tipperary had above 55 and under 60 acres: Carlow, Cavan, Cork, Dublin, Longford, Queen's, Sligo, Waterford, and Wexford had from 50 to 55 acres: Antrim, Armagh, Galway, Kerry, King's, Louth, Mayo, Monaghan, Tyrone, and Wicklow had above 40 and under 50 acres; and Donegal, Down, and Londonderry had over 30 and under 40 acres in every 100 acres under grass in 1890. Only 33·4 per cent. of the total area of Donegal was enumerated in 1890 as under grass, while Meath shows the highest percentage, 70·3.

The area of each County and Province, and the extent and percentage under grass in 1890, are given at page 84.

Division of Land, 1881–1890.

Of the total area of Ireland (20,323,738 statute acres),* the land under grass in 1890 was, as already stated, a little over one-half. It appears from the succeeding Table (II.) to have increased from 49·6 per cent. of the total area in 1881 to 50·2 in 1890, but during the ten years the proportion of grass varied from 50·9 per cent. in 1884 to 48·7 in 1888.

In Cereal Crops a decrease is shown in each year of the decade, the area in 1881 was 1,777,175 acres, and in 1890 it was 1,514,734 acres, being a decrease of 262,441 acres or 14·8 per cent.

The area under Green Crops in 1881 was 1,270,026 acres, and in 1890 it was 1,214,462 acres, showing a decrease of 55,564 acres in the decade.

Flax decreased from 147,145 acres in 1881 to 96,896 acres in 1890.

There were 2,001,039 acres in 1881 under Meadow and Clover, and 2,098,624 acres in 1890: the acreage varied from 1,931,784 in 1883 to 2,221,980 in 1888.

Fallow or uncropped arable land amounted to 21,204 acres in 1881, and to 14,695 acres in 1890.

Comparing the first and the last years of the decade, Woods and Plantations exhibit a decrease from 328,708 acres to 327,461 acres.

In "Bog, Waste, Water, &c." an increase is shown—from 4,708,047 acres in 1881, to 4,854,715 acres in 1890, the difference being equivalent to 0·8 per cent. of the total area.

* See note (†) page 5.

TABLE II.—The Extent of Land in Statute Acres, and the proportional Area, under Cereal Crops, Green Crops, Flax, Meadow and Clover, Grass, Woods and Plantation, Fallow, Bog, Waste, Water, &c., in each Year from 1881 to 1890, also the Number of Holdings exceeding 1 acre.

Years.	Number of Holdings exceeding 1 Acre.	Cereal Crops.	Green Crops.	Flax.	Meadow and Clover.	Grass.	All Land in use for Agriculture.	Woods and Plantations.	Fallow.	Bog, Waste, Water, Roads, &c.	Total.
		Acres.	Acres.	Acres.	Acres.	Acres.	Acres.	Acres.	Acres.	Acres.	
1881, .	[illegible]	1,777,173	1,270,[illegible]	147,145	[illegible]	[illegible]	[illegible]	[illegible]	[illegible]	4,790,[illegible]	[illegible] Statute Acres.
1882, .	[illegible]	[illegible]	[illegible]	[illegible]	[illegible]	[illegible]	[illegible]	[illegible]	[illegible]	[illegible]	
1883, .	[illegible]	[illegible]	[illegible]	[illegible]	[illegible]	[illegible]	[illegible]	[illegible]	[illegible]	[illegible]	
1884, .	[illegible]	[illegible]	[illegible]	[illegible]	[illegible]	[illegible]	[illegible]	[illegible]	[illegible]	[illegible]	
1885, .	[illegible]	[illegible]	[illegible]	[illegible]	[illegible]	[illegible]	[illegible]	[illegible]	[illegible]	[illegible]	
1886, .	[illegible]	[illegible]	[illegible]	[illegible]	[illegible]	[illegible]	[illegible]	[illegible]	[illegible]	[illegible]	
1887, .	[illegible]	[illegible]	[illegible]	[illegible]	[illegible]	[illegible]	[illegible]	[illegible]	[illegible]	[illegible]	
1888, .	[illegible]	[illegible]	[illegible]	[illegible]	[illegible]	[illegible]	[illegible]	[illegible]	[illegible]	[illegible]	
1889, .	[illegible]	[illegible]	[illegible]	[illegible]	[illegible]	[illegible]	[illegible]	[illegible]	[illegible]	[illegible]	
1890, .	[illegible]	[illegible]	[illegible]	[illegible]	[illegible]	[illegible]	[illegible]	[illegible]	[illegible]	[illegible]	
Average 1881–90,	617,[illegible]	[illegible]	[illegible]	[illegible]	[illegible]	[illegible]	[illegible]	[illegible]	[illegible]	4,[illegible]	

Years.	—	Cereal Crops.	Green Crops.	Flax.	Meadow and Clover.	Grass.	All Land in use for Agriculture.	Woods and Plantations.	Fallow.	Bog, Waste, Water, Roads, &c.	Total.
1881, .	–	[illegible]	[illegible]	0·7	9·9	[illegible]	[illegible]	1·6	0·1	[illegible]	100·0
1882, .	–	[illegible]	[illegible]	0·6	[illegible]	[illegible]	[illegible]	1·6	0·1	[illegible]	
1883, .	–	[illegible]	[illegible]	[illegible]	[illegible]	[illegible]	[illegible]	1·7	0·1	[illegible]	
1884, .	–	[illegible]	[illegible]	[illegible]	9·7	[illegible]	[illegible]	1·7	0·1	[illegible]	
1885, .	–	[illegible]	[illegible]	[illegible]	[illegible]	[illegible]	[illegible]	[illegible]	0·1	[illegible]	
1886, .	–	[illegible]	[illegible]	[illegible]	[illegible]	[illegible]	[illegible]	[illegible]	0·1	[illegible]	
1887, .	–	[illegible]	[illegible]	[illegible]	[illegible]	[illegible]	[illegible]	[illegible]	0·1	[illegible]	
1888, .	–	[illegible]	[illegible]	[illegible]	[illegible]	[illegible]	[illegible]	[illegible]	0·1	[illegible]	
1889, .	–	[illegible]	[illegible]	[illegible]	[illegible]	[illegible]	[illegible]	[illegible]	0·1	[illegible]	
1890, .	–	[illegible]	[illegible]	[illegible]	[illegible]	[illegible]	[illegible]	[illegible]	0·1	[illegible]	
Average 1881–90,	–	[illegible]	[illegible]	[illegible]	[illegible]	[illegible]	[illegible]	[illegible]	[illegible]	[illegible]	

Tables showing the extent and the proportionate area under Crops, Grass, Fallow, Woods and Plantations, Bog and Marsh, Barren Mountain Land, and Water, Roads, Fences, &c., in 1890, by counties and provinces, will be found at page 34. From these it appears that there are five counties with upwards of 100,000 acres under "Bog and Marsh,"* viz. :—Mayo, with 250,948 acres, or 20·7 per cent. of its entire area; Galway, 232,842 acres, or 15·3 per cent.; Donegal, 157,781 acres, or 14·1 per cent.; King's, 112,266 acres, or 22·7 per cent., and Kerry, 127,112 acres, or 11·0 per cent. The following counties contain the smallest areas under "Bog and Marsh," viz. :—Dublin, 324 acres, or 0·1 per cent. of its entire area; Louth, 2,904 acres, or 1·4 per cent.; Down, 5,166 acres, or 0·8 per cent.; and Carlow, 5,091 acres, or 2·2 per cent.; 735,837 acres in the province of Connaught, being 17·4 per cent. of its entire area, are returned as under "Bog and Marsh," including 83,198 acres, or 14·2 per cent. of the County Roscommon, in addition to the large extent in Mayo and Galway as before mentioned.

* See note (1) page 5.

The following statement, extracted from a paper laid by me before the Statistical and Social Enquiry Society of Ireland, on the 23rd June, 1891, shows in a concise manner the extent of Meadow, Clover and Pasture in Ireland during the past 10 years:—

Year.	Meadow and Clover.	Pasture.	Total Grass Land.
	Acres.	Acres.	Acres.
1881,	2,001,029	10,075,424	12,076,453
1882,	1,908,183	10,199,594	12,071,777
1883,	1,981,144	10,192,417	12,134,521
1884,	1,943,487	10,518,876	12,302,363
1885,	2,034,748	10,751,120	12,785,868
1886,	2,091,975	10,113,707	12,754,916
1887,	2,143,818	10,048,807	12,192,335
1888,	2,221,980	9,905,027	12,127,007
1889,	2,187,521	9,996,797	12,183,319
1890,	2,004,636	10,311,254	12,305,890
Average 1881–90,	2,063,858	10,139,330	12,103,474

It will be observed that the total area of grass lands has increased from 12,076,453 acres in 1881 to 12,305,890 acres in 1890, being an increase of 229,437 or 1·9 per cent. The cattle and sheep, however, have increased in a greater proportion than the area of pasture lands, so that these are more fully stocked than they were 10 years ago.

"Barren Mountain Land" covers an area of 100,000 acres and upwards in each of the following seven counties, viz.:—Donegal, 322,626 acres, or 27·1 per cent. of its entire area; Kerry, 284,619 acres, or 24·3 per cent.; Galway, 228,815 acres, or 15·1 per cent.; Cork, 242,150 acres, or 13·2 per cent.; Mayo, 198,279 acres, or 15·1 per cent.; Tyrone, 118,014 acres, or 14·5 per cent.; and Wicklow, 120,753 acres, or 24·2 per cent.

Fourteen per cent. of Sligo, or 63,106 acres, 6·3 per cent., or 71,260 acres of Tipperary, and 17·0 per cent., or 77,696 acres of Waterford are under "Barren Mountain Land." The counties containing the smallest areas under "Barren Mountain Land" are Meath with 793 acres, or 0·1 per cent. of its entire area; Longford, 504 acres, or 0·2 per cent.; Westmeath, 637 acres, or 0·2 per cent.; Kildare, 1,879 acres, or 0·3 per cent.; and Monaghan, 5,536 acres, or 1·1 per cent. Only 215,046 acres, or 4·4 per cent. of Leinster are returned as being under "Barren Mountain Land," while 786,064 acres, or 13·2 per cent. of Munster; 655,446 acres, or 12·3 per cent. of Ulster; and 528,981 acres or 12·5 per cent. of Connaught are so returned.*

Very little variation is exhibited in the proportionate area under "Water, Roads, Fences, &c." in the several counties and provinces. In the counties the highest percentage is 7·5 in Dublin, and the lowest 3·1 in Wicklow. 884,543 acres (including 189,035 acres under water), or 4·4 per cent. of the entire area of the country, were returned in 1890 as "Water, Roads, Fences, &c." This, however, does not include the acreage under the larger rivers, lakes and tideways. See note (†), page 5.

A table showing the division of land by Poor Law Unions is given at pages 35 and 36.

* With reference to the question whether waste land is increasing or decreasing in Ireland, the following from a Paper read by Dr. Grimshaw before the Statistical and Social Inquiry Society of Ireland on the 19th of April, 1884, may be of interest:—

"The following Table shows that so far from the waste land of Ireland being on the increase, an immense amount of waste land has been reclaimed during the past forty years.

"DIVISION OF LAND IN 1841, '51, '61, '71, AND '81.

Division of Land.	1841.	1851.	1861.	1871.	1881.	
	Statute Acres.	Statute Acres.	Statute Acres.	Statute Acres.	Statute Acres.	
Under Crops (including Meadow),	[illegible]	[illegible]	[illegible]	[illegible]		[illegible]
Grass,		[illegible]	[illegible]	[illegible]		[illegible]
Woods and Plantations,	[illegible]	[illegible]	[illegible]	[illegible]		[illegible]
Barren Mountain Land,	[illegible]	[illegible]	[illegible]	[illegible]	[illegible]	[illegible]
Bog and Marsh,					[illegible]	
Waste Land, &c.,					[illegible]	
Total,	[illegible]					

NOTE.—The information for 1841 and 1851, respectively, has been obtained from the Census Reports for those years; and that for the subsequent periods from the Agricultural Returns.

A more extended Extract from the Paper above referred to was printed in the Agricultural Statistics Reports for 1881 and 1885.

NUMBER OF HOLDINGS AND NUMBER OF OCCUPIERS.

Number and size of holdings, 1889 and 1890.

According to the returns for 1890, the number of separate holdings was 561,808, being 1,172 less than in the previous year. The holdings which *increased* in number were—those "not exceeding 1 acre" by 680; those "above 30 and not exceeding 50 acres" by 284; those "above 50 and not exceeding 100 acres" by 31; those "above 100 and not exceeding 200 acres" by 100; those "above 200 and not exceeding 500 acres" by 6; and those "above 500 acres" by 9. The holdings which *decreased* in number were those "above 1 and not exceeding 5 acres" by 823; those "above 5 and not exceeding 15 acres" by 798; and "above 15 and not exceeding 30 acres" by 881.

Size of Holdings.	Number in 1889.	Number in 1890.	Increase or Decrease in 1890.	
			Increase.	Decrease.
Not exceeding 1 Acre,	48,990	49,670	680	–
Above 1 and not exceeding 5 Acres,	61,590	60,767	–	823
" 5 " 15 "	156,561	155,763	–	798
" 15 " 30 "	135,096	134,215	–	881
" 30 " 50 "	73,402	73,686	284	–
" 50 " 100 "	66,640	66,671	31	–
" 100 " 200 "	32,925	33,025	100	–
" 200 " 500 "	8,367	8,373	6	–
Above 500 Acres,	1,585	1,594	9	–
Total,	562,980	561,808	–	1,172

A table showing the number of holdings, by classes, for each Poor Law Union, in 1890, will be found on pp. 35 and 36.

The number of separate holdings in each county and province, in 1889 and 1890, is given by classes in Table III. at page 11.

Number of separate Holdings and of Occupiers, 1889 and 1890.

As in many instances landholders occupy more than one farm, and as, in other cases, farms extend into two or more townlands—*the portion in each townland being enumerated and classified as a separate holding*—it has been considered desirable, with the view of ascertaining the number of *Occupiers*, and of classifying them according to the total extent of land held by each, to obtain a Return of the number of persons having more than one farm or holding. Each Enumerator is, therefore, required to furnish the name of every landholder residing in his district who has two or more farms, or whose farm extends into two or more townlands, together with the area of each portion, and the locality in which it is situated. The number of actual occupiers in 1890 thus arrived at is given in Table IV., page 12, by counties and provinces. On comparing the results in this Table with the figures given in Table III., it appears that in 1890 there were 561,808 holdings in the hands of 524,910 occupiers.

The number of separate holdings and the number of occupiers in each Province in 1889 and 1890 were :—

Provinces.	Number of Separate Holdings.		Number of Occupiers.	
	1889.	1890.	1889.	1890.
Leinster,	133,904	133,169	108,791	108,961
Munster,	126,365	125,770	112,334	112,448
Ulster,	200,604	199,425	189,418	188,040
Connaught,	101,209	100,448	114,606	115,461
Total,	562,918	561,808	525,152	524,910

The number of occupiers of land in 1890 was 524,910, being 942 less than in the previous year.

Excluding those holding land "not exceeding one acre," who are to a great extent merely occupiers of small gardens, they numbered 474,009 in 1890, or 1,808 less than in 1889. There was a decrease in Leinster of 156—from 92,727 in 1889 to 92,571 in 1890; in Munster of 147—from 99,761 in 1889 to 99,614 in 1890; in Ulster of 915—from 174,021 in 1889 to 173,106 in 1890; and in Connaught of 590—from 109,308 in 1889 to 108,718 in 1890. The decrease in occupiers holding land above 1 and not exceeding 50 acres was 1,924 and the number holding land exceeding that acreage increased by 116.

TABLE III.—The number of Holdings, by classes, for each County and Province, in 1889 and 1890, and the increase or decrease in the latter year:—

COUNTIES.	[illegible]	[illegible]	[illegible]	[illegible]	[illegible]	[illegible]	[illegible]	[illegible]	[illegible]	Total.
Antrim,	[illegible]	[illegible]	[illegible]	[illegible]	[illegible]	[illegible]	[illegible]	[illegible]	[illegible]	[illegible]
Armagh,	[illegible]	[illegible]	[illegible]	[illegible]	[illegible]	[illegible]	[illegible]	[illegible]	[illegible]	[illegible]
Carlow,	[illegible]	[illegible]	[illegible]	[illegible]	[illegible]	[illegible]	[illegible]	[illegible]	[illegible]	[illegible]
Cavan,	[illegible]	[illegible]	[illegible]	[illegible]	[illegible]	[illegible]	[illegible]	[illegible]	[illegible]	[illegible]
Clare,	[illegible]	[illegible]	[illegible]	[illegible]	[illegible]	[illegible]	[illegible]	[illegible]	[illegible]	[illegible]
Cork,	[illegible]	[illegible]	[illegible]	[illegible]	[illegible]	[illegible]	[illegible]	[illegible]	[illegible]	[illegible]
Donegal,	[illegible]	[illegible]	[illegible]	[illegible]	[illegible]	[illegible]	[illegible]	[illegible]	[illegible]	[illegible]
Down,	[illegible]	[illegible]	[illegible]	[illegible]	[illegible]	[illegible]	[illegible]	[illegible]	[illegible]	[illegible]
Dublin,	[illegible]	[illegible]	[illegible]	[illegible]	[illegible]	[illegible]	[illegible]	[illegible]	[illegible]	[illegible]
Fermanagh,	[illegible]	[illegible]	[illegible]	[illegible]	[illegible]	[illegible]	[illegible]	[illegible]	[illegible]	[illegible]
Galway,	[illegible]	[illegible]	[illegible]	[illegible]	[illegible]	[illegible]	[illegible]	[illegible]	[illegible]	[illegible]
Kerry,	[illegible]	[illegible]	[illegible]	[illegible]	[illegible]	[illegible]	[illegible]	[illegible]	[illegible]	[illegible]
Kildare,	[illegible]	[illegible]	[illegible]	[illegible]	[illegible]	[illegible]	[illegible]	[illegible]	[illegible]	[illegible]
Kilkenny,	[illegible]	[illegible]	[illegible]	[illegible]	[illegible]	[illegible]	[illegible]	[illegible]	[illegible]	[illegible]
King's,	[illegible]	[illegible]	[illegible]	[illegible]	[illegible]	[illegible]	[illegible]	[illegible]	[illegible]	[illegible]
Leitrim,	[illegible]	[illegible]	[illegible]	[illegible]	[illegible]	[illegible]	[illegible]	[illegible]	[illegible]	[illegible]
Limerick,	[illegible]	[illegible]	[illegible]	[illegible]	[illegible]	[illegible]	[illegible]	[illegible]	[illegible]	[illegible]
Londonderry,	[illegible]	[illegible]	[illegible]	[illegible]	[illegible]	[illegible]	[illegible]	[illegible]	[illegible]	[illegible]
Longford,	[illegible]	[illegible]	[illegible]	[illegible]	[illegible]	[illegible]	[illegible]	[illegible]	[illegible]	[illegible]
Louth & Drogheda Co. of Town,	[illegible]	[illegible]	[illegible]	[illegible]	[illegible]	[illegible]	[illegible]	[illegible]	[illegible]	[illegible]
Mayo,	[illegible]	[illegible]	[illegible]	[illegible]	[illegible]	[illegible]	[illegible]	[illegible]	[illegible]	[illegible]
Meath,	[illegible]	[illegible]	[illegible]	[illegible]	[illegible]	[illegible]	[illegible]	[illegible]	[illegible]	[illegible]
Monaghan,	[illegible]	[illegible]	[illegible]	[illegible]	[illegible]	[illegible]	[illegible]	[illegible]	[illegible]	[illegible]
Queen's,	[illegible]	[illegible]	[illegible]	[illegible]	[illegible]	[illegible]	[illegible]	[illegible]	[illegible]	[illegible]
Roscommon,	[illegible]	[illegible]	[illegible]	[illegible]	[illegible]	[illegible]	[illegible]	[illegible]	[illegible]	[illegible]
Sligo,	[illegible]	[illegible]	[illegible]	[illegible]	[illegible]	[illegible]	[illegible]	[illegible]	[illegible]	[illegible]
Tipperary,	[illegible]	[illegible]	[illegible]	[illegible]	[illegible]	[illegible]	[illegible]	[illegible]	[illegible]	[illegible]
Tyrone,	[illegible]	[illegible]	[illegible]	[illegible]	[illegible]	[illegible]	[illegible]	[illegible]	[illegible]	[illegible]
Waterford,	[illegible]	[illegible]	[illegible]	[illegible]	[illegible]	[illegible]	[illegible]	[illegible]	[illegible]	[illegible]
Westmeath,	[illegible]	[illegible]	[illegible]	[illegible]	[illegible]	[illegible]	[illegible]	[illegible]	[illegible]	[illegible]
Wexford,	[illegible]	[illegible]	[illegible]	[illegible]	[illegible]	[illegible]	[illegible]	[illegible]	[illegible]	[illegible]
Wicklow,	[illegible]	[illegible]	[illegible]	[illegible]	[illegible]	[illegible]	[illegible]	[illegible]	[illegible]	[illegible]

SUMMARY OF IRELAND.

PROVINCES.	[illegible]	[illegible]	[illegible]	[illegible]	[illegible]	[illegible]	[illegible]	[illegible]	[illegible]	[illegible]
Leinster,	[illegible]	[illegible]	[illegible]	[illegible]	[illegible]	[illegible]	[illegible]	[illegible]	[illegible]	[illegible]
Munster,	[illegible]	[illegible]	[illegible]	[illegible]	[illegible]	[illegible]	[illegible]	[illegible]	[illegible]	[illegible]
Ulster,	[illegible]	[illegible]	[illegible]	[illegible]	[illegible]	[illegible]	[illegible]	[illegible]	[illegible]	[illegible]
Connaught,	[illegible]	[illegible]	[illegible]	[illegible]	[illegible]	[illegible]	[illegible]	[illegible]	[illegible]	[illegible]
Total of Ireland,	[illegible]	[illegible]	[illegible]	[illegible]	[illegible]	[illegible]	[illegible]	[illegible]	[illegible]	[illegible]
Increase or Decrease in 1890,	Increase, [illegible]	Decrease, [illegible]	Decrease, [illegible]	Decrease, [illegible]	Increase, [illegible]	Decrease, [illegible]	Increase, [illegible]	Increase, 4	[illegible]	Decrease, [illegible]

TABLE IV.—Return of the number of Occupiers resident in each County and Province in 1890, classified according to the *total extent* of land held, without reference to the Townland, Poor Law Union, County, or Province in which the portions of land are situated:—

Counties.	Not exceeding 1 Acre.	Above 1 and not exceeding 5 Acres.	Above 5 and not exceeding 15 Acres.	Above 15 and not exceeding 30 Acres.	Above 30 and not exceeding 50 Acres.	Above 50 and not exceeding 100 Acres.	Above 100 and not exceeding 200 Acres.	Above 200 and not exceeding 500 Acres.	Above 500 Acres.	Total.
Antrim,	[illegible]	[illegible]	[illegible]	[illegible]	[illegible]	[illegible]	[illegible]	[illegible]	[illegible]	[illegible]
Armagh,	[illegible]	[illegible]	[illegible]	[illegible]	[illegible]	[illegible]	[illegible]	[illegible]	[illegible]	[illegible]
Carlow,	[illegible]	[illegible]	[illegible]	[illegible]	[illegible]	[illegible]	[illegible]	[illegible]	[illegible]	[illegible]
Cavan,	[illegible]	[illegible]	[illegible]	[illegible]	[illegible]	[illegible]	[illegible]	[illegible]	[illegible]	[illegible]
Clare,	[illegible]	[illegible]	[illegible]	[illegible]	[illegible]	[illegible]	[illegible]	[illegible]	[illegible]	[illegible]
Cork,	[illegible]	[illegible]	[illegible]	[illegible]	[illegible]	[illegible]	[illegible]	[illegible]	[illegible]	[illegible]
Donegal,	[illegible]	[illegible]	[illegible]	[illegible]	[illegible]	[illegible]	[illegible]	[illegible]	[illegible]	[illegible]
Down,	[illegible]	[illegible]	[illegible]	[illegible]	[illegible]	[illegible]	[illegible]	[illegible]	[illegible]	[illegible]
Dublin,	[illegible]	[illegible]	[illegible]	[illegible]	[illegible]	[illegible]	[illegible]	[illegible]	[illegible]	[illegible]
Fermanagh,	[illegible]	[illegible]	[illegible]	[illegible]	[illegible]	[illegible]	[illegible]	[illegible]	[illegible]	[illegible]
Galway,	[illegible]	[illegible]	[illegible]	[illegible]	[illegible]	[illegible]	[illegible]	[illegible]	[illegible]	[illegible]
Kerry,	[illegible]	[illegible]	[illegible]	[illegible]	[illegible]	[illegible]	[illegible]	[illegible]	[illegible]	[illegible]
Kildare,	[illegible]	[illegible]	[illegible]	[illegible]	[illegible]	[illegible]	[illegible]	[illegible]	[illegible]	[illegible]
Kilkenny,	[illegible]	[illegible]	[illegible]	[illegible]	[illegible]	[illegible]	[illegible]	[illegible]	[illegible]	[illegible]
King's,	[illegible]	[illegible]	[illegible]	[illegible]	[illegible]	[illegible]	[illegible]	[illegible]	[illegible]	[illegible]
Leitrim,	[illegible]	[illegible]	[illegible]	[illegible]	[illegible]	[illegible]	[illegible]	[illegible]	[illegible]	[illegible]
Limerick,	[illegible]	[illegible]	[illegible]	[illegible]	[illegible]	[illegible]	[illegible]	[illegible]	[illegible]	[illegible]
Londonderry,	[illegible]	[illegible]	[illegible]	[illegible]	[illegible]	[illegible]	[illegible]	[illegible]	[illegible]	[illegible]
Longford,	[illegible]	[illegible]	[illegible]	[illegible]	[illegible]	[illegible]	[illegible]	[illegible]	[illegible]	[illegible]
Louth and Drogheda, Co. of Town,	[illegible]	[illegible]	[illegible]	[illegible]	[illegible]	[illegible]	[illegible]	[illegible]	[illegible]	[illegible]
Mayo,	[illegible]	[illegible]	[illegible]	[illegible]	[illegible]	[illegible]	[illegible]	[illegible]	[illegible]	[illegible]
Meath,	[illegible]	[illegible]	[illegible]	[illegible]	[illegible]	[illegible]	[illegible]	[illegible]	[illegible]	[illegible]
Monaghan,	[illegible]	[illegible]	[illegible]	[illegible]	[illegible]	[illegible]	[illegible]	[illegible]	[illegible]	[illegible]
Queen's,	[illegible]	[illegible]	[illegible]	[illegible]	[illegible]	[illegible]	[illegible]	[illegible]	[illegible]	[illegible]
Roscommon,	[illegible]	[illegible]	[illegible]	[illegible]	[illegible]	[illegible]	[illegible]	[illegible]	[illegible]	[illegible]
Sligo,	[illegible]	[illegible]	[illegible]	[illegible]	[illegible]	[illegible]	[illegible]	[illegible]	[illegible]	[illegible]
Tipperary,	[illegible]	[illegible]	[illegible]	[illegible]	[illegible]	[illegible]	[illegible]	[illegible]	[illegible]	[illegible]
Tyrone,	[illegible]	[illegible]	[illegible]	[illegible]	[illegible]	[illegible]	[illegible]	[illegible]	[illegible]	[illegible]
Waterford,	[illegible]	[illegible]	[illegible]	[illegible]	[illegible]	[illegible]	[illegible]	[illegible]	[illegible]	[illegible]
Westmeath,	[illegible]	[illegible]	[illegible]	[illegible]	[illegible]	[illegible]	[illegible]	[illegible]	[illegible]	[illegible]
Wexford,	[illegible]	[illegible]	[illegible]	[illegible]	[illegible]	[illegible]	[illegible]	[illegible]	[illegible]	[illegible]
Wicklow,	[illegible]	[illegible]	[illegible]	[illegible]	[illegible]	[illegible]	[illegible]	[illegible]	[illegible]	[illegible]
SUMMARY OF IRELAND.										
Provinces.										
Leinster,	[illegible]	[illegible]	[illegible]	[illegible]	[illegible]	[illegible]	[illegible]	[illegible]	[illegible]	[illegible]
Munster,	[illegible]	[illegible]	[illegible]	[illegible]	[illegible]	[illegible]	[illegible]	[illegible]	[illegible]	[illegible]
Ulster,	[illegible]	[illegible]	[illegible]	[illegible]	[illegible]	[illegible]	[illegible]	[illegible]	[illegible]	[illegible]
Connaught,	[illegible]	[illegible]	[illegible]	[illegible]	[illegible]	[illegible]	[illegible]	[illegible]	[illegible]	[illegible]
Total of Ireland,	[illegible]	[illegible]	[illegible]	[illegible]	[illegible]	[illegible]	[illegible]	[illegible]	[illegible]	[illegible]

Number of Occupiers of Land, 1884 to 1890.

The following statement shows the number of occupiers of land in each year from 1884 to 1890, by Provinces:—

Provinces.	Number of Occupiers in the Years						
	1884.	1885.	1886.	1887.	1888.	1889.	1890.
Leinster,	105,800	107,676	108,627	106,661	108,594	106,791	108,631
Munster,	109,342	110,166	110,318	111,613	111,168	112,331	112,858
Ulster,	167,896	168,378	168,517	167,826	167,160	156,418	158,140
Connaught,	114,036	115,023	114,806	116,503	114,483	114,600	116,851
IRELAND,	530,734	531,546	532,377	511,181	531,465	518,163	516,210

Increase or decrease in Holdings by Classes between 1841 and 1890.

The number of holdings "above 1 and not exceeding 5 acres" diminished greatly between 1841 and 1890. In Leinster the decrease was 65·3 per cent.; in Munster 81·6; in Ulster 80·1; in Connaught 87·6; and in all Ireland 80·4 per cent.

In the same period holdings "above 5 and not exceeding 15 acres" also diminished in number; the decrease in all Ireland was 38·4 per cent.; it was—in Leinster 44·7 per cent.; in Munster 69·4; and in Ulster 31·3; while in Connaught these holdings increased 1·6 per cent.

Holdings "above 15 and not exceeding 30 acres" increased 7·9 per cent. in Leinster; 115·1 per cent. in Ulster; and 475·3 per cent. in Connaught. They decreased 12·6 per cent. in Munster; while in all Ireland they increased 66·2 per cent.

Holdings "above 30 acres" increased 119·6 per cent. in Leinster; 340·3 in Munster; 354·6 in Ulster; 432·8 in Connaught; and 235·7 per cent. in all Ireland.

The total number of holdings "above 1 acre" decreased between 1841 and 1890 by 22·4 per cent. in Leinster; 32·6 per cent. in Munster; 22·3 in Ulster; and 26·1 in Connaught.

The total number of holdings in Ireland "above 1 acre" was 691,202 in 1841; 570,338 in 1851; 568,484 in 1861; 544,149 in 1871; 526,743 in 1881; and 513,994 in 1890, showing a decrease of 177,208 or 25·6 per cent. in the period between 1841 and 1890.

TABLE V.—The number of Holdings above 1 acre in each Province in 1841, 1851, 1861, 1871, 1881, and 1890, according to the classification used by the Census Commissioners of 1841 (in which "above 30 acres" was the maximum); the increase or decrease in the numbers in each class, and the difference per cent., between 1841 and 1890:— Number of Holdings in 1841, 1851, 1861, 1871, 1881, and 1890.

Size of Holdings.		Leinster.	Munster.	Ulster.	Connaught.	Total.
		Number.	Number.	Number.	Number.	Number.
Above 1 and not exceeding 5 Acres,	1841,	50,170	97,557	102,215	100,254	310,436
	1851,	18,711	14,900	29,703	18,103	88,083
	1861,	23,848	13,136	28,158	19,137	85,469
	1871,	21,429	12,191	24,151	16,836	74,809
	1881,	19,304	11,098	21,971	14,700	67,071
	1890,	17,372	10,446	20,303	12,447	60,567
		Decrease.	Decrease.	Decrease.	Decrease.	Decrease.
Decrease in number between 1841 and 1890,		32,798	47,323	81,812	87,797	249,869
Rate per cent.,		65·3	81·6	80·1	87·8	80·4
Above 5 and not exceeding 15 Acres,	1841,	46,059	81,763	80,806	46,403	252,799
	1851,	33,046	24,368	68,176	40,386	191,854
	1861,	29,618	21,969	61,053	30,404	183,931
	1871,	27,278	20,409	73,847	50,049	171,383
	1881,	25,048	19,747	67,362	49,888	164,045
	1890,	25,481	18,916	53,624	46,865	185,763
		Decrease.	Decrease.	Decrease.	Increase.	Decrease.
Increase or Decrease in number between 1841 and 1890,		20,578	62,846	34,161	462	87,036
Rate per cent.,		44·7	69·4	34·3	1·0	35·4
Above 15 and not exceeding 30 Acres,	1841,	20,888	27,611	25,218	6,324	79,342
	1851,	28,006	38,256	57,631	28,799	161,311
	1861,	24,276	36,603	57,460	22,880	141,221
	1871,	23,143	33,074	56,878	24,709	138,647
	1881,	22,654	30,630	63,297	32,918	165,783
	1890,	22,223	24,133	54,261	33,607	134,918
		Increase.	Decrease.	Increase.	Increase.	Increase.
Increase or Decrease in number between 1841 and 1890,		1,525	3,478	29,043	27,283	64,578
Rate per cent.,		7·9	12·6	115·1	430·2	67·3
Above 30 Acres,	1841,	17,943	19,665	9,656	4,863	48,625
	1851,	33,096	52,076	37,818	20,107	149,090
	1861,	33,384	55,533	33,164	23,160	157,833
	1871,	30,631	56,418	41,071	23,378	159,303
	1881,	39,679	56,111	43,210	21,708	157,834
	1890,	39,409	60,717	43,889	22,341	163,360
		Increase.	Increase.	Increase.	Increase.	Increase.
Increase in number between 1841 and 1890,		21,460	40,088	34,233	18,579	114,635
Rate per cent.,		119·6	340·3	354·6	432·8	235·7
TOTAL ABOVE 1 ACRE,	1841,	134,700	162,386	236,634	155,842	691,202
	1851,	129,871	160,194	210,349	116,684	570,338
	1861,	116,973	118,333	207,630	125,343	568,484
	1871,	111,678	116,763	195,996	121,683	544,143
	1881,	106,880	112,014	188,078	119,708	526,743
	1890,	104,528	110,886	183,887	115,170	513,994
		Decrease.	Decrease.	Decrease.	Decrease.	Decrease.
Decrease in number between 1841 and 1890,		30,251	51,460	52,837	40,378	177,208
Rate per cent.,		23·4	32·6	22·3	26·1	25·6

PRODUCE OF THE CROPS.

Mode of collecting the Returns of Produce.

The Tables relating to the produce of the crops have been carefully compiled from information obtained by members of the Royal Irish Constabulary and of the Metropolitan Police from practical farmers and other persons qualified to form an opinion as to the yield in that *Poor Law Electoral Division* (adopted since 1856, instead of Constabulary Districts), for which they were requested to afford the information. The names and residences of the parties so co-operating and assisting are stated by the Enumerators on the Returns.

CONDITIONS INFLUENCING THE PRODUCE OF THE CROPS.

Notes of Superintendents of Enumeration.

On pp. 79 to 90 will be found the observations of the District Inspectors of the Royal Irish Constabulary and of the Sergeants of the Metropolitan Police, who acted as Superintendents of Enumeration, in reply to a circular requesting their opinion on the probable cause to which the good or bad yield of the various crops, in each of their districts, may be attributed.

The Weather.

The Weather.

The Weather being a potent factor in influencing the produce of the crops, both as to quantity and quality, the following particulars and those given on pages 147-163 are inserted by the kind permission of the Editor of the Dublin Journal of Medical Science: they have been derived from Returns of Meteorological Observations taken in Dublin City during the years 1870-90, by J. W. Moore, Esq., M.D., F.R.C.P.I., F.R. MET. SOC.; and published in the Journal during the years 1890-91. The Tables on pages 164-166 also, are founded on Dr. Moore's observations:—

The mean Atmospherical Pressure has been obtained from daily readings of the barometer at 9 A.M. and 9 P.M., corrected and reduced to 32° Fahrenheit at the mean sea level. The Mean Temperature values have been deduced from the maximal and minimal readings of the thermometer in the shade. The Rainfall is that measured daily at 9 A.M. A rainy day is one on which at least one-hundredth (·01) of an inch of rain falls within the twenty-four hours from 9 A.M. to 9 A.M.

The *Mean Height of the Barometer* during the year 1890 was 29·927 inches. The highest observed reading was 30·744 inches at 11 A.M. on February 23rd. The lowest observed reading was 28·483 inches, at 7·45 A.M. on January 22nd. The extreme range of atmospherical pressure was 2·081 inches compared with 1·940 inches in 1889.

The *Mean Temperature* of the year, deduced from the maximal and minimal readings of the thermometer in the shade was 49·8°. The highest reading was 74·8° on August 4th; the lowest reading was 24·1° on December 31st. The average mean temperature for the years 1870-89 calculated in the same way, was 48·6°. The mean temperature deduced from the daily readings of the dry bulb thermometer at 9 A.M. and 9 P.M. was 49·5°.

Rain fell on 200 days, including snow or sleet on 21 days, and hail on 23 days. The average number of rainy days in the years 1870-89 was 190·0. The total rainfall measured 27·562 inches, compared with an average of 27·068 inches in the twenty years 1870-89. During the first half of 1890 (January to June, inclusive) the rainfall was 12·413 inches on 94 days; during the second half (July to December, inclusive) 14·149 inches fell on 106 days.

As regards the *Direction of the Wind*, 730 observations were made during the year, with this result—N., 60; N.E., 41; E., 67; S.E., 61; S., 65; S.W., 119; W., 197; N.W., 96; Calm, 24.

Noxious Insects.

Noxious Insects.

The "Special Report on Insects, Fungi, and Weeds injurious to crops" by Mr. Matheson, the Secretary of this Department, mentioned in the report for 1889, was not issued until the autumn of last year. Several references to the injuries caused to crops by noxious Insects, &c., will be found in the Notes of the Superintendents of Enumeration.

As regards injury from insects, &c., to fruit and forest trees, it appears from the report of Mr. George H. Carpenter, Consulting Entomologist to the Royal Dublin Society, that the Millepede, *Julus guttatus*, Fab., has been observed causing injury to strawberries, and that the Wood Wasp, *Sirex gigas*, Linn., has been specially injurious during the year to firs and pines. Ravages on pine shoots by the grub of the Saw-fly, *Lophyrus pini*, Curt., and the Pine Weevil, *Hylobius abietis*, Linn., have also been noticed. In an interesting paper read before the Royal Dublin Society, Mr. Carpenter describes a new species of Moth, *Tortrix donelana*, found by Mr. D. O'C. Donelan, of Sylan, Tuam, the caterpillars of which caused much damage in the summers of 1889 and 1890 to a plantation of firs.

Comparing the produce of the crops in 1890 with 1889, Cereal Crops show an increase in oats of 163,667 cwts.; in beans of 9,528 cwts.; and in pease of 8,142 cwts.; while there was a decrease in wheat of 22,199 cwts.; in barley of 185,265 cwts.; in bere of 1,019 cwts.; and in rye of 34,305 cwts. Total produce in 1889 and 1890.

In Green Crops, there was a decrease in potatoes of 1,037,198 tons in 1890 compared with 1889, while there was an increase of 844,888 tons in turnips, of 41,449 tons in mangel wurzel and beet root, and of 1,594 tons in cabbage.

Flax shows an increase of 133,706 stones of 14 lbs.; hay on clover, sainfoin, and grasses under rotation, a decrease of 120,535 tons; and hay on permanent pasture or grass not broken up in rotation, a decrease of 139,678 tons.

The yield per acre of cereal crops in 1890 compared with that of 1889 shows an increase in oats of 0·4 cwt.; in bere of 0·5 cwt.; in beans of 5·2 cwts.; and in pease of 3·5 cwts.; while there was a decrease in barley of 0·7 cwt.; in wheat of 0·7 cwt., and in rye of 1·3 cwts. In other crops—potatoes show a decrease of 1·3 tons; and cabbage of 0·3 ton. Hay on clover, sainfoin, and grasses under rotation decreased by 0·1 ton, and hay on permanent pasture or grass not broken up in rotation, shows the same rate in both years. Flax shows an increase of 6·1 stones. Estimated average produce per acre in 1889 and 1890.

The *total produce* of the principal crops in 1889 and 1890, and the increase or decrease in the latter year, are given in Table VI.; the *average produce* per statute acre in Table VII.; and in Table VIII. are given the total extent under each of the principal crops, the *estimated average* yield per statute acre, and the total produce, for each year from 1881 to 1890, inclusive.

TABLE VI.—The *total produce* of the principal Crops in 1889 and 1890, and the increase or decrease in the latter year:— Produce of the Crops, 1889–90.

Crops.	Produce 1889.	Produce 1890.	Increase in 1890.	Decrease in 1890.
Wheat, Cwts. of 112 lbs.,	1,436,163	1,413,764	—	22,199
Oats, " "	17,[illegible]	17,[illegible]	163,667	—
Barley, " "	[illegible]	[illegible]	—	185,815
Bere, " "	[illegible]	[illegible]	—	1,019
Rye, " "	[illegible]	[illegible]	—	34,[illegible]
Beans, " "	67,370	[illegible]	9,[illegible]	—
Pease, " "	8,139	16,[illegible]	8,142	—
Potatoes, in Tons,	2,847,[illegible]	1,810,[illegible]	—	1,037,193
Turnips, "	3,[illegible]	4,[illegible],710	844,[illegible]	—
Mangel Wurzel and Beet Root, "	[illegible]	[illegible]	41,449	—
Cabbage, "	431,[illegible]	433,[illegible]	1,594	—
Flax, in Stones of 14 lbs.,	[illegible]	[illegible]	133,706	—
Hay, in Tons. Clover, Sainfoin, and Grasses under Rotation,	1,478,344	1,358,[illegible]	—	120,535
Hay, in Tons. Permanent Pasture or Grass not broken up in Rotation,	[illegible]	[illegible]	—	139,678

Average produce of Crops in 1889 and 1890.

TABLE VII.—The *estimated average produce* per statute acre of the principal crops in 1889 and 1890, and the *increase* or *decrease* in 1890 compared with 1889:—

Crops.		Produce per Statute Acre		Increase in 1890.	Decrease in 1890.
		1889.	1890.		
Wheat, in Cwts. of 112 lbs.,		16·0	15·3	—	0·7
Oats, " "		14·7	15·3	0·6	—
Barley, " "		17·5	16·8	—	0·7
Bere, " "		13·0	13·5	0·5	—
Rye, " "		13·4	11·6	—	1·8
Beans, " "		18·2	23·4	5·2	—
Peas, " "		12·1	15·7	3·6	—
Potatoes, in Tons,		3·5	2·3	—	1·2
Turnips, "		13·1	14·1	1·0	—
Mangel Wurzel and Beet Root, "		14·1	14·3	0·2	—
Cabbage, "		10·2	9·4	—	0·8
Flax, in Stones of 14 lbs.,		27·3	33·4	6·1	—
Hay, in Tons.	Clover, Sainfoin, and Grasses under Rotation,	2·2	2·1	—	0·1
	Permanent Pasture or Grass not broken up in Rotation,	2·2	2·2	—	—

Extent under Crops, produce, &c., 1881–90.

The further statement contained in Table VIII. gives a general view of the state of agriculture during the year 1890 as compared with preceding years.

Tables showing the total produce of the Crops in 1890, by counties and provinces, will be found at page 40, and by poor law unions at page 46. The average rates by counties and provinces for each year from 1881 to 1890, are given at pages 55 to 59.

TABLE VIII.—The extent under each of the principal Crops—the average Yield per Statute Acre, and the total Produce for all Ireland, in each year from 1881 to 1890, inclusive.

Years.	Wheat.	Oats.	Barley.	Bere.	Rye.	Potatoes.	Turnips.	Mangel Wurzel and Beet Root.	Cabbage.	Flax.	Hay.
	EXTENT UNDER CROPS IN STATUTE MEASURE.										
	Acres.	Acres.	Acres.	Acres.	Acres.	Acres.	Acres.	Acres.	Acres.	Acres.	Acres.
[illegible]	[illegible]	[illegible]	[illegible]	[illegible]	[illegible]	[illegible]	[illegible]	[illegible]	[illegible]	[illegible]	[illegible]
[illegible]	[illegible]	[illegible]	[illegible]	[illegible]	[illegible]	[illegible]	[illegible]	[illegible]	[illegible]	[illegible]	[illegible]
[illegible]	[illegible]	[illegible]	[illegible]	[illegible]	[illegible]	[illegible]	[illegible]	[illegible]	[illegible]	[illegible]	[illegible]
[illegible]	[illegible]	[illegible]	[illegible]	[illegible]	[illegible]	[illegible]	[illegible]	[illegible]	[illegible]	[illegible]	[illegible]
[illegible]	[illegible]	[illegible]	[illegible]	[illegible]	[illegible]	[illegible]	[illegible]	[illegible]	[illegible]	[illegible]	[illegible]
[illegible]	[illegible]	[illegible]	[illegible]	[illegible]	[illegible]	[illegible]	[illegible]	[illegible]	[illegible]	[illegible]	[illegible]
[illegible]	[illegible]	[illegible]	[illegible]	[illegible]	[illegible]	[illegible]	[illegible]	[illegible]	[illegible]	[illegible]	[illegible]
[illegible]	[illegible]	[illegible]	[illegible]	[illegible]	[illegible]	[illegible]	[illegible]	[illegible]	[illegible]	[illegible]	[illegible]
[illegible]	[illegible]	[illegible]	[illegible]	[illegible]	[illegible]	[illegible]	[illegible]	[illegible]	[illegible]	[illegible]	[illegible]
[illegible]	[illegible]	[illegible]	[illegible]	[illegible]	[illegible]	[illegible]	[illegible]	[illegible]	[illegible]	[illegible]	[illegible]
—	**ESTIMATED AVERAGE PRODUCE PER STATUTE ACRE.**										
	Cwts.	Cwts.	Cwts.	Cwts.	Cwts.	Tons.	Tons.	Tons.	Tons.	Stones of 14 lbs.	Tons.
[illegible]	[illegible]	[illegible]	[illegible]	[illegible]	[illegible]	[illegible]	[illegible]	[illegible]	[illegible]	[illegible]	[illegible]
[illegible]	[illegible]	[illegible]	[illegible]	[illegible]	[illegible]	[illegible]	[illegible]	[illegible]	[illegible]	[illegible]	[illegible]
[illegible]	[illegible]	[illegible]	[illegible]	[illegible]	[illegible]	[illegible]	[illegible]	[illegible]	[illegible]	[illegible]	[illegible]
[illegible]	[illegible]	[illegible]	[illegible]	[illegible]	[illegible]	[illegible]	[illegible]	[illegible]	[illegible]	[illegible]	[illegible]
[illegible]	[illegible]	[illegible]	[illegible]	[illegible]	[illegible]	[illegible]	[illegible]	[illegible]	[illegible]	[illegible]	[illegible]
[illegible]	[illegible]	[illegible]	[illegible]	[illegible]	[illegible]	[illegible]	[illegible]	[illegible]	[illegible]	[illegible]	[illegible]
[illegible]	[illegible]	[illegible]	[illegible]	[illegible]	[illegible]	[illegible]	[illegible]	[illegible]	[illegible]	[illegible]	[illegible]
[illegible]	[illegible]	[illegible]	[illegible]	[illegible]	[illegible]	[illegible]	[illegible]	[illegible]	[illegible]	[illegible]	[illegible]
[illegible]	[illegible]	[illegible]	[illegible]	[illegible]	[illegible]	[illegible]	[illegible]	[illegible]	[illegible]	[illegible]	[illegible]
[illegible]	[illegible]	[illegible]	[illegible]	[illegible]	[illegible]	[illegible]	[illegible]	[illegible]	[illegible]	[illegible]	[illegible]
—	**TOTAL PRODUCE.**										
	[illegible]	[illegible]	[illegible]	[illegible]	[illegible]	Tons.	Tons.	Tons.	Tons.	Tons.	Tons.
[illegible]	[illegible]	[illegible]	[illegible]	[illegible]	[illegible]	[illegible]	[illegible]	[illegible]	[illegible]	[illegible]	[illegible]
[illegible]	[illegible]	[illegible]	[illegible]	[illegible]	[illegible]	[illegible]	[illegible]	[illegible]	[illegible]	[illegible]	[illegible]
[illegible]	[illegible]	[illegible]	[illegible]	[illegible]	[illegible]	[illegible]	[illegible]	[illegible]	[illegible]	[illegible]	[illegible]
[illegible]	[illegible]	[illegible]	[illegible]	[illegible]	[illegible]	[illegible]	[illegible]	[illegible]	[illegible]	[illegible]	[illegible]
[illegible]	[illegible]	[illegible]	[illegible]	[illegible]	[illegible]	[illegible]	[illegible]	[illegible]	[illegible]	[illegible]	[illegible]
[illegible]	[illegible]	[illegible]	[illegible]	[illegible]	[illegible]	[illegible]	[illegible]	[illegible]	[illegible]	[illegible]	[illegible]
[illegible]	[illegible]	[illegible]	[illegible]	[illegible]	[illegible]	[illegible]	[illegible]	[illegible]	[illegible]	[illegible]	[illegible]
[illegible]	[illegible]	[illegible]	[illegible]	[illegible]	[illegible]	[illegible]	[illegible]	[illegible]	[illegible]	[illegible]	[illegible]
[illegible]	[illegible]	[illegible]	[illegible]	[illegible]	[illegible]	[illegible]	[illegible]	[illegible]	[illegible]	[illegible]	[illegible]
[illegible]	[illegible]	[illegible]	[illegible]	[illegible]	[illegible]	[illegible]	[illegible]	[illegible]	[illegible]	[illegible]	[illegible]

LIVE STOCK.

TABLE IX.—The Number and Ages of the Live Stock in Ireland, in 1889 and 1890, and the Increase or Decrease in each description :—

Number and Ages of Live Stock, 1889 and 1890.

Description of Stock.		Number in 1889.	Number in 1890.	Increase in 1890.	Decrease in 1890.
Horses,	Two years old and upwards,	497,307	498,832	1,525	—
	One year old and under two,	77,062	80,417	3,355	—
	Under one year,	61,895	76,933	6,028	—
Total No. of Horses,		574,264	584,872	10,608	—
Mules,		29,838	30,012	174	—
Asses,		208,236	213,018	4,782	—
Cattle,	Two years old and upwards,	2,274,058	2,317,706	43,648	—
	One year old and under two,	866,526	899,256	32,731	—
	Under one year,	953,601	1,023,304	69,703	—
Total No. of Cattle,		4,094,174	4,240,316	146,142	—
Sheep,	One year old and upwards,	2,363,446	2,620,286	256,840	—
	Under one year,	1,536,341	1,783,209	248,868	—
Total No. of Sheep,		3,899,787	4,403,495	504,808	—
Pigs,	One year old and upwards,	162,646	182,843	20,197	—
	Under one year,	1,218,024	1,381,023	163,899	—
Total No. of Pigs,		1,380,670	1,570,366	189,696	—
Goats,		303,933	337,144	33,211	—
Poultry,		14,858,517	15,408,428	551,911	—

Number of Live Stock.

At the period of the enumeration in 1890, the total number of horses in Ireland was 584,872, being an *increase* of 10,608 compared with 1889. There was an *increase* of 1,825 in the number "two years old and upwards," of 3,355 in the "one year old, and under two," and of 6,028 in those "under one year."

Mules numbered 30,012, being 174 more than in 1889, and asses 213,018, being an *increase* of 4,782 as compared with the previous year.

Horses, Mules and Asses taken together numbered 761,889 in 1881, and 827,902 in 1890, being an *increase* of 66,013 or 8·7 per cent.

Cattle numbered 4,240,316 in 1890, showing a total *increase* of 146,142 as compared with the number enumerated in 1889; there was an *increase* of 43,658 in the "two years old and upwards;" of 32,731 in the "one year old and under two," and of 69,703 in the number "under one year." Taking the ten years 1881 to 1890, cattle *increased* in number from 3,956,595 in 1881, to 4,928,851 in 1885, *decreased* in each of the four following years, but *increased* in 1890, the number being 4,240,316 as already stated.

Number of Live Stock.

Sheep amounted to 4,322,395 in 1890, showing an increase of 534,208, as compared with the previous year; the "one year old and upwards" increased by 265,540, and those "under one year" by 218,668.

Comparing 1881 with 1890 there has been an increase in the number of sheep from 3,256,185 in the former, to 4,322,395 in the latter year.

Pigs were returned as 1,570,366 in 1890, showing an increase of 189,696, or 13·7 per cent. as compared with the previous year. The "one year old and upwards" increased by 20,697, and those "under one year" by 168,999.

Comparing the number of pigs returned in the ten years from 1881 to 1890, the highest number, 1,570,366, was enumerated in 1890, and the lowest, 1,095,830, in 1881.

Goats numbered 327,144 in 1890, being 23,311 more than in 1889, and 61,066 more than in 1881.

Poultry

The number of poultry in 1890 was 15,408,428, being 553,911 more than in 1889, and 1,436,009 more than in 1881. Of the 15,408,428 poultry in 1890, 1,026,646 were turkeys; 2,211,135 geese; 3,001,611 ducks; and 9,169,036 ordinary fowl.

Compared with 1889, turkeys increased by 41,192, geese by 60,551, ducks by 89,674, and ordinary fowl by 360,291.

Number of Live Stock, 1881 to 1890.

TABLE X.—The Number of Live Stock in Ireland, in each year from 1881 to 1890, inclusive:—

Years.	Horses and Mules.	Asses.	Cattle.	Sheep.	Pigs.	Goats.	Poultry.
1881, . .	574,746	187,143	3,956,595	3,256,185	1,095,830	266,078	13,972,494
1882, . .	568,925	187,762	3,987,211	3,071,786	1,430,189	243,579	13,299,098
1883, . .	561,437	180,760	4,096,938	3,219,311	1,346,584	265,160	13,982,430
1884, . .	549,430	181,330	4,118,769	3,048,919	1,326,850	254,411	13,717,460
1885, . .	578,630	187,170	4,228,611	3,478,056	1,269,093	264,477	13,640,532
1886, . .	578,850	189,346	4,183,914	3,364,045	1,263,145	258,174	13,909,025
1887, . .	587,834	190,613	4,167,404	3,377,685	1,408,434	271,720	14,460,448
1888, . .	596,368	203,187	4,089,103	3,618,669	1,387,893	286,870	14,186,409
1889, . .	604,103	208,336	4,094,174	3,788,187	1,380,670	303,833	14,854,517
1890, . .	614,686	213,016	4,240,318	4,322,395	1,570,366	327,144	15,408,428

Number of Live Stock, 1881 to 1890.

TABLE XI.—The proportion per cent. of Horses, Cattle, Sheep, and Pigs in Ireland according to Age, for the years 1881 to 1890, inclusive:—

Years.	Horses.			Cattle.			Sheep.		Pigs.	
	Percentage at each age.			Percentage at each age.			Percentage at each age.		Percentage at each age.	
	Two Years old and upwards.	One Year old and under Two.	Under One Year.	Two Years old and upwards.	One Year old and under Two.	Under One Year.	One Year old and upwards.	Under One Year.	One Year old and upwards.	Under One Year.
1881, .	79·2	11·4	9·4	57·9	19·9	22·2	64·5	35·5	13·7	86·3
1882, .	79·6	10·4	10·0	57·0	19·9	23·1	63·0	37·0	13·2	86·8
1883, .	79·2	10·5	10·3	55·3	20·6	24·1	61·7	38·3	13·4	86·6
1884, .	78·0	11·1	10·9	55·9	21·5	22·6	62·5	37·5	12·5	87·5
1885, .	76·5	11·9	11·6	56·0	20·6	23·4	61·6	38·4	12·7	87·3
1886, .	76·3	12·3	11·4	56·7	21·0	22·3	61·7	38·3	12·7	87·3
1887, .	75·5	12·8	11·7	55·7	20·8	23·5	60·2	39·8	12·8	87·2
1888, .	74·6	13·1	12·3	55·3	21·3	23·4	59·6	40·4	12·2	87·8
1889, .	74·4	13·4	12·2	55·5	21·3	23·2	59·5	40·5	12·4	87·6
1890, .	73·3	13·7	13·0	54·7	21·2	24·1	58·7	41·3	12·1	87·9

ENTIRE HORSES.

In connexion with the Agricultural Statistics for 1890, a return was received from each Enumerator, but on former occasions only one return was received from each District. Entire Horses.

As the classification of the sires in the Return for 1890 differs in several details from that used in former years, the numbers are not in all cases directly comparable.

Table A. (pages 74–5) shows by counties and provinces the number of sires serving mares in Ireland.

The total number of sires returned in 1890 is 1,925, against 1,230 in 1886, being an increase of 695.

The number for 1890 comprises 667 Thoroughbreds, 464 Halfbreds, 25 Hackneys, 6 Shires, 221 Clydesdales, 472 Agricultural, and 80 of all other breeds.* 1,637 were bred in Ireland, and 288 were imported.

The number of "Thoroughbred" horses (667) exhibits an increase of 336 between 1886 and 1890.

Those returned as Half-bred (464) show an increase of 31 between 1886 and 1890.

The Clydesdale class shows a decrease of 69 between 1886 and 1890.

MILCH COWS.

TABLE XII.—The following statement shows the number of Milch Cows in Ireland in each year from 1854—the first year in which Milch Cows were separately enumerated—to 1890. The average number for the first five years of the period was 1,579,851, and for the last five years 1,392,372, being a decline of 187,479 or 11·9 per cent. The highest number in any one year was 1,690,369 in 1859, and the lowest 1,316,856 in 1884. Milch Cows.

Years.	No. of Milch Cows.	Years.	No. of Milch Cows.	Years.	No. of Milch Cows.	Years.	No. of Milch Cows.
1854, .	1,517,677	1864, .	1,348,696	1873, .	1,575,138	1882, .	1,379,065
1855, .	1,381,796	1865, .	1,387,448	1874, .	1,421,375	1883, .	1,402,314
1856, .	1,579,839	1866, .	1,482,616	1875, .	1,530,358	1884, .	1,316,856
1857, .	1,606,350	1867, .	1,531,035	1876, .	1,532,774	1885, .	1,417,439
1858, .	1,635,109	1868, .	1,476,359	1877, .	1,572,511	1886, .	1,416,644
1859, .	1,690,369	1869, .	1,506,038	1878, .	1,484,616	1887, .	1,394,133
1860, .	1,576,453	1870, .	1,519,094	1879, .	1,464,618	1888, .	1,364,771
1861, .	1,545,166	1871, .	1,543,469	1880, .	1,329,067	1889, .	1,363,781
1862, .	1,486,835	1872, .	1,561,714	1881, .	1,393,012	1890, .	[illegible]
1863, .	1,396,974						

* Under the heading "All other Breeds" in this Return are included—

One Arab and 1 Cleveland in Carlow; 1 Pony in Dublin; 1 Pony, 1 Cleveland, 1 Common Breed, and 6 Irish Breed in Kilkenny; 1 Connemara Pony, 1 Half Bred Norwegian Pony, 1 Thoroughbred Norwegian Pony, and 1 pedigree unknown in King's County; 1 "Lotherian" in Longford; 1 Norfolk Trotter in Louth; 1 Pony and 1 "not known" in Meath; 1 Pony in Queen's County; 1 Arab Pony in Wexford; 3 Half Bred Suffolk, 1 Suffolk Punch and 1 Pure Bred Welsh in Wicklow; 1 Connemara Pony in Clare; 2 Suffolk Punch and 1 English in Cork, E.R.; 2 Suffolk Punch in Cork, W.R.; 1 Suffolk Punch in Kerry; 3 Trotting, 1 Shetland, and 1 Connemara Pony in Tipperary, N.R.; 1 Highland Stallion in Antrim; 1 Norfolk and 1 Suffolk Punch in Armagh; 1 "Coaching Horse" in Donegal; 1 Half Bred Cleveland in Down; 1 "Forester" in Fermanagh; 3 "Coaching" in Londonderry; 1 Thoroughbred Welsh and 4 unspecified in Tyrone; 2 Connemara Ponies and 1 unspecified in Galway; 1 Scotch and 1 Half Bred Cleveland in Mayo.

BULLS.

It having been considered desirable to ascertain the number of Bulls serving cows in Ireland in 1890, a circular was issued asking for the following particulars:—Name of Bull; Breed—whether "Shorthorn," "Hereford," "Aberdeen Angus," "Norfolk and Suffolk Red Polled," "Kerry," "Dexter," "Jersey," "Guernsey," "cross-Bred," &c.; Age; whether imported or bred in Ireland; the place where the Bull is kept, and name and address of owner.

Table D (pages 76–7) shows by counties and provinces the number of such Bulls returned.

It appears from this Table that there were 6,714 bulls serving cows in Ireland in 1890; of these 1,630 were in Leinster, 2,024 in Munster, 2,125 in Ulster, and 935 in Connaught.

The numbers of the various breeds are as follow:—"Shorthorn," 4,273; "Hereford," 117; "Aberdeen-Angus," 131; Norfolk and Suffolk Red Polled," 19; "Kerry," 107; "Dexter," 21; "Jersey," 44; "Guernsey," 19; "Cross-bred," 1,662; and "All other Breeds," 338.*

Tables showing the number of Live Stock in 1890, by counties and provinces, will be found at page 60; by Poor Law Unions at pages 61–4; and by counties and provinces for each year from 1881 to 1890 at page 65.

DISEASES OF CATTLE.

The following information is extracted from returns compiled in pursuance of the provisions of the 39th section of the Contagious Diseases (Animals) Act, 1878, for the year ended the 31st December, 1890.

The returns show a decrease in the number of outbreaks of Pleuro-Pneumonia in the year 1890, there having been 240 outbreaks in 1887, 181 in 1888, 108 in 1889, and 95 in 1890.

Ireland continues to be free from Foot-and-Mouth Disease. No case has occurred since the year 1884.

There has been an increase in the number of outbreaks of Swine Fever reported in 1890, as compared with the previous year, the figures being 365 in the year 1890, and 273 in 1889. The number of outbreaks in the year 1890, however, was less than in 1888, in which year there were 392 outbreaks.

Nineteen cases of Glanders were reported during the year.

No case of Farcy was reported.

There were 17 outbreaks of Anthrax during the year, as compared with 21 in the previous year, and 25 in 1888.

The returns show that 838 cases of Rabies were reported in 1890, as compared with 405 in 1889, and 561 in 1888.

* Under the heading "All other Breeds" in this Return are included—

Four Common and 1 unknown in Carlow; 3 Devon, 3 Polled, 1 Dutch, 1 Ayrshire, and 1 Anglesey in Dublin; 9 not known, 1 Irish Breed, and 1 Devonshire in Kildare; 1 Devonshire and 1 "Thoroughbred" in Kilkenny; 1 Longhorn, 1 unknown, 1 unspecified, and 1 Polled Anglesey in King's County; 2 Durhams in Longford; 7 Ayrshire, 1 Berkshire, 1 Shorthorned Durham, 1 Alderney, and 1 unspecified in Louth; 2 Durham, 1 Dutch, and 4 unspecified in Meath; 1 Durham and 1 unspecified in Westmeath; 1 Common and 3 not known in Wicklow; 4 Common, 2 Durham, 8 Dutch, 1 Ayrshire, 1 Alderney, and 1 not known in Clare; 2 Dutch and 3 Common in Cork, E.R.; 4 Ayrshire, 1 Yorkshire, 1 Durham, 1 Common, and 4 not known in Cork, W.R.; 3 Ayrshire and 1 Crosby Herd in Kerry; 3 Durham, 1 Devon, 1 Alderney, 1 Polled, 1 Crosby, and 17 not known in Limerick; 1 Polled, 4 Ordinary, 9 unknown, and 1 unspecified in Tipperary, N.R.; 2 Red Old Irish Breed, 1 Thoroughbred, and 4 not known in Tipperary, S.R.; 3 Common in Waterford; 13 Durham, 4 Ayrshire, 8 Galloway, 1 Polled Galloway, 1 Black Galloway, 1 Normandy, 1 Polled, 1 Common Irish and 5 not known in Antrim; 2 Devon, 3 Ayrshire, 2 Alderney, 1 Polled, and 2 unspecified in Armagh; 23 Durham, 8 Ayrshire, 1 Devon, and 6 unknown in Cavan; 8 Ayrshire, 3 Durham, 1 Longhorn, 1 Half Bred Yorkshire, 1 Half Bred Highland, 1 Galloway, 1 Polled Galloway, 1 Black Polled and 1 Common in Donegal; 3 Durham, 2 Alderney, 2 Devon, 1 Ayrshire, and 6 not known in Down; 1 Devon Red, 1 Devon Gray, 1 Durham, and 8 unknown in Fermanagh; 6 Durham, 7 Galloway, 4 Ayrshire and 3 Polled in Londonderry; 3 Devon, 1 Durham, 1 Alderney, and 1 unspecified in Monaghan; 7 Ayrshire, 4 Black Polled, 3 Durham, 9 Devon, 8 Galloway, 1 Durham, 1 Highland, and 3 unknown in Tyrone; 5 Old Irish, 4 Galloway, 4 Polled, 6 Black Polled, 1 Durham, 1 Commons, and 3 unspecified in Galway; 3 Durham, 1 Yorkshire, 1 Polled, 1 Black Polled, and 2 unknown in Leitrim; 7 Kyloes, 4 Common, 5 Polled, 5 Galloway, 8 Scotch Breed, and 1 unspecified in Mayo; 3 Devonshire, 1 Polled, and 4 unknown in Roscommon; 2 unknown in Sligo.

PRICES OF AGRICULTURAL PRODUCE.

The following Table is taken from Returns of the Average Prices of Agricultural Produce collected by the Irish Land Commission for the years 1887, 1888, 1889, and 1890, respectively :—

Produce.	Average Price for the year 1887.	Average Price for the year 1888.	Average Price for the year 1889.	Average Prices for the Year 1890: Quarter ending 31 March.	Quarter ending 30 June.	Quarter ending 30 Sept.	Quarter ending 31 Dec.	Whole Year 1890.
	s. d.	s. d.	s.	s. d.	s. d.	s. d.	s. d.	s. d.
CROPS :—								
Wheat, per cwt.,	[illegible]	[illegible]	[illegible]	[illegible]	[illegible]	[illegible]	[illegible]	[illegible]
Oats, „	[illegible]	[illegible]	[illegible]	[illegible]	[illegible]	[illegible]	[illegible]	[illegible]
Barley, „	[illegible]	[illegible]	[illegible]	[illegible]	[illegible]	[illegible]	[illegible]	[illegible]
Flax, per stone,	[illegible]	[illegible]	[illegible]	[illegible]	[illegible]	[illegible]	[illegible]	[illegible]
Potatoes, per cwt.,	[illegible]	[illegible]	[illegible]	[illegible]	[illegible]	[illegible]	[illegible]	[illegible]
Hay, „	[illegible]	[illegible]	[illegible]	[illegible]	[illegible]	[illegible]	[illegible]	[illegible]
BUTTER,	[illegible]	[illegible]	[illegible]	[illegible]	[illegible]	[illegible]	[illegible]	[illegible]
BEEF,	[illegible]	[illegible]	[illegible]	[illegible]	[illegible]	[illegible]	[illegible]	[illegible]
MUTTON,	[illegible]	[illegible]	[illegible]	[illegible]	[illegible]	[illegible]	[illegible]	[illegible]
PORK (Fresh),	[illegible]	[illegible]	[illegible]	[illegible]	[illegible]	[illegible]	[illegible]	[illegible]
WOOL, per lb.,	[illegible]	[illegible]	[illegible]	[illegible]	[illegible]	[illegible]	[illegible]	[illegible]
	£ s. d.	£ s. d.	£ s. d.	£ s. d.	£ s. d.	£ s. d.	£ s. d.	£ s. d.
CATTLE :—	[illegible]							
1st Class—One year old,		[illegible]	[illegible]	[illegible]	[illegible]	[illegible]	[illegible]	[illegible]
„ Two years old,		[illegible]	[illegible]	[illegible]	[illegible]	[illegible]	[illegible]	[illegible]
„ Three years old,		[illegible]	[illegible]	[illegible]	[illegible]	[illegible]	[illegible]	[illegible]
„ Springers,		[illegible]	[illegible]	[illegible]	[illegible]	[illegible]	[illegible]	[illegible]
2nd Class—One year old,		[illegible]	[illegible]	[illegible]	[illegible]	[illegible]	[illegible]	[illegible]
„ Two years old,		[illegible]	[illegible]	[illegible]	[illegible]	[illegible]	[illegible]	[illegible]
„ Three years old,		[illegible]	[illegible]	[illegible]	[illegible]	[illegible]	[illegible]	[illegible]
„ Springers,		[illegible]	[illegible]	[illegible]	[illegible]	[illegible]	[illegible]	[illegible]
3rd Class—One year old,		[illegible]	[illegible]	[illegible]	[illegible]	[illegible]	[illegible]	[illegible]
„ Two years old,		[illegible]	[illegible]	[illegible]	[illegible]	[illegible]	[illegible]	[illegible]
„ Three years old,		[illegible]	[illegible]	[illegible]	[illegible]	[illegible]	[illegible]	[illegible]
„ Springers,		[illegible]	[illegible]	[illegible]	[illegible]	[illegible]	[illegible]	[illegible]
	s. d.	s. d.	s. d.	s. d.	s. d.	s. d.	s. d.	s. d.
SHEEP :—								
Lambs,	[illegible]	[illegible]	[illegible]	—	[illegible]	[illegible]	[illegible]	[illegible]
Hoggets,	—	—	—	—	[illegible]	[illegible]	[illegible]	[illegible]
Two years old and over,	—	—	—	—	[illegible]	[illegible]	[illegible]	[illegible]

EXPORTS AND IMPORTS OF LIVE STOCK.

Exports of Live Stock. With the view of giving a more accurate idea of the number of live stock produced in Ireland the following statement has been extracted from the Statistical Returns published in the Report for 1890 under the "Contagious Diseases (Animals) Act, 1878."

Number of Cattle, Sheep, and Swine, exported from Ireland to Great Britain during each of the sixteen years, 1875–90:—

Years.	Cattle.						Sheep.			Swine.			Years.
	Oxen, Bulls, and Cows.				Calves.	Total.	Sheep.	Lambs.	Total.	Fat Swine.	Store Swine.	Total.	
	Fat Cattle.	Store Cattle for fattening or breeding purposes.	Other Cattle.	Total.									
1875,	[illegible]	[illegible]	[illegible]	[illegible]	[illegible]	[illegible]	[illegible]	[illegible]	[illegible]	[illegible]	[illegible]	[illegible]	1875.
1876,	[illegible]	[illegible]	[illegible]	[illegible]	[illegible]	[illegible]	[illegible]	[illegible]	[illegible]	[illegible]	[illegible]	[illegible]	1876.
1877,	[illegible]	[illegible]	[illegible]	[illegible]	[illegible]	[illegible]	[illegible]	[illegible]	[illegible]	[illegible]	[illegible]	[illegible]	1877.
1878,	[illegible]	[illegible]	[illegible]	[illegible]	[illegible]	[illegible]	[illegible]	[illegible]	[illegible]	[illegible]	[illegible]	[illegible]	1878.
1879,	[illegible]	[illegible]	[illegible]	[illegible]	[illegible]	[illegible]	[illegible]	[illegible]	[illegible]	[illegible]	[illegible]	[illegible]	1879.
1880,	[illegible]	[illegible]	[illegible]	[illegible]	[illegible]	[illegible]	[illegible]	[illegible]	[illegible]	[illegible]	[illegible]	[illegible]	1880.
1881,	[illegible]	[illegible]	[illegible]	[illegible]	[illegible]	[illegible]	[illegible]	[illegible]	[illegible]	[illegible]	[illegible]	[illegible]	1881.
1882,	[illegible]	[illegible]	[illegible]	[illegible]	[illegible]	[illegible]	[illegible]	[illegible]	[illegible]	[illegible]	[illegible]	[illegible]	1882.
1883,	[illegible]	[illegible]	[illegible]	[illegible]	[illegible]	[illegible]	[illegible]	[illegible]	[illegible]	[illegible]	[illegible]	[illegible]	1883.
1884,	[illegible]	[illegible]	[illegible]	[illegible]	[illegible]	[illegible]	[illegible]	[illegible]	[illegible]	[illegible]	[illegible]	[illegible]	1884.
1885,	[illegible]	[illegible]	[illegible]	[illegible]	[illegible]	[illegible]	[illegible]	[illegible]	[illegible]	[illegible]	[illegible]	[illegible]	1885.
1886,	[illegible]	[illegible]	[illegible]	[illegible]	[illegible]	[illegible]	[illegible]	[illegible]	[illegible]	[illegible]	[illegible]	[illegible]	1886.
1887,	[illegible]	[illegible]	[illegible]	[illegible]	[illegible]	[illegible]	[illegible]	[illegible]	[illegible]	[illegible]	[illegible]	[illegible]	1887.
1888,	[illegible]	[illegible]	[illegible]	[illegible]	[illegible]	[illegible]	[illegible]	[illegible]	[illegible]	[illegible]	[illegible]	[illegible]	1888.
1889,	[illegible]	[illegible]	[illegible]	[illegible]	[illegible]	[illegible]	[illegible]	[illegible]	[illegible]	[illegible]	[illegible]	[illegible]	1889.
1890,	[illegible]	[illegible]	[illegible]	[illegible]	[illegible]	[illegible]	[illegible]	[illegible]	[illegible]	[illegible]	[illegible]	[illegible]	1890.

From the foregoing it is evident that some of the younger animals included in the Statistics of Exports must of necessity escape enumeration in June of each year when the returns of live stock are collected for this Department. Viewing the number of animals exported in relation to those enumerated, it is found that in cattle the number exported bears a relation of 14·9 per cent. to those enumerated in 1890, as compared with 15·4 per cent. in 1889; in sheep 14·7 per cent. as compared with 16·9 per cent. in 1889; and in pigs 38·4 per cent. as compared with 34·3 per cent. in 1889.

From the same Report it appears that the number of horses exported in 1890 amounted to 34,152, equal to 5·8 per cent. of those enumerated.

Imports of Live Stock. It also appears that during the same period there were imported into Ireland, 3,913 horses, 432 cattle, 34,287 sheep, and 189 pigs.

HONEY PRODUCED IN 1889.

Honey produced in 1889. In connexion with the Agricultural Statistics for 1890, Returns were obtained of the amount of Honey produced in the year 1889, and of the number of swarms at work. Tables compiled from the information contained in these Returns are given in the Produce Report presented to Parliament in December of last year.

According to the returns received there would appear to have been an increase of 11·3 per cent. in the number of swarms of bees at work, the respective numbers for 1888 and 1889 being 26,447 and 29,396; and an increase of 29·4 per cent. in the quantity of Honey (424,588 lbs.), produced in 1889, as compared with that produced in 1888 (328,098 lbs.)

Of the 424,588 lbs. of Honey produced in 1889, 218,508 lbs. were produced "in hives having movable frames," and 206,080 lbs. "in other hives." It was stated that 237,046 lbs. was "run honey," and 187,542 lbs. "section honey."

The average number of lbs. of honey to each hive having a movable frame was 20 lbs., the average number of lbs. to each of the other hives was 11 lbs., and the average quantity produced in all hives was 14 lbs. Honey produced in 1889.

The number of stocks brought through the winter of 1889–90 amounted to 24,665, of which 9,994 were in hives having movable frames, and 14,671 in other hives; the stocks brought through the winter of 1888–9 numbered 21,486, showing an increase in 1889–90 of 3,179 stocks.

According to the returns collected there were 7,536 lbs. of wax manufactured in 1889, of which 2,681 lbs. were from hives having movable frames, and 4,855 lbs. from other hives; in 1888 the quantity manufactured was 7,751 lbs., showing a decrease of 215 lbs. in 1889 as compared with 1888.

AGRICULTURAL MACHINERY.

Agricultural Machines.—A return of the number of Agricultural Machines in Ireland was taken in connexion with the Agricultural Statistics for 1890. On page 78 will be found a table showing the number of the different kinds of these Implements in 1865, 1875, 1881, 1880, and 1890. From this table it will be seen that churning machines (2,796) show an increase of 1,948 between 1865 and 1890. Mowing machines and combined mowing and reaping machines numbered 11,530 in 1890, being an increase of 10,445 since 1865, when the number was 1,085. Reaping machines increased by 1,644 between 1865 and 1890, the respective numbers for these years being 412 and 2,056. Threshing machines numbered 9,180 in 1865, 12,410 in 1875, 18,295 in 1881, 7,048 in 1886, and 7,894 in 1890. Agricultural Machinery.

SCUTCHING MILLS.

The number of Mills for scutching Flax in Ireland in 1890 was 1,059, being a decrease of 8 compared with 1889, and a decrease of 119 since the year 1881. 1,043 of these Mills in 1890 were in Ulster, 6 in Munster, 3 in Connaught, and 7 in Leinster. There were 429 Mills with from 1 to 4 stocks; 335 having 5 or 6; 266 with from 7 to 12; 29 having from 13 to 18, and 3 having above 18 stocks; 838 were worked by water power; 150 by steam; and 71 by water and steam. The total number of Stocks in Ireland in 1890 amounted to 6,470, and of this number 6,363 were in Mills situated in Ulster. Scutching Mills, 1890.

The following is the number of Scutching Mills, in each year, from 1881 to 1890, inclusive, by Provinces:— Scutching Mills, 1881 to 1890.

Provinces.	1881.	1882.	1883.	1884.	1885.	1886.	1887.	1888.	1889.	1890.
Leinster, . .	9	7	5	9	7	7	7	6	7	7
Munster, . .	16	19	16	13	8	8	8	4	4	5
Ulster, . .	1,138	1,114	1,089	1,050	1,007	1,033	1,053	1,058	1,048	1,045
Connaught, . .	13	12	10	4	9	5	8	8	5	8
Ireland, .	1,178	1,152	1,123	1,116	1,025	1,063	1,078	1,070	1,063	1,059

Scutching Mills, 1890.

Number of Scutching Mills in 1890, by Counties and Provinces, classified according to the number of Stocks in each Mill, and the Power used in working them; with the Total Number of Stocks in each County:—

Provinces and Counties in which there were Scutching Mills.	Power Employed.					Total No. of Mills.	Classification of Mills.					Total No. of Stocks.
	Water.	Steam.	Water and Steam.	Horse.	Wind.		Having 1, 2, 3 or 4 Stocks.	Having 5 to 8 Stocks.	Having above 8 and not exceeding 12 Stocks.	Having above 12 and not exceeding 16 Stocks.	Having above 16 Stocks.	
Leinster:												
Longford, . .	1	.	.	.	.	1	.	.	.	1	.	14
Louth & Drogheda,												
Co. of Town, .	3	3	.	.	.	6	.	.	6	.	.	50
Meath, . .	1	.	1	.	.	2	.	1	1	.	.	14
Total, . .	4	3	1	.	.	7	.	1	6	1	.	64
Munster:												
Cork, . . .	6	.	1	.	.	8	3	1	1	.	.	33
Total, . .	6	.	1	.	.	8	3	1	1	.	.	33
Ulster:												
Antrim, . .	119	6	6	.	.	133	65	66	53	1	.	749
Armagh, . .	77	16	4	.	.	97	6	45	38	8	1	763
Cavan, . .	38	7	.	.	.	45	9	20	15	.	1	311
Donegal, . .	151	8	8	.	.	163	124	24	15	.	.	850
Down, . .	107	39	24	.	.	170	29	64	76	8	.	1,360
Fermanagh, .	31	2	2	.	.	35	13	6	5	8	.	143
Londonderry, .	167	8	9	.	.	184	68	87	19	.	.	888
Monaghan, . .	49	13	7	.	.	78	23	30	33	3	.	634
Tyrone, . .	133	31	9	.	.	173	85	46	37	8	.	978
Total, . .	819	127	89	.	.	1,045	425	336	256	37	2	6,383
Connaught:												
Leitrim, . .	1	.	.	.	.	1	.	.	1	.	.	8
Mayo, . .	.	1	.	.	.	1	.	.	1	.	.	11
Total, . .	1	1	.	.	.	2	.	.	2	.	.	19
Total of Ireland,	839	130	71	.	.	1,059	429	338	260	39	5	6,470

SILOS AND ENSILAGE.

Silos and Ensilage.

Following the course adopted in the three previous years relative to Ensilage, I communicated with those Landed Proprietors and Landholders, throughout the country, having Silos or otherwise making Ensilage, requesting them to favour me with certain details regarding the methods followed and the results obtained in the year 1890. I received replies to 261 out of 378 circulars issued by me, and I beg to express my obligations to my correspondents for the valuable and interesting information afforded. It will be found set forth in the Appendix, pp. 92 to 145.

The following Table shows, by Counties and Provinces, the number of Silos or Stacks mentioned in the communications received from the persons who forwarded replies to the circular above referred to:—

Counties.	Number in [illegible]	Number in [illegible]	Counties.	Number in [illegible]	Number in [illegible]
Antrim,	27	22	Mayo,	14	9
Armagh,	1	1	Meath,	63	67
Carlow,	6	1	Monaghan,	2	1
Cavan,	3	6	Queen's,	12	19
Clare,	9	8	Roscommon,	8	8
			Sligo,	8	1
Cork,	24	18			
Donegal,	13	10	Tipperary,	24	19
Down,	3	7	Tyrone,	18	13
Dublin,	10	8	Waterford,	10	9
Fermanagh,	8	4	Westmeath,	4	14
			Wexford,	10	2
Galway,	16	14	Wicklow,	10	7
Kerry,	8	5			
Kildare,	14	17	Provinces.		
Kilkenny,	15	16			
King's,	29	25	Leinster,	175	186
			Munster,	91	78
Leitrim,	8	19	Ulster,	93	82
Limerick,	16	31	Connaught,	45	45
Londonderry,	31	17			
Longford,	4	10			
Louth,	6	3	Total of Ireland,	404	401

FORESTRY OPERATIONS.

Forestry Operations.

In view of the interest attaching to this subject in later years, inquiries into Forestry Operations were instituted in 1890: the details are set forth in the General Abstract of Forestry Operations in Ireland during the year ended 30th June, 1890. The subjects of investigation were—I. Planting—The area planted during the year ended 30th June, 1890, the total number of trees planted in that period, and the number of each description; II. Felling—The area cleared and the number of trees of each description felled; III. Ages of trees felled; IV. Disposal of timber. The inquiry did not extend to the planting or felling of isolated trees.

It appears that during the period 1851–90 there was some slight fluctuation in the acreage, and that comparing 1890 with 1851 there has been an increase of about 7 per cent., the extent under woods and plantations in 1851 being 304,906 statute acres, and in last year 327,461 acres.

During the year ended 30th June, 1890, 1,488 acres were planted with trees. Larch trees constituted more than one-third, and fir trees about 12 per cent. of the total number planted.

In connection with this subject it may be here mentioned that 109 loans for £74,270 have been sanctioned for planting for shelter since the passing of the Act, 29 & 30 Vict., cap. 40, and of this number 3, amounting to £2,050, were sanctioned in the year ended 31st March, 1890.

The number of trees felled both for clearance and for thinning plantations amounted to 1,256,887. It would appear that about one-half of the total number felled consisted of larch trees. The area returned as cleared is 1,899 acres.

Of the 1,256,887 trees felled, 798,805 were used for "propping," which appears to have been the chief purpose to which the timber of almost all descriptions was applied. The numbers applied to the principal specified uses comprise also:—64,104 trees (including 80,434 larch and 12,033 oak), for sleepers, 60,598 (chiefly larch) for paling, 23,288 for spools, &c., 80,808 for furniture and building purposes, 19,348 for carts, wagons, &c., 10,374 for clog soles, 11,590 (mainly oak from the County Wicklow), for ship-building, and 5,750 for telegraph and telephone poles.

WAGES OF AGRICULTURAL LABOURERS IN 1890.

Enquiries were made as to the Wages paid to Agricultural Labourers in 1890, and the information received from the District Inspectors of the Royal Irish Constabulary with reference to their respective districts is shown in the following Table and notes appended thereto.

I.—PROVINCE OF LEINSTER.

Counties and Constabulary Districts.	Summer.								Winter.							
	Men.		Boys.		Women.		Girls.		Men.		Boys.		Women.		Girls.	
	From	To	From	To	From	To	From	To	From	To	From	To	From	To	From	To
	s. d.	s. d.	s. d.	s. d.	s. d.	s. d.	s. d.	s. d.	s. d.	s. d.	s. d.	s. d.	s. d.	s. d.	s. d.	s. d.
Carlow County.																
[illegible]	[illegible]	[illegible]	[illegible]	[illegible]	[illegible]	[illegible]	[illegible]	[illegible]	[illegible]	[illegible]	[illegible]	[illegible]	[illegible]	[illegible]	[illegible]	[illegible]
Carlow,	[illegible]	[illegible]	[illegible]	[illegible]	[illegible]	[illegible]	[illegible]	[illegible]	[illegible]	[illegible]	[illegible]	[illegible]	[illegible]	[illegible]	[illegible]	[illegible]
Dublin County.																
[illegible]	[illegible]	[illegible]	[illegible]	[illegible]	[illegible]	[illegible]	[illegible]	[illegible]	[illegible]	[illegible]	[illegible]	[illegible]	[illegible]	[illegible]	[illegible]	[illegible]
[illegible]	[illegible]	[illegible]	[illegible]	[illegible]	[illegible]	[illegible]	None employed		[illegible]	[illegible]	[illegible]	[illegible]	[illegible]	[illegible]	None employed	
[illegible]	[illegible]	[illegible]	[illegible]	[illegible]	[illegible]	[illegible]	[illegible]	[illegible]	[illegible]	[illegible]	[illegible]	[illegible]	[illegible]	[illegible]	[illegible]	[illegible]
[illegible]	[illegible]	[illegible]	[illegible]	[illegible]	[illegible]	[illegible]	[illegible]	[illegible]	[illegible]	[illegible]	[illegible]	[illegible]	[illegible]	[illegible]	[illegible]	[illegible]
Kildare County.																
Athy,	[illegible]	[illegible]	[illegible]	[illegible]	[illegible]	[illegible]	[illegible]	[illegible]	[illegible]	[illegible]	[illegible]	[illegible]	[illegible]	[illegible]	[illegible]	[illegible]
Kildare,	[illegible]	[illegible]	[illegible]	[illegible]	[illegible]	[illegible]	[illegible]	[illegible]	[illegible]	[illegible]	[illegible]	[illegible]	[illegible]	[illegible]	[illegible]	[illegible]
Naas,	[illegible]	[illegible]	[illegible]	[illegible]	[illegible]	[illegible]	[illegible]	[illegible]	[illegible]	[illegible]	[illegible]	[illegible]	[illegible]	[illegible]	[illegible]	[illegible]
[illegible]	[illegible]	[illegible]	[illegible]	[illegible]	[illegible]	[illegible]	[illegible]	[illegible]	[illegible]	[illegible]	[illegible]	[illegible]	[illegible]	[illegible]	[illegible]	[illegible]
Kilkenny County.																
Callan,	[illegible]	[illegible]	[illegible]	[illegible]	[illegible]	[illegible]	[illegible]	[illegible]	[illegible]	[illegible]	[illegible]	–	[illegible]	–	–	–
[illegible]	[illegible]	[illegible]	[illegible]	[illegible]	[illegible]	[illegible]	[illegible]	[illegible]	[illegible]	[illegible]	[illegible]	[illegible]	[illegible]	[illegible]	[illegible]	[illegible]
[illegible]	[illegible]	[illegible]	[illegible]	[illegible]	[illegible]	[illegible]	[illegible]	[illegible]	[illegible]	[illegible]	[illegible]	[illegible]	[illegible]	[illegible]	[illegible]	[illegible]
Kilkenny,	[illegible]	[illegible]	[illegible]	[illegible]	[illegible]	[illegible]	[illegible]	[illegible]	[illegible]	[illegible]	[illegible]	[illegible]	[illegible]	[illegible]	[illegible]	[illegible]
[illegible]	[illegible]	[illegible]	[illegible]	[illegible]	[illegible]	[illegible]	[illegible]	[illegible]	[illegible]	[illegible]	[illegible]	[illegible]	[illegible]	[illegible]	[illegible]	[illegible]
[illegible]	[illegible]	[illegible]	[illegible]	[illegible]	[illegible]	[illegible]	[illegible]	[illegible]	[illegible]	[illegible]	[illegible]	[illegible]	[illegible]	[illegible]	[illegible]	[illegible]
King's County.																
[illegible]	[illegible]	[illegible]	[illegible]	[illegible]	[illegible]	[illegible]	[illegible]	[illegible]	[illegible]	[illegible]	[illegible]	[illegible]	[illegible]	[illegible]	[illegible]	[illegible]
[illegible]	[illegible]	[illegible]	[illegible]	[illegible]	[illegible]	[illegible]	[illegible]	[illegible]	[illegible]	[illegible]	[illegible]	[illegible]	[illegible]	[illegible]	[illegible]	[illegible]
[illegible]	[illegible]	[illegible]	[illegible]	[illegible]	[illegible]	[illegible]	[illegible]	[illegible]	[illegible]	[illegible]	[illegible]	[illegible]	[illegible]	[illegible]	[illegible]	[illegible]
[illegible]	[illegible]	[illegible]	[illegible]	[illegible]	[illegible]	[illegible]	[illegible]	[illegible]	[illegible]	[illegible]	[illegible]	[illegible]	[illegible]	[illegible]	[illegible]	[illegible]
[illegible]	[illegible]	[illegible]	[illegible]	[illegible]	[illegible]	[illegible]	[illegible]	[illegible]	[illegible]	[illegible]	[illegible]	[illegible]	[illegible]	[illegible]	[illegible]	[illegible]
Longford County.																
[illegible]	[illegible]	–	[illegible]	–	[illegible]	–	[illegible]	–	[illegible]	–	[illegible]	–	[illegible]	–	[illegible]	–
[illegible]	[illegible]	[illegible]	[illegible]	[illegible]	[illegible]	[illegible]	[illegible]	[illegible]	[illegible]	[illegible]	[illegible]	[illegible]	–	–	–	–
Longford,	[illegible]	[illegible]	[illegible]	[illegible]	[illegible]	[illegible]	[illegible]	[illegible]	[illegible]	[illegible]	[illegible]	[illegible]	[illegible]	[illegible]	[illegible]	[illegible]
Louth County.																
[illegible]	[illegible]	[illegible]	[illegible]	[illegible]	[illegible]	[illegible]	[illegible]	[illegible]	[illegible]	[illegible]	[illegible]	[illegible]	[illegible]	–	[illegible]	–
[illegible]	[illegible]	[illegible]	[illegible]	[illegible]	[illegible]	[illegible]	[illegible]	[illegible]	[illegible]	[illegible]	[illegible]	[illegible]	[illegible]	[illegible]	[illegible]	[illegible]
[illegible]	[illegible]	[illegible]	[illegible]	[illegible]	[illegible]	[illegible]	[illegible]	[illegible]	[illegible]	[illegible]	[illegible]	[illegible]	[illegible]	[illegible]	[illegible]	[illegible]
[illegible]	[illegible]	[illegible]	[illegible]	[illegible]	[illegible]	[illegible]	[illegible]	[illegible]	[illegible]	[illegible]	[illegible]	[illegible]	[illegible]	[illegible]	[illegible]	[illegible]

I.—PROVINCE OF LEINSTER—continued.

Counties and Poor-Law Unions	Summer								Winter							
	Men		Boys		Women		Girls		Men		Boys		Women		Girls	
	From	To	From	To	From	To	From	To	From	To	From	To	From	To	From	To
	s. d.	s. d.	s. d.	s. d.	s. d.	s. d.	s. d.	s. d.	s. d.	s. d.	s. d.	s. d.	s. d.	s. d.	s. d.	s. d.
KING'S COUNTY.																
[illegible]	[illegible]	[illegible]	[illegible]	[illegible]	[illegible]	[illegible]	[illegible]	[illegible]	[illegible]	[illegible]	[illegible]	[illegible]	[illegible]	[illegible]	[illegible]	[illegible]
[illegible]	[illegible]	[illegible]	[illegible]	[illegible]	[illegible]	[illegible]	[illegible]	[illegible]	[illegible]	[illegible]	[illegible]	[illegible]	[illegible]	[illegible]	[illegible]	[illegible]
[illegible]	[illegible]	[illegible]	–	–	[illegible]	[illegible]	[illegible]	[illegible]	[illegible]	[illegible]	–	–	[illegible]	[illegible]	[illegible]	[illegible]
[illegible]	[illegible]	[illegible]	[illegible]	[illegible]	[illegible]	[illegible]	[illegible]	[illegible]	[illegible]	[illegible]	[illegible]	[illegible]	[illegible]	[illegible]	[illegible]	[illegible]
[illegible]	[illegible]	[illegible]	[illegible]	[illegible]	[illegible]	[illegible]	[illegible]	[illegible]	[illegible]	[illegible]	[illegible]	[illegible]	[illegible]	[illegible]	[illegible]	[illegible]
[illegible]	[illegible]	[illegible]	[illegible]	[illegible]	[illegible]	[illegible]	[illegible]	[illegible]	[illegible]	[illegible]	[illegible]	[illegible]	[illegible]	[illegible]	[illegible]	[illegible]
QUEEN'S COUNTY.																
[illegible]	[illegible]	[illegible]	[illegible]	[illegible]	[illegible]	[illegible]	[illegible]	[illegible]	[illegible]	[illegible]	[illegible]	[illegible]	–	–	–	–
[illegible]	[illegible]	[illegible]	[illegible]	[illegible]	[illegible]	[illegible]	[illegible]	[illegible]	[illegible]	[illegible]	[illegible]	[illegible]	[illegible]	[illegible]	[illegible]	[illegible]
[illegible]	[illegible]	[illegible]	[illegible]	[illegible]	[illegible]	[illegible]	[illegible]	[illegible]	[illegible]	[illegible]	[illegible]	[illegible]	[illegible]	[illegible]	[illegible]	[illegible]
[illegible]	[illegible]	[illegible]	[illegible]	[illegible]	[illegible]	[illegible]	[illegible]	[illegible]	[illegible]	[illegible]	[illegible]	[illegible]	[illegible]	[illegible]	[illegible]	[illegible]
WESTMEATH COUNTY.																
[illegible]	[illegible]	[illegible]	[illegible]	[illegible]	[illegible]	[illegible]	[illegible]	[illegible]	[illegible]	[illegible]	[illegible]	[illegible]	[illegible]	[illegible]	[illegible]	[illegible]
[illegible]	–	[illegible]	–	–	–	–	–	–	–	[illegible]	–	–	–	–	–	–
[illegible]	[illegible]	[illegible]	[illegible]	[illegible]	[illegible]	[illegible]	[illegible]	[illegible]	[illegible]	[illegible]	[illegible]	[illegible]	[illegible]	[illegible]	[illegible]	[illegible]
[illegible]	[illegible]	[illegible]	[illegible]	[illegible]	[illegible]	[illegible]	[illegible]	[illegible]	[illegible]	[illegible]	[illegible]	[illegible]	[illegible]	[illegible]	[illegible]	[illegible]
[illegible]	[illegible]	[illegible]	[illegible]	[illegible]	[illegible]	[illegible]	[illegible]	[illegible]	[illegible]	[illegible]	[illegible]	[illegible]	[illegible]	[illegible]	[illegible]	[illegible]
[illegible]	[illegible]	[illegible]	[illegible]	[illegible]	[illegible]	[illegible]	[illegible]	[illegible]	[illegible]	[illegible]	–	–	–	–	–	–
WEXFORD COUNTY.																
[illegible]	[illegible]	[illegible]	[illegible]	[illegible]	[illegible]	[illegible]	[illegible]	[illegible]	[illegible]	[illegible]	[illegible]	[illegible]	[illegible]	[illegible]	[illegible]	[illegible]
[illegible]	[illegible]	[illegible]	[illegible]	[illegible]	[illegible]	[illegible]	[illegible]	[illegible]	[illegible]	[illegible]	[illegible]	[illegible]	[illegible]	[illegible]	[illegible]	[illegible]
[illegible]	[illegible]	[illegible]	[illegible]	[illegible]	[illegible]	[illegible]	[illegible]	[illegible]	[illegible]	[illegible]	[illegible]	[illegible]	[illegible]	[illegible]	[illegible]	[illegible]
[illegible]	[illegible]	[illegible]	[illegible]	[illegible]	[illegible]	[illegible]	[illegible]	[illegible]	[illegible]	[illegible]	[illegible]	[illegible]	[illegible]	[illegible]	–	–
[illegible]	[illegible]	[illegible]	[illegible]	[illegible]	[illegible]	[illegible]	[illegible]	[illegible]	[illegible]	[illegible]	[illegible]	[illegible]	[illegible]	[illegible]	[illegible]	[illegible]
WICKLOW COUNTY.																
[illegible]	[illegible]	[illegible]	[illegible]	[illegible]	[illegible]	[illegible]	[illegible]	[illegible]	[illegible]	[illegible]	[illegible]	[illegible]	[illegible]	[illegible]	[illegible]	[illegible]
[illegible]	[illegible]	[illegible]	[illegible]	[illegible]	[illegible]	[illegible]	[illegible]	[illegible]	[illegible]	[illegible]	[illegible]	[illegible]	[illegible]	[illegible]	[illegible]	[illegible]
[illegible]	[illegible]	[illegible]	[illegible]	[illegible]	[illegible]	[illegible]	[illegible]	[illegible]	[illegible]	[illegible]	[illegible]	[illegible]	[illegible]	[illegible]	[illegible]	[illegible]
[illegible]	[illegible]	[illegible]	[illegible]	[illegible]	[illegible]	[illegible]	–	–	[illegible]	[illegible]	[illegible]	[illegible]	[illegible]	[illegible]	–	–

32.—PROVINCE OF MUNSTER—continued.

Summer.								Winter.					
Men.		Boys.		Women.		Girls.		Men.		Boys.		Women.	
From	To	From	To	From	To	From	To	From	To	From	To	From	To
s. d.	s. d.	s. d.	s. d.	s. d.	s. d.	s. d.	s. d.	s. d.	s. d.	s. d.	s. d.	s. d.	s. d.
[illegible]	[illegible]	[illegible]	[illegible]	[illegible]	[illegible]	[illegible]	[illegible]	[illegible]	[illegible]	[illegible]	[illegible]	[illegible]	[illegible]
[illegible]	[illegible]	[illegible]	[illegible]	[illegible]	[illegible]	[illegible]	[illegible]	[illegible]	[illegible]	[illegible]	[illegible]	[illegible]	[illegible]
[illegible]	[illegible]	[illegible]	[illegible]	–	–	–	–	[illegible]	[illegible]	[illegible]	[illegible]	–	–
[illegible]	[illegible]	[illegible]	[illegible]	[illegible]	[illegible]	[illegible]	[illegible]	[illegible]	[illegible]	[illegible]	[illegible]	[illegible]	[illegible]
[illegible]	[illegible]	[illegible]	[illegible]	[illegible]	[illegible]	[illegible]	[illegible]	[illegible]	[illegible]	[illegible]	[illegible]	[illegible]	[illegible]
[illegible]	[illegible]	[illegible]	[illegible]	[illegible]	[illegible]	[illegible]	[illegible]	[illegible]	[illegible]	[illegible]	[illegible]	[illegible]	[illegible]
[illegible]	[illegible]	[illegible]	[illegible]	[illegible]	[illegible]	[illegible]	[illegible]	[illegible]	[illegible]	[illegible]	[illegible]	[illegible]	[illegible]
[illegible]	[illegible]	[illegible]	[illegible]	[illegible]	[illegible]	[illegible]	[illegible]	[illegible]	[illegible]	[illegible]	[illegible]	[illegible]	[illegible]
[illegible]	[illegible]	[illegible]	[illegible]	[illegible]	[illegible]	[illegible]	[illegible]	[illegible]	[illegible]	–	–	[illegible]	[illegible]
[illegible]	[illegible]	[illegible]	[illegible]	[illegible]	[illegible]	[illegible]	[illegible]	[illegible]	[illegible]	[illegible]	[illegible]	[illegible]	[illegible]
[illegible]	[illegible]	[illegible]	[illegible]	[illegible]	[illegible]	[illegible]	[illegible]	[illegible]	[illegible]	[illegible]	[illegible]	[illegible]	[illegible]
[illegible]	[illegible]	[illegible]	[illegible]	[illegible]	[illegible]	[illegible]	[illegible]	[illegible]	[illegible]	[illegible]	[illegible]	[illegible]	[illegible]
[illegible]	[illegible]	[illegible]	[illegible]	[illegible]	[illegible]	[illegible]	[illegible]	[illegible]	[illegible]	[illegible]	[illegible]	[illegible]	[illegible]
[illegible]	[illegible]	[illegible]	[illegible]	[illegible]	[illegible]	[illegible]	[illegible]	[illegible]	[illegible]	[illegible]	[illegible]	[illegible]	[illegible]
[illegible]	[illegible]	[illegible]	[illegible]	[illegible]	–	[illegible]	[illegible]	[illegible]	[illegible]	[illegible]	[illegible]	–	[illegible]
[illegible]	[illegible]	[illegible]	[illegible]	[illegible]	[illegible]	[illegible]	[illegible]	[illegible]	[illegible]	[illegible]	[illegible]	[illegible]	[illegible]
[illegible]	[illegible]	[illegible]	[illegible]	[illegible]	[illegible]	[illegible]	[illegible]	[illegible]	[illegible]	[illegible]	[illegible]	[illegible]	[illegible]
[illegible]	[illegible]	[illegible]	[illegible]	[illegible]	[illegible]	[illegible]	[illegible]	[illegible]	[illegible]	[illegible]	[illegible]	[illegible]	[illegible]
[illegible]	[illegible]	[illegible]	[illegible]	[illegible]	[illegible]	[illegible]	[illegible]	[illegible]	[illegible]	[illegible]	[illegible]	[illegible]	[illegible]
[illegible]	[illegible]	[illegible]	[illegible]	[illegible]	[illegible]	[illegible]	[illegible]	[illegible]	[illegible]	[illegible]	[illegible]	[illegible]	[illegible]
[illegible]	[illegible]	[illegible]	[illegible]	[illegible]	[illegible]	[illegible]	[illegible]	[illegible]	[illegible]	[illegible]	[illegible]	[illegible]	[illegible]
[illegible]	[illegible]	[illegible]	[illegible]	[illegible]	[illegible]	[illegible]	[illegible]	[illegible]	[illegible]	[illegible]	[illegible]	[illegible]	[illegible]
[illegible]	[illegible]	[illegible]	[illegible]	[illegible]	[illegible]	[illegible]	[illegible]	[illegible]	[illegible]	[illegible]	–	[illegible]	[illegible]
[illegible]	[illegible]	[illegible]	[illegible]	[illegible]	[illegible]	[illegible]	[illegible]	[illegible]	[illegible]	[illegible]	[illegible]	[illegible]	[illegible]
[illegible]	[illegible]	[illegible]	[illegible]	[illegible]	[illegible]	[illegible]	[illegible]	[illegible]	[illegible]	[illegible]	[illegible]	[illegible]	[illegible]
[illegible]	[illegible]	[illegible]	[illegible]	[illegible]	[illegible]	[illegible]	[illegible]	[illegible]	[illegible]	[illegible]	[illegible]	[illegible]	[illegible]
[illegible]	[illegible]	[illegible]	[illegible]	[illegible]	[illegible]	[illegible]	[illegible]	[illegible]	[illegible]	[illegible]	[illegible]	[illegible]	[illegible]
[illegible]	[illegible]	[illegible]	[illegible]	[illegible]	[illegible]	[illegible]	[illegible]	[illegible]	[illegible]	[illegible]	[illegible]	[illegible]	[illegible]
[illegible]	[illegible]	[illegible]	[illegible]	[illegible]	[illegible]	[illegible]	[illegible]	[illegible]	[illegible]	[illegible]	[illegible]	[illegible]	[illegible]
[illegible]	[illegible]	[illegible]	[illegible]	[illegible]	[illegible]	[illegible]	[illegible]	[illegible]	[illegible]	[illegible]	[illegible]	[illegible]	[illegible]
[illegible]	[illegible]	[illegible]	[illegible]	[illegible]	[illegible]	[illegible]	[illegible]	[illegible]	[illegible]	[illegible]	[illegible]	[illegible]	[illegible]
[illegible]	[illegible]	[illegible]	[illegible]	[illegible]	[illegible]	[illegible]	[illegible]	[illegible]	[illegible]	[illegible]	[illegible]	[illegible]	[illegible]
[illegible]	[illegible]	[illegible]	[illegible]	[illegible]	[illegible]	[illegible]	[illegible]	[illegible]	[illegible]	[illegible]	[illegible]	[illegible]	[illegible]
[illegible]	[illegible]	[illegible]	[illegible]	[illegible]	[illegible]	[illegible]	[illegible]	[illegible]	[illegible]	[illegible]	[illegible]	[illegible]	[illegible]
[illegible]	[illegible]	[illegible]	[illegible]	[illegible]	[illegible]	[illegible]	[illegible]	[illegible]	[illegible]	[illegible]	[illegible]	[illegible]	[illegible]
[illegible]	–	[illegible]	[illegible]	[illegible]	[illegible]	[illegible]	[illegible]	[illegible]	[illegible]	[illegible]	[illegible]	[illegible]	[illegible]
[illegible]	[illegible]	[illegible]	[illegible]	[illegible]	[illegible]	[illegible]	[illegible]	[illegible]	[illegible]	[illegible]	[illegible]	[illegible]	[illegible]
[illegible]	[illegible]	[illegible]	[illegible]	[illegible]	[illegible]	[illegible]	[illegible]	[illegible]	[illegible]	[illegible]	[illegible]	[illegible]	[illegible]

PROVINCE OF MUNSTER—*continued.*

Counties and Constabulary Districts.	Summer.								Winter.							
	Men.		Boys.		Women.		Girls.		Men.		Boys.		Women.		Girls.	
	From	To	From	To	From	To	From	To	From	To	From	To	From	To	From	To
	s. d.	s. d.	s. d.	s. d.	s. d.	s. d.	s. d.	s. d.	s. d.	s. d.	s. d.	s. d.	s. d.	s. d.	s. d.	s. d.
TIPPERARY CO., N.R.																
[illegible]	[illegible]	[illegible]	[illegible]	[illegible]	[illegible]	[illegible]	[illegible]	[illegible]	[illegible]	[illegible]	[illegible]	[illegible]	[illegible]	[illegible]	[illegible]	[illegible]
Nenagh,	[illegible]	[illegible]	[illegible]	[illegible]	[illegible]	[illegible]	[illegible]	[illegible]	[illegible]	[illegible]	[illegible]	[illegible]	[illegible]	[illegible]	[illegible]	[illegible]
[illegible]	[illegible]	[illegible]	[illegible]	[illegible]	[illegible]	[illegible]	—	[illegible]	[illegible]	[illegible]	—	[illegible]	[illegible]	[illegible]	[illegible]	[illegible]
[illegible]	[illegible]	[illegible]	[illegible]	[illegible]	[illegible]	[illegible]	[illegible]	[illegible]	[illegible]	[illegible]	[illegible]	[illegible]	[illegible]	[illegible]	[illegible]	[illegible]
[illegible]	[illegible]	[illegible]	[illegible]	[illegible]	[illegible]	[illegible]	[illegible]	[illegible]	[illegible]	[illegible]	[illegible]	[illegible]	[illegible]	[illegible]	[illegible]	[illegible]
Thurles (e)	[illegible]	[illegible]	[illegible]	[illegible]	[illegible]	[illegible]	[illegible]	[illegible]	[illegible]	[illegible]	—	—	—	—	—	—
TIPPERARY CO., S.R.																
[illegible]	[illegible]	[illegible]	[illegible]	[illegible]	[illegible]	[illegible]	[illegible]	[illegible]	[illegible]	[illegible]	[illegible]	[illegible]	[illegible]	[illegible]	[illegible]	[illegible]
[illegible]	[illegible]	[illegible]	[illegible]	[illegible]	[illegible]	[illegible]	[illegible]	[illegible]	[illegible]	[illegible]	[illegible]	[illegible]	[illegible]	[illegible]	[illegible]	[illegible]
Cashel,	[illegible]	[illegible]	[illegible]	[illegible]	[illegible]	[illegible]	[illegible]	[illegible]	[illegible]	[illegible]	[illegible]	[illegible]	[illegible]	[illegible]	[illegible]	[illegible]
Clonmel,	[illegible]	[illegible]	[illegible]	[illegible]	[illegible]	[illegible]	[illegible]	[illegible]	[illegible]	[illegible]	[illegible]	[illegible]	[illegible]	[illegible]	[illegible]	[illegible]
[illegible]	[illegible]	[illegible]	[illegible]	[illegible]	[illegible]	[illegible]	[illegible]	—	[illegible]	[illegible]	[illegible]	—	[illegible]	—	[illegible]	—
[illegible]	[illegible]	[illegible]	[illegible]	[illegible]	[illegible]	[illegible]	[illegible]	[illegible]	[illegible]	[illegible]	[illegible]	[illegible]	[illegible]	[illegible]	[illegible]	[illegible]
Tipperary (i),	[illegible]	[illegible]	[illegible]	[illegible]	[illegible]	[illegible]	[illegible]	[illegible]	[illegible]	[illegible]	[illegible]	[illegible]	[illegible]	[illegible]	[illegible]	[illegible]
WATERFORD CO.																
[illegible]	[illegible]	[illegible]	[illegible]	[illegible]	[illegible]	[illegible]	[illegible]	[illegible]	[illegible]	[illegible]	[illegible]	[illegible]	[illegible]	[illegible]	[illegible]	[illegible]
Dungarvan (l),	[illegible]	[illegible]	[illegible]	[illegible]	[illegible]	[illegible]	[illegible]	[illegible]	[illegible]	[illegible]	[illegible]	[illegible]	[illegible]	[illegible]	[illegible]	[illegible]
[illegible]	[illegible]	[illegible]	[illegible]	[illegible]	[illegible]	[illegible]	[illegible]	[illegible]	[illegible]	[illegible]	[illegible]	[illegible]	[illegible]	[illegible]	[illegible]	[illegible]
Waterford,	[illegible]	[illegible]	[illegible]	[illegible]	[illegible]	[illegible]	[illegible]	[illegible]	[illegible]	[illegible]	[illegible]	[illegible]	[illegible]	[illegible]	[illegible]	[illegible]

III.—PROVINCE OF ULSTER.

Counties and Constabulary Districts.	Summer Men From	Summer Men To	Summer Boys From	Summer Boys To	Summer Women From	Summer Women To	Summer Girls From	Summer Girls To	Winter Men From	Winter Men To	Winter Boys From	Winter Boys To	Winter Women From	Winter Women To	Winter Girls From	Winter Girls To
ANTRIM COUNTY.																
Antrim,	[illegible]	[illegible]	[illegible]	[illegible]	[illegible]	[illegible]	[illegible]	[illegible]	[illegible]	[illegible]	[illegible]	[illegible]	[illegible]	[illegible]	[illegible]	[illegible]
Ballymena,	[illegible]	[illegible]	[illegible]	[illegible]	[illegible]	[illegible]	[illegible]	[illegible]	[illegible]	[illegible]	[illegible]	[illegible]	[illegible]	[illegible]	[illegible]	[illegible]
Ballymoney,	[illegible]	[illegible]	[illegible]	[illegible]	[illegible]	[illegible]	[illegible]	[illegible]	[illegible]	[illegible]	[illegible]	[illegible]	[illegible]	[illegible]	[illegible]	[illegible]
Belfast South (h),	[illegible]	[illegible]	[illegible]	[illegible]	[illegible]	[illegible]	[illegible]	[illegible]	[illegible]	[illegible]	[illegible]	[illegible]	[illegible]	[illegible]	[illegible]	[illegible]
Belfast West (i),	[illegible]	[illegible]	[illegible]	[illegible]	[illegible]	[illegible]	—	—	[illegible]	[illegible]	[illegible]	[illegible]	[illegible]	[illegible]	—	—
Larne,	[illegible]	[illegible]	[illegible]	[illegible]	[illegible]	[illegible]	[illegible]	[illegible]	[illegible]	[illegible]	[illegible]	[illegible]	[illegible]	[illegible]	[illegible]	[illegible]
Lisburn,	[illegible]	[illegible]	[illegible]	[illegible]	[illegible]	[illegible]	[illegible]	[illegible]	[illegible]	[illegible]	[illegible]	[illegible]	[illegible]	[illegible]	[illegible]	[illegible]
ARMAGH COUNTY.																
Armagh,	[illegible]	[illegible]	[illegible]	[illegible]	[illegible]	[illegible]	[illegible]	[illegible]	[illegible]	[illegible]	[illegible]	[illegible]	[illegible]	[illegible]	[illegible]	[illegible]
Lurgan,	[illegible]	[illegible]	[illegible]	[illegible]	[illegible]	[illegible]	[illegible]	[illegible]	[illegible]	[illegible]	[illegible]	[illegible]	[illegible]	[illegible]	[illegible]	[illegible]
Newry (l),	[illegible]	[illegible]	[illegible]	[illegible]	[illegible]	—	[illegible]	—	[illegible]	[illegible]	[illegible]	[illegible]	[illegible]	—	—	—
[illegible]	[illegible]	[illegible]	[illegible]	[illegible]	[illegible]	[illegible]	[illegible]	[illegible]	[illegible]	[illegible]	[illegible]	[illegible]	[illegible]	[illegible]	[illegible]	[illegible]
CAVAN COUNTY.																
Bailieborough,	[illegible]	[illegible]	[illegible]	[illegible]	[illegible]	[illegible]	[illegible]	[illegible]	[illegible]	[illegible]	[illegible]	[illegible]	[illegible]	[illegible]	[illegible]	[illegible]
Cavan (l),	[illegible]	[illegible]	[illegible]	[illegible]	[illegible]	[illegible]	[illegible]	[illegible]	[illegible]	[illegible]	[illegible]	[illegible]	—	—	—	—
[illegible]	[illegible]	[illegible]	[illegible]	[illegible]	[illegible]	[illegible]	[illegible]	[illegible]	[illegible]	[illegible]	[illegible]	[illegible]	[illegible]	[illegible]	[illegible]	[illegible]
[illegible]	[illegible]	[illegible]	[illegible]	[illegible]	[illegible]	[illegible]	[illegible]	[illegible]	[illegible]	[illegible]	[illegible]	[illegible]	[illegible]	[illegible]	[illegible]	[illegible]
Virginia (m),	[illegible]	[illegible]	[illegible]	[illegible]	[illegible]	[illegible]	[illegible]	[illegible]	[illegible]	[illegible]	[illegible]	[illegible]	[illegible]	[illegible]	[illegible]	[illegible]

[illegible]

PROVINCE OF ULSTER—*continued.*

Counties and Constabulary Districts	Summer								Winter							
	Men.		Boys.		Women.		Girls.		Men.		Boys.		Women.		Girls.	
	From	To	From	To	From	To	From	To	From	To	From	To	From	To	From	To
	s. d.	s. d.	s. d.	s. d.	s. d.	s. d.	s. d.	s. d.	s. d.	s. d.	s. d.	s. d.	s. d.	s. d.	s. d.	s. d.
Donegal County.																
[illegible] (a),	[illegible]	[illegible]	[illegible]	[illegible]	[illegible]	[illegible]	[illegible]	[illegible]	[illegible]	[illegible]	[illegible]	[illegible]	–	–	–	–
Ballyshannon,	[illegible]	[illegible]	[illegible]	[illegible]	[illegible]	[illegible]	[illegible]	[illegible]	[illegible]	[illegible]	[illegible]	[illegible]	[illegible]	[illegible]	[illegible]	[illegible]
[illegible],	[illegible]	[illegible]	[illegible]	[illegible]	[illegible]	[illegible]	[illegible]	[illegible]	[illegible]	[illegible]	[illegible]	[illegible]	[illegible]	[illegible]	[illegible]	[illegible]
[illegible] (?),	[illegible]	[illegible]	[illegible]	[illegible]	[illegible]	[illegible]	[illegible]	[illegible]	[illegible]	[illegible]	[illegible]	[illegible]	[illegible]	[illegible]	[illegible]	[illegible]
[illegible],	[illegible]	[illegible]	[illegible]	[illegible]	[illegible]	[illegible]	[illegible]	[illegible]	[illegible]	[illegible]	[illegible]	[illegible]	[illegible]	[illegible]	[illegible]	[illegible]
Letterkenny,	[illegible]	[illegible]	[illegible]	[illegible]	[illegible]	[illegible]	[illegible]	[illegible]	[illegible]	[illegible]	[illegible]	[illegible]	[illegible]	[illegible]	[illegible]	[illegible]
Milford,	[illegible]	[illegible]	[illegible]	[illegible]	[illegible]	[illegible]	[illegible]	[illegible]	[illegible]	[illegible]	[illegible]	[illegible]	[illegible]	[illegible]	[illegible]	[illegible]
[illegible] (?),	[illegible]	[illegible]	[illegible]	[illegible]	[illegible]	[illegible]	[illegible]	[illegible]	[illegible]	[illegible]	[illegible]	[illegible]	[illegible]	[illegible]	[illegible]	[illegible]
[illegible] (?),	[illegible]	[illegible]	[illegible]	[illegible]	[illegible]	[illegible]	[illegible]	[illegible]	[illegible]	[illegible]	[illegible]	[illegible]	[illegible]	[illegible]	[illegible]	[illegible]
Down County.																
[illegible],	[illegible]	[illegible]	[illegible]	[illegible]	[illegible]	[illegible]	[illegible]	[illegible]	[illegible]	[illegible]	[illegible]	[illegible]	[illegible]	[illegible]	[illegible]	[illegible]
Downpatrick,	[illegible]	[illegible]	[illegible]	[illegible]	[illegible]	[illegible]	[illegible]	[illegible]	[illegible]	[illegible]	[illegible]	[illegible]	[illegible]	[illegible]	[illegible]	[illegible]
[illegible] (?),	[illegible]	[illegible]	[illegible]	[illegible]	[illegible]	[illegible]	[illegible]	[illegible]	[illegible]	[illegible]	[illegible]	[illegible]	[illegible]	[illegible]	[illegible]	[illegible]
[illegible],	[illegible]	[illegible]	[illegible]	[illegible]	[illegible]	[illegible]	[illegible]	[illegible]	[illegible]	[illegible]	[illegible]	[illegible]	[illegible]	[illegible]	[illegible]	[illegible]
Fermanagh County.																
[illegible],	[illegible]	[illegible]	[illegible]	[illegible]	[illegible]	[illegible]	[illegible]	[illegible]	[illegible]	[illegible]	[illegible]	[illegible]	[illegible]	[illegible]	[illegible]	[illegible]
[illegible] (?),	[illegible]	[illegible]	[illegible]	[illegible]	[illegible]	[illegible]	[illegible]	[illegible]	[illegible]	[illegible]	[illegible]	[illegible]	[illegible]	[illegible]	[illegible]	[illegible]
[illegible],	[illegible]	[illegible]	[illegible]	[illegible]	[illegible]	[illegible]	[illegible]	[illegible]	[illegible]	[illegible]	[illegible]	[illegible]	[illegible]	[illegible]	[illegible]	[illegible]
[illegible] (?),	[illegible]	[illegible]	[illegible]	[illegible]	[illegible]	[illegible]	[illegible]	[illegible]	[illegible]	[illegible]	[illegible]	[illegible]	–	–	–	–
Londonderry Co.																
Coleraine,	[illegible]	[illegible]	[illegible]	[illegible]	[illegible]	[illegible]	[illegible]	[illegible]	[illegible]	[illegible]	[illegible]	[illegible]	[illegible]	[illegible]	[illegible]	[illegible]
Limavady,	[illegible]	[illegible]	[illegible]	[illegible]	[illegible]	[illegible]	[illegible]	[illegible]	[illegible]	[illegible]	[illegible]	[illegible]	[illegible]	[illegible]	[illegible]	[illegible]
Londonderry,	[illegible]	[illegible]	[illegible]	[illegible]	[illegible]	[illegible]	[illegible]	[illegible]	[illegible]	[illegible]	[illegible]	[illegible]	[illegible]	[illegible]	[illegible]	[illegible]
Magherafelt,	[illegible]	[illegible]	[illegible]	[illegible]	[illegible]	[illegible]	[illegible]	[illegible]	[illegible]	[illegible]	[illegible]	[illegible]	[illegible]	[illegible]	[illegible]	[illegible]
Monaghan County.																
Carrickmacross,	[illegible]	[illegible]	[illegible]	[illegible]	[illegible]	[illegible]	[illegible]	[illegible]	[illegible]	[illegible]	[illegible]	[illegible]	[illegible]	[illegible]	[illegible]	[illegible]
Clones (h),	[illegible]	[illegible]	[illegible]	[illegible]	[illegible]	[illegible]	–	–	[illegible]	[illegible]	–	–	–	–	–	–
Monaghan,	[illegible]	[illegible]	[illegible]	[illegible]	[illegible]	[illegible]	[illegible]	[illegible]	[illegible]	[illegible]	[illegible]	[illegible]	[illegible]	[illegible]	[illegible]	[illegible]
Tyrone County.																
[illegible],	[illegible]	[illegible]	[illegible]	[illegible]	[illegible]	[illegible]	[illegible]	[illegible]	[illegible]	[illegible]	[illegible]	[illegible]	[illegible]	[illegible]	[illegible]	[illegible]
Cookstown,	[illegible]	[illegible]	[illegible]	[illegible]	[illegible]	[illegible]	[illegible]	[illegible]	[illegible]	[illegible]	[illegible]	[illegible]	[illegible]	[illegible]	[illegible]	[illegible]
Dungannon,	[illegible]	[illegible]	–	[illegible]	[illegible]	[illegible]	[illegible]	[illegible]	[illegible]	[illegible]	[illegible]	[illegible]	[illegible]	[illegible]	[illegible]	[illegible]
Newtownstewart (?),	[illegible]	[illegible]	[illegible]	[illegible]	[illegible]	[illegible]	[illegible]	[illegible]	[illegible]	[illegible]	[illegible]	[illegible]	[illegible]	[illegible]	[illegible]	[illegible]
Omagh (?),	[illegible]	[illegible]	[illegible]	[illegible]	[illegible]	[illegible]	[illegible]	[illegible]	[illegible]	[illegible]	[illegible]	[illegible]	[illegible]	[illegible]	[illegible]	[illegible]
Strabane (?),	[illegible]	[illegible]	[illegible]	[illegible]	[illegible]	[illegible]	[illegible]	[illegible]	[illegible]	[illegible]	[illegible]	[illegible]	[illegible]	[illegible]	[illegible]	[illegible]

[illegible]

IV.—PROVINCE OF CONNAUGHT.

Counties and Poor-Law Unions	Summer.								Winter.							
	Men.		Boys.		Women.		Girls.		Men.		Boys.		Women.		Girls.	
	From	To	From	To	From	To	From	To	From	To	From	To	From	To	From	To
	s. d.	s. d.	s. d.	s. d.	s. d.	s. d.	s. d.	s. d.	s. d.	s. d.	s. d.	s. d.	s. d.	s. d.	s. d.	s. d.
GALWAY COUNTY.																
[illegible]	[illegible]	[illegible]	[illegible]	[illegible]	[illegible]	[illegible]	[illegible]	[illegible]	[illegible]	[illegible]	[illegible]	[illegible]	[illegible]	[illegible]	[illegible]	[illegible]
[illegible]	[illegible]	[illegible]	[illegible]	[illegible]	[illegible]	[illegible]	[illegible]	[illegible]	[illegible]	[illegible]	[illegible]	[illegible]	[illegible]	[illegible]	[illegible]	[illegible]
[illegible]	[illegible]	[illegible]	[illegible]	[illegible]	[illegible]	[illegible]	[illegible]	[illegible]	[illegible]	[illegible]	[illegible]	[illegible]	[illegible]	[illegible]	[illegible]	[illegible]
[illegible]	[illegible]	[illegible]	[illegible]	[illegible]	[illegible]	[illegible]	[illegible]	[illegible]	[illegible]	[illegible]	[illegible]	[illegible]	[illegible]	[illegible]	[illegible]	[illegible]
[illegible]	[illegible]	[illegible]	[illegible]	[illegible]	[illegible]	[illegible]	[illegible]	[illegible]	[illegible]	[illegible]	[illegible]	[illegible]	[illegible]	[illegible]	[illegible]	[illegible]
[illegible]	[illegible]	[illegible]	[illegible]	[illegible]	[illegible]	[illegible]	[illegible]	[illegible]	[illegible]	[illegible]	[illegible]	[illegible]	[illegible]	[illegible]	[illegible]	[illegible]
[illegible]	[illegible]	[illegible]	[illegible]	[illegible]	[illegible]	[illegible]	[illegible]	[illegible]	[illegible]	[illegible]	[illegible]	[illegible]	[illegible]	[illegible]	[illegible]	[illegible]
[illegible]	[illegible]	[illegible]	[illegible]	[illegible]	[illegible]	[illegible]	[illegible]	[illegible]	[illegible]	[illegible]	[illegible]	[illegible]	[illegible]	[illegible]	[illegible]	[illegible]
[illegible]	[illegible]	[illegible]	[illegible]	[illegible]	[illegible]	[illegible]	[illegible]	[illegible]	[illegible]	[illegible]	[illegible]	[illegible]	[illegible]	[illegible]	[illegible]	[illegible]
[illegible]	[illegible]	[illegible]	[illegible]	[illegible]	[illegible]	[illegible]	-	-	[illegible]	[illegible]	[illegible]	[illegible]	-	-	-	-
[illegible]	[illegible]	[illegible]	[illegible]	[illegible]	[illegible]	[illegible]	[illegible]	[illegible]	[illegible]	[illegible]	[illegible]	[illegible]	[illegible]	[illegible]	[illegible]	[illegible]
[illegible]	[illegible]	-	[illegible]	-	[illegible]	-	-	-	[illegible]	-	[illegible]	-	[illegible]	-	-	-
[illegible]	[illegible]	[illegible]	[illegible]	[illegible]	[illegible]	[illegible]	[illegible]	[illegible]	[illegible]	[illegible]	[illegible]	[illegible]	[illegible]	[illegible]	[illegible]	[illegible]
[illegible]	[illegible]	[illegible]	[illegible]	[illegible]	[illegible]	[illegible]	[illegible]	[illegible]	[illegible]	[illegible]	[illegible]	[illegible]	[illegible]	[illegible]	[illegible]	[illegible]
[illegible]	[illegible]	[illegible]	[illegible]	[illegible]	[illegible]	[illegible]	[illegible]	[illegible]	[illegible]	[illegible]	[illegible]	[illegible]	[illegible]	[illegible]	[illegible]	[illegible]
LEITRIM COUNTY.																
[illegible]	[illegible]	[illegible]	[illegible]	[illegible]	[illegible]	[illegible]	[illegible]	[illegible]	[illegible]	[illegible]	[illegible]	[illegible]	[illegible]	[illegible]	[illegible]	[illegible]
[illegible]	[illegible]	[illegible]	[illegible]	[illegible]	[illegible]	[illegible]	[illegible]	[illegible]	[illegible]	[illegible]	[illegible]	[illegible]	[illegible]	[illegible]	[illegible]	[illegible]
[illegible]	[illegible]	[illegible]	[illegible]	[illegible]	[illegible]	[illegible]	[illegible]	[illegible]	[illegible]	[illegible]	[illegible]	[illegible]	[illegible]	[illegible]	[illegible]	[illegible]
[illegible]	[illegible]	[illegible]	[illegible]	[illegible]	-	-	-	-	[illegible]	[illegible]	[illegible]	[illegible]	-	-	-	-
[illegible]	[illegible]	[illegible]	[illegible]	[illegible]	-	-	-	-	[illegible]	[illegible]	[illegible]	[illegible]	-	-	-	-
MAYO COUNTY.																
[illegible]	[illegible]	[illegible]	[illegible]	[illegible]	[illegible]	[illegible]	[illegible]	[illegible]	[illegible]	[illegible]	[illegible]	[illegible]	[illegible]	[illegible]	[illegible]	[illegible]
[illegible]	[illegible]	[illegible]	[illegible]	[illegible]	[illegible]	[illegible]	[illegible]	[illegible]	[illegible]	[illegible]	[illegible]	[illegible]	[illegible]	[illegible]	[illegible]	[illegible]
[illegible]	[illegible]	[illegible]	[illegible]	[illegible]	[illegible]	[illegible]	[illegible]	[illegible]	[illegible]	[illegible]	[illegible]	[illegible]	[illegible]	[illegible]	[illegible]	[illegible]
[illegible]	[illegible]	-	[illegible]	-	[illegible]	-	[illegible]	-	[illegible]	-	[illegible]	-	[illegible]	-	[illegible]	-
[illegible]	[illegible]	[illegible]	[illegible]	[illegible]	[illegible]	[illegible]	[illegible]	[illegible]	[illegible]	[illegible]	[illegible]	[illegible]	[illegible]	[illegible]	[illegible]	[illegible]
[illegible]	[illegible]	[illegible]	[illegible]	[illegible]	[illegible]	[illegible]	[illegible]	[illegible]	[illegible]	[illegible]	[illegible]	[illegible]	[illegible]	[illegible]	[illegible]	[illegible]
[illegible]	[illegible]	[illegible]	[illegible]	[illegible]	[illegible]	[illegible]	[illegible]	[illegible]	[illegible]	[illegible]	[illegible]	[illegible]	[illegible]	[illegible]	[illegible]	[illegible]
[illegible]	[illegible]	[illegible]	[illegible]	[illegible]	[illegible]	[illegible]	[illegible]	[illegible]	[illegible]	[illegible]	[illegible]	[illegible]	[illegible]	[illegible]	[illegible]	[illegible]
[illegible]	[illegible]	[illegible]	[illegible]	[illegible]	[illegible]	[illegible]	[illegible]	[illegible]	[illegible]	[illegible]	[illegible]	[illegible]	-	-	-	-
ROSCOMMON COUNTY.																
[illegible]	[illegible]	[illegible]	[illegible]	[illegible]	[illegible]	[illegible]	[illegible]	[illegible]	[illegible]	[illegible]	[illegible]	[illegible]	[illegible]	[illegible]	[illegible]	[illegible]
[illegible]	[illegible]	[illegible]	[illegible]	[illegible]	-	-	-	-	[illegible]	[illegible]	[illegible]	[illegible]	-	-	-	-
[illegible]	[illegible]	[illegible]	[illegible]	[illegible]	[illegible]	[illegible]	[illegible]	[illegible]	[illegible]	[illegible]	[illegible]	[illegible]	[illegible]	[illegible]	[illegible]	[illegible]
[illegible]	[illegible]	[illegible]	[illegible]	-	[illegible]	-	-	-	[illegible]	-	[illegible]	-	[illegible]	-	-	-
[illegible]	[illegible]	[illegible]	[illegible]	[illegible]	[illegible]	[illegible]	[illegible]	[illegible]	[illegible]	[illegible]	[illegible]	[illegible]	[illegible]	[illegible]	[illegible]	[illegible]
SLIGO COUNTY.																
[illegible]	[illegible]	[illegible]	[illegible]	[illegible]	[illegible]	[illegible]	[illegible]	[illegible]	[illegible]	[illegible]	[illegible]	[illegible]	[illegible]	[illegible]	[illegible]	[illegible]
[illegible]	[illegible]	[illegible]	[illegible]	[illegible]	-	-	-	-	[illegible]	[illegible]	[illegible]	[illegible]	-	-	-	-
[illegible]	[illegible]	[illegible]	[illegible]	[illegible]	[illegible]	[illegible]	[illegible]	[illegible]	[illegible]	[illegible]	[illegible]	[illegible]	[illegible]	[illegible]	[illegible]	[illegible]
[illegible]	[illegible]	[illegible]	[illegible]	[illegible]	[illegible]	[illegible]	[illegible]	[illegible]	[illegible]	[illegible]	[illegible]	[illegible]	[illegible]	[illegible]	[illegible]	[illegible]
[illegible]	[illegible]	[illegible]	[illegible]	[illegible]	[illegible]	[illegible]	[illegible]	[illegible]	[illegible]	[illegible]	[illegible]	[illegible]	[illegible]	[illegible]	[illegible]	[illegible]

[illegible]

Loans for Labourers' Dwellings under Labourers Acts.

It would appear from the report of the Local Government Board for Ireland for the year ended 31st March, 1891, that from the inception of these Acts up to that date, loans for the erection of 22,998 cottages were applied for by various Boards of Guardians, and that loans to the amount of £1,205,849 were sanctioned for the erection of 11,910 cottages.

Out of the 11,910 houses authorised, 8,063 have been provided, and 7,917 of them actually let (at weekly rents varying from 6*d*. to 2*s*.), and 916 others were in process of erection at the date of the Report.

It is also stated in the same report that further improvement schemes are about to be submitted, embracing 2,573 cottages at an estimated cost of about £314,610.

It would appear from the report of the Commissioners of Public Works for the year ended 31st March, 1891, that 692 loans to private persons, for this class of work, were sanctioned since the passing of the Act 23 Vic., c. 19, the total amount of the loans being £333,530.

Agricultural Schools.

The following information is extracted from the report of the Commissioners of National Education in Ireland for the year 1890:—

The total number of school farms in connection with ordinary National Schools on the 31st December, 1890, was 47. The total number of pupils examined in agriculture in this class of schools was 701, of whom 585 passed in the agricultural programme.

There were also 29 schools having school gardens attached; the number of pupils examined in the school gardens was 497, of whom 437 passed.

The number of pupils who attended at the Glasnevin establishment during the two sessions was 51. The Royal Dublin Society has continued its aid by offering money prizes and free studentships for competition amongst the pupils, both at this school and at that in Cork.

The dairy school at Cork has done very useful work during the year. The attendances have been—30 at the first and second and 29 at the third session.

There is also a very useful dairy school at the Marlborough-street Training College, attendance at which is voluntary, for the female Queen's scholars. A project is in contemplation by which instruction in dairying may be brought within the reach of farmers' families through the agency of travelling instructors. An experiment of this class was made in 1888 with marked success.

FRUIT CULTIVATION.—TURF BOG.

Arrangements have been made, in connection with the Agricultural Statistics for 1891 to obtain information with reference to the area planted with fruit trees, &c., and to the area occupied by turf bog.

In conclusion I have to thank the occupiers and owners of land in general for their courtesy in supplying the information required for the various Agricultural Returns to the Enumerators. I have also to express my thanks to the District Inspectors of the Royal Irish Constabulary and the Sergeants of the Metropolitan Police, who have furnished the valuable notes on the local circumstances affecting agriculture in the various parts of the country, which will be found at pages 79 to 90; and to add, as I do, with much pleasure, that the Enumerators discharged their duty with their usual efficiency.

I have the honour to remain

Your Excellency's faithful servant,

T. W. GRIMSHAW,

Registrar-General.

GENERAL REGISTER OFFICE,
CHARLEMONT HOUSE, DUBLIN,
21st *August*, 1891.

TILLAGE; MEADOW AND CLOVER; &c.

TILLAGE; MEADOW AND CLOVER; &c.

TABLE 1.—Showing, by Counties and Provinces, the Number of Holdings, their Size in Statute Acres, and the Division of Land in the Year 1890.

COUNTIES.	[illegible]
[illegible]	[illegible]

TABLE 2.—Showing the Percentage per cent. under Crops (including Meadow and Clover), Grass, Fallow, Woods and Plantations, Bog and Marsh, Barren Mountain Land, and Water, Roads, and Fences, &c., in each County and Province in Ireland in 1890.

COUNTIES.	[illegible]
[illegible]	[illegible]

TABLE 4.—Showing, by Poor Law Unions, the Percentage per cent. under Crops (including Meadow and Clover), Grass, Fallow, Woods and Plantations, Bog and Marsh, Barren Mountain Land, and Water, Roads, and Fences, &c., in 1880.

Poor Law Unions.	Percentage (under Crops, including Meadow and Clover)	Grass.	Fallow.	Woods and Plantations.	Bog and Marsh.	Barren Mountain Land.	Water, Roads, Fences, &c.	Poor Law Unions.	Percentage (under Crops, including Meadow and Clover)	Grass.	Fallow.	Woods and Plantations.	Bog and Marsh.	Barren Mountain Land.	Water, Roads, Fences, &c.
[illegible]	[illegible]	[illegible]	[illegible]	[illegible]	[illegible]	[illegible]	[illegible]	[illegible]	[illegible]	[illegible]	[illegible]	[illegible]	[illegible]	[illegible]	[illegible]

TABLE 8.—SHOWING, BY COUNTIES AND PROVINCES, THE EXTENT OF LAND

COUNTIES.	CORN, BEANS, AND PEAS.								GREEN CROPS.		
	Wheat.	Oats.	Barley.	Bere.	Rye.	Beans.	Peas.	Total.	Potatoes.	Turnips.	Other Green Crops.
	Acres.	Acres.	Acres.	Acres.	Acres.	Acres.	Acres.	Acres.	Acres.	Acres.	Acres.
Antrim,	[illegible]	[illegible]	[illegible]	[illegible]	[illegible]	[illegible]	[illegible]	[illegible]	[illegible]	[illegible]	[illegible]
Armagh,	[illegible]	[illegible]	[illegible]	[illegible]	[illegible]	[illegible]	[illegible]	[illegible]	[illegible]	[illegible]	[illegible]
Carlow,	[illegible]	[illegible]	[illegible]	[illegible]	[illegible]	[illegible]	.	[illegible]	[illegible]	[illegible]	[illegible]
Cavan,	[illegible]	[illegible]	[illegible]	[illegible]	[illegible]	[illegible]	[illegible]	[illegible]	[illegible]	[illegible]	[illegible]
Clare,	[illegible]	[illegible]	[illegible]	[illegible]	[illegible]	[illegible]	[illegible]	[illegible]	[illegible]	[illegible]	[illegible]
Cork,	[illegible]	[illegible]	[illegible]	[illegible]	[illegible]	[illegible]	[illegible]	[illegible]	[illegible]	[illegible]	[illegible]
Donegal,	[illegible]	[illegible]	[illegible]	[illegible]	[illegible]	[illegible]	[illegible]	[illegible]	[illegible]	[illegible]	[illegible]
Down,	[illegible]	[illegible]	[illegible]	[illegible]	[illegible]	[illegible]	[illegible]	[illegible]	[illegible]	[illegible]	[illegible]
Dublin,	[illegible]	[illegible]	[illegible]	[illegible]	[illegible]	[illegible]	[illegible]	[illegible]	[illegible]	[illegible]	[illegible]
Fermanagh,	[illegible]	[illegible]	[illegible]	[illegible]	[illegible]	[illegible]	[illegible]	[illegible]	[illegible]	[illegible]	[illegible]
Galway,	[illegible]	[illegible]	[illegible]	[illegible]	[illegible]	[illegible]	[illegible]	[illegible]	[illegible]	[illegible]	[illegible]
Kerry,	[illegible]	[illegible]	[illegible]	[illegible]	[illegible]	[illegible]	[illegible]	[illegible]	[illegible]	[illegible]	[illegible]
Kildare,	[illegible]	[illegible]	[illegible]	[illegible]	[illegible]	[illegible]	[illegible]	[illegible]	[illegible]	[illegible]	[illegible]
Kilkenny,	[illegible]	[illegible]	[illegible]	[illegible]	.	[illegible]	[illegible]	[illegible]	[illegible]	[illegible]	[illegible]
King's,	[illegible]	[illegible]	[illegible]	[illegible]	[illegible]	.	.	[illegible]	[illegible]	[illegible]	[illegible]
Leitrim,	[illegible]	[illegible]	[illegible]	[illegible]	[illegible]	[illegible]	.	[illegible]	[illegible]	[illegible]	[illegible]
Limerick,	[illegible]	[illegible]	[illegible]	[illegible]	[illegible]	[illegible]	.	[illegible]	[illegible]	[illegible]	[illegible]
Londonderry,	[illegible]	[illegible]	[illegible]	[illegible]	[illegible]	[illegible]	[illegible]	[illegible]	[illegible]	[illegible]	[illegible]
Longford,	[illegible]	[illegible]	[illegible]	[illegible]	[illegible]	[illegible]	.	[illegible]	[illegible]	[illegible]	[illegible]
Louth and Drogheda, County of Town,	[illegible]	[illegible]	[illegible]	[illegible]	[illegible]	[illegible]	[illegible]	[illegible]	[illegible]	[illegible]	[illegible]
Mayo,	[illegible]	[illegible]	[illegible]	[illegible]	[illegible]	.	[illegible]	[illegible]	[illegible]	[illegible]	[illegible]
Meath,	[illegible]	[illegible]	[illegible]	[illegible]	[illegible]	[illegible]	[illegible]	[illegible]	[illegible]	[illegible]	[illegible]
Monaghan,	[illegible]	[illegible]	[illegible]	[illegible]	[illegible]	[illegible]	[illegible]	[illegible]	[illegible]	[illegible]	[illegible]
Queen's,	[illegible]	[illegible]	[illegible]	[illegible]	[illegible]	[illegible]	.	[illegible]	[illegible]	[illegible]	[illegible]
Roscommon,	[illegible]	[illegible]	[illegible]	[illegible]	[illegible]	[illegible]	[illegible]	[illegible]	[illegible]	[illegible]	[illegible]
Sligo,	[illegible]	[illegible]	[illegible]	[illegible]	[illegible]	[illegible]	[illegible]	[illegible]	[illegible]	[illegible]	[illegible]
Tipperary,	[illegible]	[illegible]	[illegible]	[illegible]	[illegible]	[illegible]	[illegible]	[illegible]	[illegible]	[illegible]	[illegible]
Tyrone,	[illegible]	[illegible]	[illegible]	[illegible]	[illegible]	[illegible]	[illegible]	[illegible]	[illegible]	[illegible]	[illegible]
Waterford,	[illegible]	[illegible]	[illegible]	.	[illegible]	.	.	[illegible]	[illegible]	[illegible]	[illegible]
Westmeath,	[illegible]	[illegible]	[illegible]	[illegible]	[illegible]	[illegible]	.	[illegible]	[illegible]	[illegible]	[illegible]
Wexford,	[illegible]	[illegible]	[illegible]	.	[illegible]	[illegible]	[illegible]	[illegible]	[illegible]	[illegible]	[illegible]
Wicklow,	[illegible]	[illegible]	[illegible]	[illegible]	[illegible]	.	.	[illegible]	[illegible]	[illegible]	[illegible]
PROVINCES.											
Leinster,	[illegible]	[illegible]	[illegible]	[illegible]	[illegible]	[illegible]	[illegible]	[illegible]	[illegible]	[illegible]	[illegible]
Munster,	[illegible]	[illegible]	[illegible]	[illegible]	[illegible]	[illegible]	[illegible]	[illegible]	[illegible]	[illegible]	[illegible]
Ulster,	[illegible]	[illegible]	[illegible]	[illegible]	[illegible]	[illegible]	[illegible]	[illegible]	[illegible]	[illegible]	[illegible]
Connaught,	[illegible]	[illegible]	[illegible]	[illegible]	[illegible]	[illegible]	[illegible]	[illegible]	[illegible]	[illegible]	[illegible]
TOTAL,	[illegible]	[illegible]	[illegible]	[illegible]	[illegible]	[illegible]	[illegible]	[illegible]	[illegible]	[illegible]	[illegible]

[illegible] Crops in the Year 18[illegible], the Valuation in 18[illegible], and the Population in 18[illegible].

IN STATUTE ACRES.

[illegible]	[illegible]	[illegible]	[illegible]	[illegible]	[illegible]	[illegible]	[illegible]	[illegible]	[illegible]	[illegible]	[illegible]	COUNTIES.
Acres.	Acres.	Acres.	Acres.	Acres.	Acres.	Acres.	Acres.	Acres.	Acres.	£		
[illegible]	[illegible]	[illegible]	[illegible]	[illegible]	[illegible]	[illegible]	[illegible]	[illegible]	[illegible]	[illegible]	[illegible]	Antrim.
[illegible]	[illegible]	[illegible]	[illegible]	[illegible]	[illegible]	[illegible]	[illegible]	[illegible]	[illegible]	[illegible]	[illegible]	Armagh.
[illegible]	[illegible]	[illegible]	[illegible]	[illegible]	[illegible]	[illegible]	[illegible]	[illegible]	[illegible]	[illegible]	[illegible]	Carlow.
[illegible]	[illegible]	[illegible]	[illegible]	[illegible]	[illegible]	[illegible]	[illegible]	[illegible]	[illegible]	[illegible]	[illegible]	Cavan.
[illegible]	[illegible]	[illegible]	[illegible]	[illegible]	[illegible]	[illegible]	[illegible]	[illegible]	[illegible]	[illegible]	[illegible]	Clare.
[illegible]	[illegible]	[illegible]	[illegible]	[illegible]	[illegible]	[illegible]	[illegible]	[illegible]	[illegible]	[illegible]	[illegible]	Cork.
[illegible]	[illegible]	[illegible]	[illegible]	[illegible]	[illegible]	[illegible]	[illegible]	[illegible]	[illegible]	[illegible]	[illegible]	Donegal.
[illegible]	[illegible]	[illegible]	[illegible]	[illegible]	[illegible]	[illegible]	[illegible]	[illegible]	[illegible]	[illegible]	[illegible]	Down.
[illegible]	[illegible]	[illegible]	[illegible]	[illegible]	[illegible]	[illegible]	[illegible]	[illegible]	[illegible]	[illegible]	[illegible]	Dublin.
[illegible]	[illegible]	[illegible]	[illegible]	[illegible]	[illegible]	[illegible]	[illegible]	[illegible]	[illegible]	[illegible]	[illegible]	Fermanagh.
[illegible]	[illegible]	[illegible]	[illegible]	[illegible]	[illegible]	[illegible]	[illegible]	[illegible]	[illegible]	[illegible]	[illegible]	Galway.
[illegible]	[illegible]	[illegible]	[illegible]	[illegible]	[illegible]	[illegible]	[illegible]	[illegible]	[illegible]	[illegible]	[illegible]	Kerry.
[illegible]	[illegible]	[illegible]	[illegible]	[illegible]	[illegible]	[illegible]	[illegible]	[illegible]	[illegible]	[illegible]	[illegible]	Kildare.
[illegible]	[illegible]	[illegible]	[illegible]	[illegible]	[illegible]	[illegible]	[illegible]	[illegible]	[illegible]	[illegible]	[illegible]	Kilkenny.
[illegible]	[illegible]	[illegible]	[illegible]	[illegible]	[illegible]	[illegible]	[illegible]	[illegible]	[illegible]	[illegible]	[illegible]	King's.
[illegible]	[illegible]	[illegible]	[illegible]	[illegible]	[illegible]	[illegible]	[illegible]	[illegible]	[illegible]	[illegible]	[illegible]	Leitrim.
[illegible]	[illegible]	[illegible]	[illegible]	[illegible]	[illegible]	[illegible]	[illegible]	[illegible]	[illegible]	[illegible]	[illegible]	Limerick.
[illegible]	[illegible]	[illegible]	[illegible]	[illegible]	[illegible]	[illegible]	[illegible]	[illegible]	[illegible]	[illegible]	[illegible]	Londonderry.
[illegible]	[illegible]	[illegible]	[illegible]	[illegible]	[illegible]	[illegible]	[illegible]	[illegible]	[illegible]	[illegible]	[illegible]	Longford.
[illegible]	[illegible]	[illegible]	[illegible]	[illegible]	[illegible]	[illegible]	[illegible]	[illegible]	[illegible]	[illegible]	[illegible]	Louth & Drogheda County of Town.
[illegible]	[illegible]	[illegible]	[illegible]	[illegible]	[illegible]	[illegible]	[illegible]	[illegible]	[illegible]	[illegible]	[illegible]	Mayo.
[illegible]	[illegible]	[illegible]	[illegible]	[illegible]	[illegible]	[illegible]	[illegible]	[illegible]	[illegible]	[illegible]	[illegible]	Meath.
[illegible]	[illegible]	[illegible]	[illegible]	[illegible]	[illegible]	[illegible]	[illegible]	[illegible]	[illegible]	[illegible]	[illegible]	Monaghan.
[illegible]	[illegible]	[illegible]	[illegible]	[illegible]	[illegible]	[illegible]	[illegible]	[illegible]	[illegible]	[illegible]	[illegible]	Queen's.
[illegible]	[illegible]	[illegible]	[illegible]	[illegible]	[illegible]	[illegible]	[illegible]	[illegible]	[illegible]	[illegible]	[illegible]	Roscommon.
[illegible]	[illegible]	[illegible]	[illegible]	[illegible]	[illegible]	[illegible]	[illegible]	[illegible]	[illegible]	[illegible]	[illegible]	Sligo.
[illegible]	[illegible]	[illegible]	[illegible]	[illegible]	[illegible]	[illegible]	[illegible]	[illegible]	[illegible]	[illegible]	[illegible]	Tipperary.
[illegible]	[illegible]	[illegible]	[illegible]	[illegible]	[illegible]	[illegible]	[illegible]	[illegible]	[illegible]	[illegible]	[illegible]	Tyrone.
[illegible]	[illegible]	[illegible]	[illegible]	[illegible]	[illegible]	[illegible]	[illegible]	[illegible]	[illegible]	[illegible]	[illegible]	Waterford.
[illegible]	[illegible]	[illegible]	[illegible]	[illegible]	[illegible]	[illegible]	[illegible]	[illegible]	[illegible]	[illegible]	[illegible]	Westmeath.
[illegible]	[illegible]	[illegible]	[illegible]	[illegible]	[illegible]	[illegible]	[illegible]	[illegible]	[illegible]	[illegible]	[illegible]	Wexford.
[illegible]	[illegible]	[illegible]	[illegible]	[illegible]	[illegible]	[illegible]	[illegible]	[illegible]	[illegible]	[illegible]	[illegible]	Wicklow.
												PROVINCES.
[illegible]	[illegible]	[illegible]	[illegible]	[illegible]	[illegible]	[illegible]	[illegible]	[illegible]	[illegible]	[illegible]	[illegible]	Leinster.
[illegible]	[illegible]	[illegible]	[illegible]	[illegible]	[illegible]	[illegible]	[illegible]	[illegible]	[illegible]	[illegible]	[illegible]	Munster.
[illegible]	[illegible]	[illegible]	[illegible]	[illegible]	[illegible]	[illegible]	[illegible]	[illegible]	[illegible]	[illegible]	[illegible]	Ulster.
[illegible]	[illegible]	[illegible]	[illegible]	[illegible]	[illegible]	[illegible]	[illegible]	[illegible]	[illegible]	[illegible]	[illegible]	Connaught.
[illegible]	[illegible]	[illegible]	[illegible]	[illegible]	[illegible]	[illegible]	[illegible]	[illegible]	[illegible]	[illegible]	[illegible]	Total.

* The slight difference between the Total Valuation by Counties and that by [illegible] is accounted for by the fact that the County and Union Returns do not take effect at the same period of the year.

TABLE 6.—[illegible], BY COUNTIES AND PROVINCES [illegible]

COUNTIES.	[illegible]	[illegible]	[illegible]	[illegible]	[illegible]	[illegible]	[illegible]
Antrim,	[illegible]	1,2[illegible]	14,[illegible]	77	779	[illegible]	1,1[illegible]
Armagh,	[illegible]	[illegible]	1,[illegible]	[illegible]	3,[illegible]	4,[illegible]	1,[illegible]
Carlow,	[illegible]	[illegible]	[illegible]	[illegible]	[illegible]	[illegible]	.
Cavan,	7,[illegible]	[illegible]	[illegible]	91	2,[illegible]	[illegible]	12
Clare,	[illegible]	[illegible]	[illegible]	[illegible]	[illegible]	1,1[illegible]	[illegible]
Cork,	[illegible]	1,[illegible]	[illegible]	[illegible]	[illegible]	[illegible]	[illegible]
Donegal,	[illegible]	1,[illegible]	[illegible]	[illegible]	11,[illegible]	[illegible]	[illegible]
Down,	244,[illegible]	1,[illegible]	4,[illegible]	[illegible]	[illegible]	7,[illegible]	1,[illegible]
Dublin,	[illegible]	[illegible]	[illegible]	[illegible]	[illegible]	[illegible]	1,[illegible]
Fermanagh,	[illegible]	[illegible]	[illegible]	[illegible]	[illegible]	[illegible]	[illegible]
Galway,	74,[illegible]	[illegible]	[illegible]	[illegible]	[illegible]	[illegible]	[illegible]
Kerry,	[illegible]	[illegible]	[illegible]	[illegible]	4,[illegible]	140	[illegible]
Kildare,	[illegible]	[illegible]	[illegible]	[illegible]	4,377	[illegible]	[illegible]
Kilkenny,	[illegible]	[illegible]	[illegible]	[illegible]	.	[illegible]	[illegible]
King's,	[illegible]	[illegible]	[illegible]	[illegible]	[illegible]	.	.
Leitrim,	[illegible]	[illegible]	[illegible]	[illegible]	[illegible]	[illegible]	.
Limerick,	[illegible]	[illegible]	[illegible]	[illegible]	[illegible]	[illegible]	.
Londonderry,	[illegible]	[illegible]	[illegible]	9	4,[illegible]	[illegible]	[illegible]
Longford,	[illegible]	[illegible]	[illegible]	[illegible]	[illegible]	[illegible]	.
Louth and Drogheda, County of Town.	[illegible]	[illegible]	[illegible]	[illegible]	[illegible]	[illegible]	[illegible]
Mayo,	[illegible]	[illegible]	[illegible]	[illegible]	[illegible]	.	[illegible]
Meath,	[illegible]	[illegible]	[illegible]	[illegible]	[illegible]	[illegible]	[illegible]
Monaghan,	[illegible]	[illegible]	[illegible]	[illegible]	[illegible]	[illegible]	[illegible]
Queen's,	[illegible]	[illegible]	[illegible]	[illegible]	[illegible]	[illegible]	.
Roscommon,	[illegible]	[illegible]	[illegible]	[illegible]	[illegible]	77	[illegible]
Sligo,	[illegible]	[illegible]	[illegible]	[illegible]	[illegible]	[illegible]	[illegible]
Tipperary,	[illegible]	[illegible]	[illegible]	[illegible]	[illegible]	[illegible]	[illegible]
Tyrone,	[illegible]	[illegible]	[illegible]	[illegible]	[illegible]	[illegible]	[illegible]
Waterford,	[illegible]	[illegible]	[illegible]	.	[illegible]	.	.
Westmeath,	[illegible]	[illegible]	[illegible]	[illegible]	[illegible]	[illegible]	.
Wexford,	[illegible]	[illegible]	[illegible]	.	[illegible]	[illegible]	[illegible]
Wicklow,	[illegible]	[illegible]	[illegible]	[illegible]	[illegible]	.	.
PROVINCES.							
Leinster,	[illegible]	[illegible]	[illegible]	[illegible]	[illegible]	[illegible]	[illegible]
Munster,	[illegible]	[illegible]	[illegible]	[illegible]	[illegible]	1,[illegible]	[illegible]
Ulster,	[illegible]	[illegible]	[illegible]	[illegible]	[illegible]	[illegible]	[illegible]
Connaught,	[illegible]	[illegible]	[illegible]	[illegible]	[illegible]	[illegible]	[illegible]
TOTAL,	[illegible]	[illegible]	[illegible]	[illegible]	[illegible]	[illegible]	[illegible]

Produce of the Crops in the Year 1890.

[illegible]	[illegible]	[illegible]	[illegible]	[illegible]	[illegible]	[illegible]	[illegible]	[illegible]	[illegible]	Counties.
[illegible]	[illegible]	[illegible]	[illegible]	[illegible]	[illegible]	[illegible]	[illegible]	[illegible]	[illegible]	Antrim.
[illegible]	[illegible]	[illegible]	[illegible]	[illegible]	[illegible]	[illegible]	[illegible]	[illegible]	[illegible]	Armagh.
[illegible]	[illegible]	[illegible]	[illegible]	[illegible]	[illegible]	[illegible]	.	[illegible]	[illegible]	Carlow.
[illegible]	[illegible]	[illegible]	[illegible]	[illegible]	[illegible]	[illegible]	[illegible]	[illegible]	[illegible]	Cavan.
[illegible]	[illegible]	[illegible]	[illegible]	[illegible]	[illegible]	[illegible]	[illegible]	[illegible]	[illegible]	Clare.
[illegible]	[illegible]	[illegible]	[illegible]	[illegible]	[illegible]	[illegible]	[illegible]	[illegible]	[illegible]	Cork.
[illegible]	[illegible]	[illegible]	[illegible]	[illegible]	[illegible]	[illegible]	[illegible]	[illegible]	[illegible]	Donegal.
[illegible]	[illegible]	[illegible]	[illegible]	[illegible]	[illegible]	[illegible]	[illegible]	[illegible]	[illegible]	Down.
[illegible]	[illegible]	[illegible]	[illegible]	[illegible]	[illegible]	[illegible]	.	[illegible]	[illegible]	Dublin.
[illegible]	[illegible]	[illegible]	[illegible]	[illegible]	[illegible]	[illegible]	[illegible]	[illegible]	[illegible]	Fermanagh.
[illegible]	[illegible]	[illegible]	[illegible]	[illegible]	[illegible]	[illegible]	[illegible]	[illegible]	[illegible]	Galway.
[illegible]	[illegible]	[illegible]	[illegible]	[illegible]	[illegible]	[illegible]	[illegible]	[illegible]	[illegible]	Kerry.
[illegible]	[illegible]	[illegible]	[illegible]	[illegible]	[illegible]	[illegible]	.	[illegible]	[illegible]	Kildare.
[illegible]	[illegible]	[illegible]	[illegible]	[illegible]	[illegible]	[illegible]	.	[illegible]	[illegible]	Kilkenny.
[illegible]	[illegible]	[illegible]	[illegible]	[illegible]	[illegible]	[illegible]	.	[illegible]	[illegible]	King's.
[illegible]	[illegible]	[illegible]	[illegible]	[illegible]	[illegible]	[illegible]	[illegible]	[illegible]	[illegible]	Leitrim.
[illegible]	[illegible]	[illegible]	[illegible]	[illegible]	[illegible]	[illegible]	[illegible]	[illegible]	[illegible]	Limerick.
[illegible]	[illegible]	[illegible]	[illegible]	[illegible]	[illegible]	[illegible]	[illegible]	[illegible]	[illegible]	Londonderry.
[illegible]	[illegible]	[illegible]	[illegible]	[illegible]	[illegible]	[illegible]	[illegible]	[illegible]	[illegible]	Longford.
[illegible]	[illegible]	[illegible]	[illegible]	[illegible]	[illegible]	.	[illegible]	[illegible]	[illegible]	Louth and Drogheda, County of Town.
[illegible]	[illegible]	[illegible]	[illegible]	[illegible]	[illegible]	[illegible]	[illegible]	[illegible]	[illegible]	Mayo.
[illegible]	[illegible]	[illegible]	[illegible]	[illegible]	[illegible]	[illegible]	[illegible]	[illegible]	[illegible]	Meath.
[illegible]	[illegible]	[illegible]	[illegible]	[illegible]	[illegible]	[illegible]	[illegible]	[illegible]	[illegible]	Monaghan.
[illegible]	[illegible]	[illegible]	[illegible]	[illegible]	[illegible]	[illegible]	.	[illegible]	[illegible]	Queen's.
[illegible]	[illegible]	[illegible]	[illegible]	[illegible]	[illegible]	[illegible]	[illegible]	[illegible]	[illegible]	Roscommon.
[illegible]	[illegible]	[illegible]	[illegible]	[illegible]	[illegible]	[illegible]	[illegible]	[illegible]	[illegible]	Sligo.
[illegible]	[illegible]	[illegible]	[illegible]	[illegible]	[illegible]	[illegible]	.	[illegible]	[illegible]	Tipperary.
[illegible]	[illegible]	[illegible]	[illegible]	[illegible]	[illegible]	[illegible]	[illegible]	[illegible]	[illegible]	Tyrone.
[illegible]	[illegible]	[illegible]	[illegible]	[illegible]	[illegible]	[illegible]	.	[illegible]	[illegible]	Waterford.
[illegible]	[illegible]	[illegible]	[illegible]	[illegible]	[illegible]	[illegible]	[illegible]	[illegible]	[illegible]	Westmeath.
[illegible]	[illegible]	[illegible]	[illegible]	[illegible]	[illegible]	[illegible]	[illegible]	[illegible]	[illegible]	Wexford.
[illegible]	[illegible]	[illegible]	[illegible]	[illegible]	[illegible]	[illegible]	[illegible]	[illegible]	[illegible]	Wicklow.
										PROVINCES.
[illegible]	[illegible]	[illegible]	[illegible]	[illegible]	[illegible]	[illegible]	[illegible]	[illegible]	[illegible]	Leinster.
[illegible]	[illegible]	[illegible]	[illegible]	[illegible]	[illegible]	[illegible]	[illegible]	[illegible]	[illegible]	Munster.
[illegible]	[illegible]	[illegible]	[illegible]	[illegible]	[illegible]	[illegible]	[illegible]	[illegible]	[illegible]	Ulster.
[illegible]	[illegible]	[illegible]	[illegible]	[illegible]	[illegible]	[illegible]	[illegible]	[illegible]	[illegible]	Connaught.
[illegible]	[illegible]	[illegible]	[illegible]	[illegible]	[illegible]	[illegible]	[illegible]	[illegible]	[illegible]	Total.

TABLE V.—SHOWING BY POOR LAW UNIONS, THE EXTENT OF LAND

EXTENT UNDER CROPS										
CORN, BEANS, AND PEAS.										
Wheat.	[illegible]	[illegible]	[illegible]	[illegible]	[illegible]	[illegible]	[illegible]	[illegible]	[illegible]	[illegible]
Acres.	Acres.	Acres.	Acres.	Acres.	Acres.	Acres.	Acres.	Acres.	Acres.	Acres.

[illegible] Crops in the Year 1890, the Valuation in 1890, and the Population in 1891.

[illegible] Crops in the Year 1890, the Valuation in 1890, and the Population in 1891—continued.

In Statute Acres.												
[illegible]							[illegible]	[illegible]		[illegible]	Valuation in 1890.	Population in 1891.
[illegible]	[illegible]	[illegible]	[illegible]	[illegible]	[illegible]	[illegible]		[illegible]	[illegible]			
Acres.	Acres.	Acres.	Acres.	Acres.	Acres.	Acres.		Acres.	Acres.	Acres.	£	
[illegible]												

POOR LAW UNIONS	[illegible]
[illegible]	[illegible]

TABLE 3.—SHOWING, BY POOR LAW UNIONS, THE

Produce of the Crops in the Year 1850—continued.

TABLE 2.—Showing the Number of Holdings exceeding one Acre, and Extent of Land under Crops in each Year from 1851 to 1890, by Counties and Provinces.

Counties	Year	No. of Holdings	Extent under Crops in Statute Acres in each Year from 1851 to 1890 — Corn, Beans, and Peas							Green Crops							Total
Antrim — Area [illegible] Acres	[illegible]	[illegible]	[illegible]	[illegible]	[illegible]	[illegible]	[illegible]	[illegible]	[illegible]	[illegible]	[illegible]	[illegible]	[illegible]	[illegible]	[illegible]	[illegible]	[illegible]
Armagh — Area [illegible] Acres	[illegible]	[illegible]	[illegible]	[illegible]	[illegible]	[illegible]	[illegible]	[illegible]	[illegible]	[illegible]	[illegible]	[illegible]	[illegible]	[illegible]	[illegible]	[illegible]	[illegible]
Carlow — Area [illegible] Acres	[illegible]	[illegible]	[illegible]	[illegible]	[illegible]	[illegible]	[illegible]	[illegible]	[illegible]	[illegible]	[illegible]	[illegible]	[illegible]	[illegible]	[illegible]	[illegible]	[illegible]
Cavan — Area [illegible] Acres	[illegible]	[illegible]	[illegible]	[illegible]	[illegible]	[illegible]	[illegible]	[illegible]	[illegible]	[illegible]	[illegible]	[illegible]	[illegible]	[illegible]	[illegible]	[illegible]	[illegible]
Clare — Area [illegible] Acres	[illegible]	[illegible]	[illegible]	[illegible]	[illegible]	[illegible]	[illegible]	[illegible]	[illegible]	[illegible]	[illegible]	[illegible]	[illegible]	[illegible]	[illegible]	[illegible]	[illegible]
Cork — Area [illegible] Acres	[illegible]	[illegible]	[illegible]	[illegible]	[illegible]	[illegible]	[illegible]	[illegible]	[illegible]	[illegible]	[illegible]	[illegible]	[illegible]	[illegible]	[illegible]	[illegible]	[illegible]
Donegal — Area [illegible] Acres	[illegible]	[illegible]	[illegible]	[illegible]	[illegible]	[illegible]	[illegible]	[illegible]	[illegible]	[illegible]	[illegible]	[illegible]	[illegible]	[illegible]	[illegible]	[illegible]	[illegible]
Down — Area [illegible] Acres	[illegible]	[illegible]	[illegible]	[illegible]	[illegible]	[illegible]	[illegible]	[illegible]	[illegible]	[illegible]	[illegible]	[illegible]	[illegible]	[illegible]	[illegible]	[illegible]	[illegible]

Table 8.—Showing the Number of Holdings exceeding One Acre, and Extent of Land under Crops in each Year from 1881 to 1890, by Counties and Provinces—continued.

Counties.	Years.	No. of Holdings exceeding 1 Acre.	Extent under Crops in Statute Acres in each Year from 1881 to 1890. — Corn, Beans, and Peas.	Green Crops.	Total Extent under Crops.
Longford: Area, [illegible] Acres.	[illegible]	[illegible]	[illegible]	[illegible]	[illegible]
Londonderry: Area, [illegible] Acres.	[illegible]	[illegible]	[illegible]	[illegible]	[illegible]
Limerick: Area, [illegible] Acres.	[illegible]	[illegible]	[illegible]	[illegible]	[illegible]
Louth and Drogheda Co. of Town: Area, [illegible] Acres.	[illegible]	[illegible]	[illegible]	[illegible]	[illegible]
Mayo: Area, [illegible] Acres.	[illegible]	[illegible]	[illegible]	[illegible]	[illegible]
Meath: Area, [illegible] Acres.	[illegible]	[illegible]	[illegible]	[illegible]	[illegible]
Monaghan: Area, [illegible] Acres.	[illegible]	[illegible]	[illegible]	[illegible]	[illegible]
Queen's: Area, [illegible] Acres.	[illegible]	[illegible]	[illegible]	[illegible]	[illegible]

TABLE 2.—SHOWING THE EXTENT OF HOLDINGS EXCEEDING ONE ACRE, AND EXTENT OF LAND UNDER CROPS IN EACH YEAR FROM 1851 TO 1880, BY COUNTIES AND PROVINCES—continued.

COUNTIES.	Years.	No. of Holdings exceeding 1 acre.	Corn, Beans, and Peas.							Green Crops.							Total under Crops.
			[illegible]	[illegible]	[illegible]	[illegible]	[illegible]	[illegible]	[illegible]	[illegible]	[illegible]	[illegible]	[illegible]	[illegible]	[illegible]	[illegible]	
ROSCOMMON: Area, [illegible] Acres.	[illegible]	[illegible]	[illegible]	[illegible]	[illegible]	[illegible]	[illegible]	[illegible]	[illegible]	[illegible]	[illegible]	[illegible]	[illegible]	[illegible]	[illegible]	[illegible]	[illegible]
SLIGO: Area, [illegible] Acres.	[illegible]	[illegible]	[illegible]	[illegible]	[illegible]	[illegible]	[illegible]	[illegible]	[illegible]	[illegible]	[illegible]	[illegible]	[illegible]	[illegible]	[illegible]	[illegible]	[illegible]
TIPPERARY: Area, [illegible] Acres.	[illegible]	[illegible]	[illegible]	[illegible]	[illegible]	[illegible]	[illegible]	[illegible]	[illegible]	[illegible]	[illegible]	[illegible]	[illegible]	[illegible]	[illegible]	[illegible]	[illegible]
TYRONE: Area, [illegible] Acres.	[illegible]	[illegible]	[illegible]	[illegible]	[illegible]	[illegible]	[illegible]	[illegible]	[illegible]	[illegible]	[illegible]	[illegible]	[illegible]	[illegible]	[illegible]	[illegible]	[illegible]
WATERFORD: Area, [illegible] Acres.	[illegible]	[illegible]	[illegible]	[illegible]	[illegible]	[illegible]	[illegible]	[illegible]	[illegible]	[illegible]	[illegible]	[illegible]	[illegible]	[illegible]	[illegible]	[illegible]	[illegible]
WESTMEATH: Area, [illegible] Acres.	[illegible]	[illegible]	[illegible]	[illegible]	[illegible]	[illegible]	[illegible]	[illegible]	[illegible]	[illegible]	[illegible]	[illegible]	[illegible]	[illegible]	[illegible]	[illegible]	[illegible]
WEXFORD: Area, [illegible] Acres.	[illegible]	[illegible]	[illegible]	[illegible]	[illegible]	[illegible]	[illegible]	[illegible]	[illegible]	[illegible]	[illegible]	[illegible]	[illegible]	[illegible]	[illegible]	[illegible]	[illegible]
WICKLOW: Area, [illegible] Acres.	[illegible]	[illegible]	[illegible]	[illegible]	[illegible]	[illegible]	[illegible]	[illegible]	[illegible]	[illegible]	[illegible]	[illegible]	[illegible]	[illegible]	[illegible]	[illegible]	[illegible]

PROVINCES.

TOTAL OF IRELAND.

TABLE 10.—Showing the Average Rates of Produce of Crops to the Statute Acre, in each Year, from 1881 to 1890.

Counties	[illegible]	[illegible]	[illegible]	[illegible]	[illegible]	[illegible]	[illegible]	[illegible]	[illegible]	[illegible]	[illegible]	[illegible]	[illegible]	[illegible]
ANTRIM,	[illegible]	[illegible]	[illegible]	[illegible]	[illegible]	[illegible]	[illegible]	[illegible]	[illegible]	[illegible]	[illegible]	[illegible]	[illegible]	[illegible]
ARMAGH,	[illegible]	[illegible]	[illegible]	[illegible]	[illegible]	[illegible]	[illegible]	[illegible]	[illegible]	[illegible]	[illegible]	[illegible]	[illegible]	[illegible]
CARLOW,	[illegible]	[illegible]	[illegible]	[illegible]	[illegible]	[illegible]	[illegible]	[illegible]	[illegible]	[illegible]	[illegible]	[illegible]	[illegible]	[illegible]
CAVAN,	[illegible]	[illegible]	[illegible]	[illegible]	[illegible]	[illegible]	[illegible]	[illegible]	[illegible]	[illegible]	[illegible]	[illegible]	[illegible]	[illegible]
CLARE,	[illegible]	[illegible]	[illegible]	[illegible]	[illegible]	[illegible]	[illegible]	[illegible]	[illegible]	[illegible]	[illegible]	[illegible]	[illegible]	[illegible]
CORK,	[illegible]	[illegible]	[illegible]	[illegible]	[illegible]	[illegible]	[illegible]	[illegible]	[illegible]	[illegible]	[illegible]	[illegible]	[illegible]	[illegible]
DONEGAL,	[illegible]	[illegible]	[illegible]	[illegible]	[illegible]	[illegible]	[illegible]	[illegible]	[illegible]	[illegible]	[illegible]	[illegible]	[illegible]	[illegible]
DOWN,	[illegible]	[illegible]	[illegible]	[illegible]	[illegible]	[illegible]	[illegible]	[illegible]	[illegible]	[illegible]	[illegible]	[illegible]	[illegible]	[illegible]

TABLE 10.—Showing the Average Rates of Produce to the Statute Acre—continued.

Counties.	[illegible]
Limerick,	[illegible]
Londonderry,	[illegible]
Longford,	[illegible]
Louth and Drogheda, Co. of Town.	[illegible]
Mayo,	[illegible]
Meath,	[illegible]
Monaghan,	[illegible]
Queen's,	[illegible]

AVERAGE OF PROVINCES.

AVERAGE OF IRELAND.

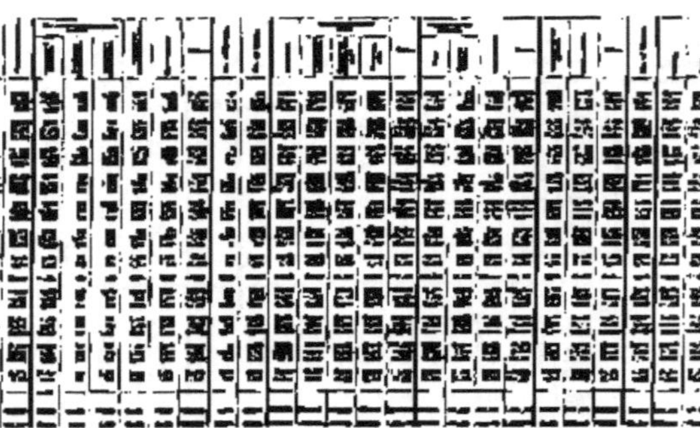

TABLE [illegible].—Showing [illegible] Quantity of Stock in each Poor Law Union of Ireland, in [illegible]—continued.

[illegible]

Total, [illegible]

TABLE 13.—SHOWING THE QUANTITY OF LIVE STOCK IN EACH YEAR FROM 1881 to 1890, BY COUNTIES AND PROVINCES.

COUNTIES.	Years.	No. of Horses.			Mules and Asses.		No. of Cattle.			No. of Sheep.		No. of Pigs.		[illegible]	[illegible]
		[illegible]	[illegible]	[illegible]	[illegible]	[illegible]	[illegible]	[illegible]	[illegible]	[illegible]	[illegible]	[illegible]	[illegible]		
[illegible]	[illegible]	[illegible]	[illegible]	[illegible]	[illegible]	[illegible]	[illegible]	[illegible]	[illegible]	[illegible]	[illegible]	[illegible]	[illegible]	[illegible]	[illegible]

TABLE 16.—SHOWING THE QUANTITY OF LIVE STOCK IN EACH YEAR FROM 1881 TO 1890, BY COUNTIES AND PROVINCES—continued.

COUNTIES.	Years	No. of Horses			Mules and Asses		No. of Cattle			No. of Sheep		No. of Pigs		No. of Goats	No. of Poultry
[illegible]	[illegible]	[illegible]	[illegible]	[illegible]	[illegible]	[illegible]	[illegible]	[illegible]	[illegible]	[illegible]	[illegible]	[illegible]	[illegible]	[illegible]	[illegible]

AGRICULTURAL STATISTICS FOR THE YEAR [illegible].

13.—Showing the Quantity of Live Stock in each Year from [illegible] to [illegible], by Counties and Provinces—continued.

Years.	No. of Horses.			Mules and Asses.		No. of Cattle.			No. of Sheep.		No. of Pigs.		No. of Goats.
	[illegible]	[illegible]	[illegible]	[illegible]	[illegible]	[illegible]	[illegible]	[illegible]	[illegible]	[illegible]	[illegible]	[illegible]	
[illegible]	[illegible]	[illegible]	[illegible]	[illegible]	[illegible]	[illegible]	[illegible]	[illegible]	[illegible]	[illegible]	[illegible]	[illegible]	[illegible]
[illegible]	[illegible]	[illegible]	[illegible]	[illegible]	[illegible]	[illegible]	[illegible]	[illegible]	[illegible]	[illegible]	[illegible]	[illegible]	[illegible]
[illegible]	[illegible]	[illegible]	[illegible]	[illegible]	[illegible]	[illegible]	[illegible]	[illegible]	[illegible]	[illegible]	[illegible]	[illegible]	[illegible]
[illegible]	[illegible]	[illegible]	[illegible]	[illegible]	[illegible]	[illegible]	[illegible]	[illegible]	[illegible]	[illegible]	[illegible]	[illegible]	[illegible]
[illegible]	[illegible]	[illegible]	[illegible]	[illegible]	[illegible]	[illegible]	[illegible]	[illegible]	[illegible]	[illegible]	[illegible]	[illegible]	[illegible]
[illegible]	[illegible]	[illegible]	[illegible]	[illegible]	[illegible]	[illegible]	[illegible]	[illegible]	[illegible]	[illegible]	[illegible]	[illegible]	[illegible]
[illegible]	[illegible]	[illegible]	[illegible]	[illegible]	[illegible]	[illegible]	[illegible]	[illegible]	[illegible]	[illegible]	[illegible]	[illegible]	[illegible]
[illegible]	[illegible]	[illegible]	[illegible]	[illegible]	[illegible]	[illegible]	[illegible]	[illegible]	[illegible]	[illegible]	[illegible]	[illegible]	[illegible]
[illegible]	[illegible]	[illegible]	[illegible]	[illegible]	[illegible]	[illegible]	[illegible]	[illegible]	[illegible]	[illegible]	[illegible]	[illegible]	[illegible]
[illegible]	[illegible]	[illegible]	[illegible]	[illegible]	[illegible]	[illegible]	[illegible]	[illegible]	[illegible]	[illegible]	[illegible]	[illegible]	[illegible]

TABLE 13.—SHOWING THE QUANTITY OF LIVE STOCK IN EACH YEAR FROM 1881 TO 1890, BY COUNTIES AND PROVINCES—continued.

PROVINCES.

PROVINCES.	Years.	No. of Horses.			Mules and Asses.		No. of Cattle.			No. of Sheep.		No. of Pigs.		No. of Goats.	No. of Poultry.
		[illegible]	[illegible]	[illegible]	No. of Mules.	No. of Asses.	[illegible]	[illegible]	[illegible]	[illegible]	[illegible]	[illegible]	[illegible]		
LEINSTER:	1881	[illegible]	[illegible]	[illegible]	[illegible]	[illegible]	[illegible]	[illegible]	[illegible]	[illegible]	[illegible]	[illegible]	[illegible]	[illegible]	[illegible]
	1882	[illegible]	[illegible]	[illegible]	[illegible]	[illegible]	[illegible]	[illegible]	[illegible]	[illegible]	[illegible]	[illegible]	[illegible]	[illegible]	[illegible]
	1883	[illegible]	[illegible]	[illegible]	[illegible]	[illegible]	[illegible]	[illegible]	[illegible]	[illegible]	[illegible]	[illegible]	[illegible]	[illegible]	[illegible]
Area, [illegible] Acres.	1884	[illegible]	[illegible]	[illegible]	[illegible]	[illegible]	[illegible]	[illegible]	[illegible]	[illegible]	[illegible]	[illegible]	[illegible]	[illegible]	[illegible]
	1885	[illegible]	[illegible]	[illegible]	[illegible]	[illegible]	[illegible]	[illegible]	[illegible]	[illegible]	[illegible]	[illegible]	[illegible]	[illegible]	[illegible]
	1886	[illegible]	[illegible]	[illegible]	[illegible]	[illegible]	[illegible]	[illegible]	[illegible]	[illegible]	[illegible]	[illegible]	[illegible]	[illegible]	[illegible]
	1887	[illegible]	[illegible]	[illegible]	[illegible]	[illegible]	[illegible]	[illegible]	[illegible]	[illegible]	[illegible]	[illegible]	[illegible]	[illegible]	[illegible]
	1888	[illegible]	[illegible]	[illegible]	[illegible]	[illegible]	[illegible]	[illegible]	[illegible]	[illegible]	[illegible]	[illegible]	[illegible]	[illegible]	[illegible]
	1889	[illegible]	[illegible]	[illegible]	[illegible]	[illegible]	[illegible]	[illegible]	[illegible]	[illegible]	[illegible]	[illegible]	[illegible]	[illegible]	[illegible]
	1890	[illegible]	[illegible]	[illegible]	[illegible]	[illegible]	[illegible]	[illegible]	[illegible]	[illegible]	[illegible]	[illegible]	[illegible]	[illegible]	[illegible]
MUNSTER:	1881	[illegible]	[illegible]	[illegible]	[illegible]	[illegible]	[illegible]	[illegible]	[illegible]	[illegible]	[illegible]	[illegible]	[illegible]	[illegible]	[illegible]
	1882	[illegible]	[illegible]	[illegible]	[illegible]	[illegible]	[illegible]	[illegible]	[illegible]	[illegible]	[illegible]	[illegible]	[illegible]	[illegible]	[illegible]
	1883	[illegible]	[illegible]	[illegible]	[illegible]	[illegible]	[illegible]	[illegible]	[illegible]	[illegible]	[illegible]	[illegible]	[illegible]	[illegible]	[illegible]
Area, [illegible] Acres.	1884	[illegible]	[illegible]	[illegible]	[illegible]	[illegible]	[illegible]	[illegible]	[illegible]	[illegible]	[illegible]	[illegible]	[illegible]	[illegible]	[illegible]
	1885	[illegible]	[illegible]	[illegible]	[illegible]	[illegible]	[illegible]	[illegible]	[illegible]	[illegible]	[illegible]	[illegible]	[illegible]	[illegible]	[illegible]
	1886	[illegible]	[illegible]	[illegible]	[illegible]	[illegible]	[illegible]	[illegible]	[illegible]	[illegible]	[illegible]	[illegible]	[illegible]	[illegible]	[illegible]
	1887	[illegible]	[illegible]	[illegible]	[illegible]	[illegible]	[illegible]	[illegible]	[illegible]	[illegible]	[illegible]	[illegible]	[illegible]	[illegible]	[illegible]
	1888	[illegible]	[illegible]	[illegible]	[illegible]	[illegible]	[illegible]	[illegible]	[illegible]	[illegible]	[illegible]	[illegible]	[illegible]	[illegible]	[illegible]
	1889	[illegible]	[illegible]	[illegible]	[illegible]	[illegible]	[illegible]	[illegible]	[illegible]	[illegible]	[illegible]	[illegible]	[illegible]	[illegible]	[illegible]
	1890	[illegible]	[illegible]	[illegible]	[illegible]	[illegible]	[illegible]	[illegible]	[illegible]	[illegible]	[illegible]	[illegible]	[illegible]	[illegible]	[illegible]
ULSTER:	1881	[illegible]	[illegible]	[illegible]	[illegible]	[illegible]	[illegible]	[illegible]	[illegible]	[illegible]	[illegible]	[illegible]	[illegible]	[illegible]	[illegible]
	1882	[illegible]	[illegible]	[illegible]	[illegible]	[illegible]	[illegible]	[illegible]	[illegible]	[illegible]	[illegible]	[illegible]	[illegible]	[illegible]	[illegible]
	1883	[illegible]	[illegible]	[illegible]	[illegible]	[illegible]	[illegible]	[illegible]	[illegible]	[illegible]	[illegible]	[illegible]	[illegible]	[illegible]	[illegible]
Area, [illegible] Acres.	1884	[illegible]	[illegible]	[illegible]	[illegible]	[illegible]	[illegible]	[illegible]	[illegible]	[illegible]	[illegible]	[illegible]	[illegible]	[illegible]	[illegible]
	1885	[illegible]	[illegible]	[illegible]	[illegible]	[illegible]	[illegible]	[illegible]	[illegible]	[illegible]	[illegible]	[illegible]	[illegible]	[illegible]	[illegible]
	1886	[illegible]	[illegible]	[illegible]	[illegible]	[illegible]	[illegible]	[illegible]	[illegible]	[illegible]	[illegible]	[illegible]	[illegible]	[illegible]	[illegible]
	1887	[illegible]	[illegible]	[illegible]	[illegible]	[illegible]	[illegible]	[illegible]	[illegible]	[illegible]	[illegible]	[illegible]	[illegible]	[illegible]	[illegible]
	1888	[illegible]	[illegible]	[illegible]	[illegible]	[illegible]	[illegible]	[illegible]	[illegible]	[illegible]	[illegible]	[illegible]	[illegible]	[illegible]	[illegible]
	1889	[illegible]	[illegible]	[illegible]	[illegible]	[illegible]	[illegible]	[illegible]	[illegible]	[illegible]	[illegible]	[illegible]	[illegible]	[illegible]	[illegible]
	1890	[illegible]	[illegible]	[illegible]	[illegible]	[illegible]	[illegible]	[illegible]	[illegible]	[illegible]	[illegible]	[illegible]	[illegible]	[illegible]	[illegible]
CONNAUGHT:	1881	[illegible]	[illegible]	[illegible]	[illegible]	[illegible]	[illegible]	[illegible]	[illegible]	[illegible]	[illegible]	[illegible]	[illegible]	[illegible]	[illegible]
	1882	[illegible]	[illegible]	[illegible]	[illegible]	[illegible]	[illegible]	[illegible]	[illegible]	[illegible]	[illegible]	[illegible]	[illegible]	[illegible]	[illegible]
	1883	[illegible]	[illegible]	[illegible]	[illegible]	[illegible]	[illegible]	[illegible]	[illegible]	[illegible]	[illegible]	[illegible]	[illegible]	[illegible]	[illegible]
Area, [illegible] Acres.	1884	[illegible]	[illegible]	[illegible]	[illegible]	[illegible]	[illegible]	[illegible]	[illegible]	[illegible]	[illegible]	[illegible]	[illegible]	[illegible]	[illegible]
	1885	[illegible]	[illegible]	[illegible]	[illegible]	[illegible]	[illegible]	[illegible]	[illegible]	[illegible]	[illegible]	[illegible]	[illegible]	[illegible]	[illegible]
	1886	[illegible]	[illegible]	[illegible]	[illegible]	[illegible]	[illegible]	[illegible]	[illegible]	[illegible]	[illegible]	[illegible]	[illegible]	[illegible]	[illegible]
	1887	[illegible]	[illegible]	[illegible]	[illegible]	[illegible]	[illegible]	[illegible]	[illegible]	[illegible]	[illegible]	[illegible]	[illegible]	[illegible]	[illegible]
	1888	[illegible]	[illegible]	[illegible]	[illegible]	[illegible]	[illegible]	[illegible]	[illegible]	[illegible]	[illegible]	[illegible]	[illegible]	[illegible]	[illegible]
	1889	[illegible]	[illegible]	[illegible]	[illegible]	[illegible]	[illegible]	[illegible]	[illegible]	[illegible]	[illegible]	[illegible]	[illegible]	[illegible]	[illegible]
	1890	[illegible]	[illegible]	[illegible]	[illegible]	[illegible]	[illegible]	[illegible]	[illegible]	[illegible]	[illegible]	[illegible]	[illegible]	[illegible]	[illegible]

TOTAL OF IRELAND.

IRELAND.	Years.	No. of Horses.			Mules and Asses.		No. of Cattle.			No. of Sheep.		No. of Pigs.		No. of Goats.	No. of Poultry.
		[illegible]	[illegible]	[illegible]	No. of Mules.	No. of Asses.	[illegible]	[illegible]	[illegible]	[illegible]	[illegible]	[illegible]	[illegible]		
Total of Ireland,	1881	[illegible]	[illegible]	[illegible]	[illegible]	[illegible]	[illegible]	[illegible]	[illegible]	[illegible]	[illegible]	[illegible]	[illegible]	[illegible]	[illegible]
	1882	[illegible]	[illegible]	[illegible]	[illegible]	[illegible]	[illegible]	[illegible]	[illegible]	[illegible]	[illegible]	[illegible]	[illegible]	[illegible]	[illegible]
	1883	[illegible]	[illegible]	[illegible]	[illegible]	[illegible]	[illegible]	[illegible]	[illegible]	[illegible]	[illegible]	[illegible]	[illegible]	[illegible]	[illegible]
	1884	[illegible]	[illegible]	[illegible]	[illegible]	[illegible]	[illegible]	[illegible]	[illegible]	[illegible]	[illegible]	[illegible]	[illegible]	[illegible]	[illegible]
Area, [illegible] Acres.	1885	[illegible]	[illegible]	[illegible]	[illegible]	[illegible]	[illegible]	[illegible]	[illegible]	[illegible]	[illegible]	[illegible]	[illegible]	[illegible]	[illegible]
	1886	[illegible]	[illegible]	[illegible]	[illegible]	[illegible]	[illegible]	[illegible]	[illegible]	[illegible]	[illegible]	[illegible]	[illegible]	[illegible]	[illegible]
	1887	[illegible]	[illegible]	[illegible]	[illegible]	[illegible]	[illegible]	[illegible]	[illegible]	[illegible]	[illegible]	[illegible]	[illegible]	[illegible]	[illegible]
	1888	[illegible]	[illegible]	[illegible]	[illegible]	[illegible]	[illegible]	[illegible]	[illegible]	[illegible]	[illegible]	[illegible]	[illegible]	[illegible]	[illegible]
	1889	[illegible]	[illegible]	[illegible]	[illegible]	[illegible]	[illegible]	[illegible]	[illegible]	[illegible]	[illegible]	[illegible]	[illegible]	[illegible]	[illegible]
	1890	[illegible]	[illegible]	[illegible]	[illegible]	[illegible]	[illegible]	[illegible]	[illegible]	[illegible]	[illegible]	[illegible]	[illegible]	[illegible]	[illegible]

TABLE 14.—SHOWING, by COUNTIES and PROVINCES, the Total Area under POTATOES in 1880, and the Extent in Statute Acres under each description of that crop.

COUNTIES.	Total Area	SEVERAL NAMES OF THE DIFFERENT KINDS OF POTATOES PLANTED.													All others
	[illegible]	[illegible]	[illegible]	[illegible]	[illegible]	[illegible]	[illegible]	[illegible]	[illegible]	[illegible]	[illegible]	[illegible]	[illegible]	[illegible]	[illegible]
	Acres.	Acres.	Acres.	Acres.	Acres.	Acres.	Acres.	Acres.	Acres.	Acres.	Acres.	Acres.	Acres.	Acres.	Acres.
ANTRIM,	[illegible]	[illegible]	[illegible]	[illegible]	[illegible]	[illegible]	[illegible]	[illegible]	[illegible]	[illegible]	[illegible]	[illegible]	[illegible]	[illegible]	[illegible]
ARMAGH,	[illegible]	[illegible]	[illegible]	[illegible]	[illegible]	[illegible]	[illegible]	[illegible]	[illegible]	[illegible]	[illegible]	[illegible]	[illegible]	[illegible]	[illegible]
CARLOW,	[illegible]	[illegible]	[illegible]	[illegible]	[illegible]	[illegible]	[illegible]	[illegible]	[illegible]	[illegible]	[illegible]	[illegible]	[illegible]	[illegible]	[illegible]
CAVAN,	[illegible]	[illegible]	[illegible]	[illegible]	[illegible]	[illegible]	[illegible]	[illegible]	[illegible]	[illegible]	[illegible]	[illegible]	[illegible]	[illegible]	[illegible]
CLARE,	[illegible]	[illegible]	[illegible]	[illegible]	[illegible]	[illegible]	[illegible]	[illegible]	[illegible]	[illegible]	[illegible]	[illegible]	[illegible]	[illegible]	[illegible]
CORK,	[illegible]	[illegible]	[illegible]	[illegible]	[illegible]	[illegible]	[illegible]	[illegible]	[illegible]	[illegible]	[illegible]	[illegible]	[illegible]	[illegible]	[illegible]
DONEGAL,	[illegible]	[illegible]	[illegible]	[illegible]	[illegible]	[illegible]	[illegible]	[illegible]	[illegible]	[illegible]	[illegible]	[illegible]	[illegible]	[illegible]	[illegible]
DOWN,	[illegible]	[illegible]	[illegible]	[illegible]	[illegible]	[illegible]	[illegible]	[illegible]	[illegible]	[illegible]	[illegible]	[illegible]	[illegible]	[illegible]	[illegible]
DUBLIN,	[illegible]	[illegible]	[illegible]	[illegible]	[illegible]	[illegible]	[illegible]	[illegible]	[illegible]	[illegible]	[illegible]	[illegible]	[illegible]	[illegible]	[illegible]
FERMANAGH,	[illegible]	[illegible]	[illegible]	[illegible]	[illegible]	[illegible]	[illegible]	[illegible]	[illegible]	[illegible]	[illegible]	[illegible]	[illegible]	[illegible]	[illegible]
GALWAY,	[illegible]	[illegible]	[illegible]	[illegible]	[illegible]	[illegible]	[illegible]	[illegible]	[illegible]	[illegible]	[illegible]	[illegible]	[illegible]	[illegible]	[illegible]
KERRY,	[illegible]	[illegible]	[illegible]	[illegible]	[illegible]	[illegible]	[illegible]	[illegible]	[illegible]	[illegible]	[illegible]	[illegible]	[illegible]	[illegible]	[illegible]
KILDARE,	[illegible]	[illegible]	[illegible]	[illegible]	[illegible]	[illegible]	[illegible]	[illegible]	[illegible]	[illegible]	[illegible]	[illegible]	[illegible]	[illegible]	[illegible]
KILKENNY,	[illegible]	[illegible]	[illegible]	[illegible]	[illegible]	[illegible]	[illegible]	[illegible]	[illegible]	[illegible]	[illegible]	[illegible]	[illegible]	[illegible]	[illegible]
KING'S,	[illegible]	[illegible]	[illegible]	[illegible]	[illegible]	[illegible]	[illegible]	[illegible]	[illegible]	[illegible]	[illegible]	[illegible]	[illegible]	[illegible]	[illegible]
LEITRIM,	[illegible]	[illegible]	[illegible]	[illegible]	[illegible]	[illegible]	[illegible]	[illegible]	[illegible]	[illegible]	[illegible]	[illegible]	[illegible]	[illegible]	[illegible]
LIMERICK,	[illegible]	[illegible]	[illegible]	[illegible]	[illegible]	[illegible]	[illegible]	[illegible]	[illegible]	[illegible]	[illegible]	[illegible]	[illegible]	[illegible]	[illegible]
LONDONDERRY,	[illegible]	[illegible]	[illegible]	[illegible]	[illegible]	[illegible]	[illegible]	[illegible]	[illegible]	[illegible]	[illegible]	[illegible]	[illegible]	[illegible]	[illegible]
LONGFORD,	[illegible]	[illegible]	[illegible]	[illegible]	[illegible]	[illegible]	[illegible]	[illegible]	[illegible]	[illegible]	[illegible]	[illegible]	[illegible]	[illegible]	[illegible]
LOUTH and DROGHEDA, County of Town,	[illegible]	[illegible]	[illegible]	[illegible]	[illegible]	[illegible]	[illegible]	[illegible]	[illegible]	[illegible]	[illegible]	[illegible]	[illegible]	[illegible]	[illegible]
MAYO,	[illegible]	[illegible]	[illegible]	[illegible]	[illegible]	[illegible]	[illegible]	[illegible]	[illegible]	[illegible]	[illegible]	[illegible]	[illegible]	[illegible]	[illegible]
MEATH,	[illegible]	[illegible]	[illegible]	[illegible]	[illegible]	[illegible]	[illegible]	[illegible]	[illegible]	[illegible]	[illegible]	[illegible]	[illegible]	[illegible]	[illegible]
MONAGHAN,	[illegible]	[illegible]	[illegible]	[illegible]	[illegible]	[illegible]	[illegible]	[illegible]	[illegible]	[illegible]	[illegible]	[illegible]	[illegible]	[illegible]	[illegible]
QUEEN'S,	[illegible]	[illegible]	[illegible]	[illegible]	[illegible]	[illegible]	[illegible]	[illegible]	[illegible]	[illegible]	[illegible]	[illegible]	[illegible]	[illegible]	[illegible]
ROSCOMMON,	[illegible]	[illegible]	[illegible]	[illegible]	[illegible]	[illegible]	[illegible]	[illegible]	[illegible]	[illegible]	[illegible]	[illegible]	[illegible]	[illegible]	[illegible]
SLIGO,	[illegible]	[illegible]	[illegible]	[illegible]	[illegible]	[illegible]	[illegible]	[illegible]	[illegible]	[illegible]	[illegible]	[illegible]	[illegible]	[illegible]	[illegible]
TIPPERARY,	[illegible]	[illegible]	[illegible]	[illegible]	[illegible]	[illegible]	[illegible]	[illegible]	[illegible]	[illegible]	[illegible]	[illegible]	[illegible]	[illegible]	[illegible]
TYRONE,	[illegible]	[illegible]	[illegible]	[illegible]	[illegible]	[illegible]	[illegible]	[illegible]	[illegible]	[illegible]	[illegible]	[illegible]	[illegible]	[illegible]	[illegible]
WATERFORD,	[illegible]	[illegible]	[illegible]	[illegible]	[illegible]	[illegible]	[illegible]	[illegible]	[illegible]	[illegible]	[illegible]	[illegible]	[illegible]	[illegible]	[illegible]
WESTMEATH,	[illegible]	[illegible]	[illegible]	[illegible]	[illegible]	[illegible]	[illegible]	[illegible]	[illegible]	[illegible]	[illegible]	[illegible]	[illegible]	[illegible]	[illegible]
WEXFORD,	[illegible]	[illegible]	[illegible]	[illegible]	[illegible]	[illegible]	[illegible]	[illegible]	[illegible]	[illegible]	[illegible]	[illegible]	[illegible]	[illegible]	[illegible]
WICKLOW,	[illegible]	[illegible]	[illegible]	[illegible]	[illegible]	[illegible]	[illegible]	[illegible]	[illegible]	[illegible]	[illegible]	[illegible]	[illegible]	[illegible]	[illegible]
PROVINCES.															
LEINSTER,	[illegible]	[illegible]	[illegible]	[illegible]	[illegible]	[illegible]	[illegible]	[illegible]	[illegible]	[illegible]	[illegible]	[illegible]	[illegible]	[illegible]	[illegible]
MUNSTER,	[illegible]	[illegible]	[illegible]	[illegible]	[illegible]	[illegible]	[illegible]	[illegible]	[illegible]	[illegible]	[illegible]	[illegible]	[illegible]	[illegible]	[illegible]
ULSTER,	[illegible]	[illegible]	[illegible]	[illegible]	[illegible]	[illegible]	[illegible]	[illegible]	[illegible]	[illegible]	[illegible]	[illegible]	[illegible]	[illegible]	[illegible]
CONNAUGHT,	[illegible]	[illegible]	[illegible]	[illegible]	[illegible]	[illegible]	[illegible]	[illegible]	[illegible]	[illegible]	[illegible]	[illegible]	[illegible]	[illegible]	[illegible]
Total of Ireland, 1880,	[illegible]	[illegible]	[illegible]	[illegible]	[illegible]	[illegible]	[illegible]	[illegible]	[illegible]	[illegible]	[illegible]	[illegible]	[illegible]	[illegible]	[illegible]
Percentage in 1880,	[illegible]	[illegible]	[illegible]	[illegible]	[illegible]	[illegible]	[illegible]	[illegible]	[illegible]						
Total of Ireland, 1879,	[illegible]	[illegible]	[illegible]	[illegible]	[illegible]	[illegible]	[illegible]	[illegible]	[illegible]	[illegible]	[illegible]	[illegible]	[illegible]	[illegible]	[illegible]
Percentage in 1879,	[illegible]	[illegible]	[illegible]	[illegible]	[illegible]	[illegible]	[illegible]	[illegible]	[illegible]						

TABLE 15.—SHOWING, by POOR LAW UNIONS, the Total extent in STATUTE ACRES under POTATOES in 18[illegible], and the extent under each description of that Crop—continued.

POOR LAW UNIONS	[illegible]	EXTENT UNDER [illegible]
[illegible]	[illegible]	[illegible]
Total	[illegible]	[illegible]

TABLE 16.—SHOWING, by COUNTIES, the average rate of Produce per statute acre of the principal descriptions of POTATOES planted in Ireland in 185[illegible].

COUNTIES.	GENERAL NAMES OF THE DIFFERENT KINDS OF POTATOES PLANTED IN EACH COUNTY.															
	[illegible]	[illegible]	[illegible]	[illegible]	[illegible]	[illegible]	[illegible]	[illegible]	[illegible]	[illegible]	[illegible]	[illegible]	[illegible]	[illegible]	[illegible]	[illegible]
	[illegible]	[illegible]	[illegible]	[illegible]	[illegible]	[illegible]	[illegible]	[illegible]	[illegible]	[illegible]	[illegible]	[illegible]	[illegible]	[illegible]	[illegible]	[illegible]
ANTRIM,	57	[illegible]	[illegible]	[illegible]	[illegible]	[illegible]	[illegible]	55	-	[illegible]	-	-	-	-	72	-
ARMAGH,	[illegible]	45	[illegible]	[illegible]	71	[illegible]	[illegible]	[illegible]	-	[illegible]	-	-	-	-	-	-
CARLOW,	[illegible]	[illegible]	-	-	74	[illegible]	64	-	-	-	-	-	-	-	-	-
CAVAN,	[illegible]	[illegible]	45	[illegible]	-	[illegible]	[illegible]	-	-	54	-	-	-	-	-	-
CLARE,	[illegible]	[illegible]	45	51	-	[illegible]	[illegible]	-	-	-	[illegible]	-	-	-	-	-
CORK,	[illegible]	[illegible]	[illegible]	[illegible]	-	[illegible]	[illegible]	-	-	-	-	-	-	-	-	-
DONEGAL,	[illegible]	[illegible]	[illegible]	51	[illegible]	[illegible]	[illegible]	[illegible]	43	[illegible]	-	[illegible]	-	-	-	[illegible]
DOWN,	[illegible]	[illegible]	71	75	[illegible]	[illegible]	48	74	-	46	-	-	-	-	-	-
DUBLIN,	[illegible]	[illegible]	[illegible]	62	[illegible]	[illegible]	[illegible]	-	-	[illegible]	-	-	-	-	-	-
FERMANAGH,	[illegible]	[illegible]	[illegible]	11	-	-	-	-	-	-	-	-	-	-	-	-
GALWAY,	[illegible]	41	[illegible]	51	-	[illegible]	[illegible]	-	-	-	-	-	-	41	-	-
KERRY,	[illegible]	74	[illegible]	[illegible]	-	[illegible]	[illegible]	-	-	-	-	-	-	-	-	-
KILDARE,	[illegible]	[illegible]	[illegible]	[illegible]	54	44	[illegible]	-	-	[illegible]	-	-	-	-	-	-
KILKENNY,	61	44	-	-	[illegible]	[illegible]	[illegible]	-	-	[illegible]	-	-	-	-	-	-
KING'S,	61	41	[illegible]	[illegible]	-	[illegible]	[illegible]	-	[illegible]	[illegible]	-	-	-	-	-	-
LEITRIM,	[illegible]	[illegible]	[illegible]	[illegible]	-	[illegible]	[illegible]	-	-	[illegible]	-	-	-	-	-	-
LIMERICK,	67	[illegible]	[illegible]	[illegible]	-	[illegible]	[illegible]	-	-	-	77	-	[illegible]	-	-	-
LONDONDERRY,	[illegible]	[illegible]	[illegible]	64	71	[illegible]	71	[illegible]	[illegible]	[illegible]	-	[illegible]	[illegible]	-	77	-
LONGFORD,	[illegible]	54	[illegible]	[illegible]	[illegible]	45	[illegible]	-	-	44	-	-	-	-	-	-
LOUTH and DROGHEDA, County of Town.	[illegible]	[illegible]	71	[illegible]	11	72	61	-	-	-	-	-	-	-	-	-
MAYO,	[illegible]	[illegible]	[illegible]	[illegible]	-	[illegible]	48	-	-	-	-	-	-	-	-	-
MEATH,	[illegible]	[illegible]	47	[illegible]	44	[illegible]	[illegible]	-	-	[illegible]	-	-	-	-	-	-
MONAGHAN,	[illegible]	[illegible]	[illegible]	[illegible]	[illegible]	-	[illegible]	-	-	[illegible]	-	-	-	-	-	-
QUEEN'S,	[illegible]	[illegible]	-	[illegible]	-	[illegible]	47	-	-	-	-	-	-	-	-	-
ROSCOMMON,	61	[illegible]	[illegible]	[illegible]	-	[illegible]	[illegible]	-	-	[illegible]	-	-	-	[illegible]	-	-
SLIGO,	61	[illegible]	[illegible]	[illegible]	-	31	40	-	-	-	-	-	-	-	-	-
TIPPERARY,	44	47	[illegible]	[illegible]	-	[illegible]	[illegible]	-	-	[illegible]	-	-	-	-	-	-
TYRONE,	[illegible]	[illegible]	54	62	[illegible]	[illegible]	[illegible]	-	[illegible]	-	-	-	[illegible]	-	-	-
WATERFORD,	[illegible]	[illegible]	-	[illegible]	-	[illegible]	[illegible]	-	-	-	-	-	-	-	-	-
WESTMEATH,	[illegible]	41	[illegible]	[illegible]	[illegible]	[illegible]	[illegible]	-	-	[illegible]	-	-	-	[illegible]	-	-
WEXFORD,	61	[illegible]	[illegible]	[illegible]	[illegible]	[illegible]	[illegible]	-	-	[illegible]	-	-	-	-	-	-
WICKLOW,	[illegible]	[illegible]	[illegible]	[illegible]	[illegible]	[illegible]	[illegible]	-	-	[illegible]	-	-	-	-	-	-

TABLE A.—Showing, by Counties and Provinces, the

COUNTIES AND PROVINCES	[illegible]			[illegible]			[illegible]			[illegible]		
	[illegible]	[illegible]	Total.	[illegible]	[illegible]	Total.	[illegible]	[illegible]	Total.	[illegible]	[illegible]	Total.
LEINSTER.												
Carlow,	[illegible]	[illegible]	[illegible]	[illegible]	[illegible]	[illegible]	[illegible]	[illegible]	[illegible]	[illegible]	[illegible]	[illegible]
Dublin,	[illegible]	[illegible]	[illegible]	[illegible]	[illegible]	[illegible]	[illegible]	[illegible]	[illegible]	[illegible]	[illegible]	[illegible]
Kildare,	[illegible]	[illegible]	[illegible]	[illegible]	[illegible]	[illegible]	[illegible]	[illegible]	[illegible]	[illegible]	[illegible]	[illegible]
Kilkenny,	[illegible]	[illegible]	[illegible]	[illegible]	[illegible]	[illegible]	[illegible]	[illegible]	[illegible]	[illegible]	[illegible]	[illegible]
King's,	[illegible]	[illegible]	[illegible]	[illegible]	[illegible]	[illegible]	[illegible]	[illegible]	[illegible]	[illegible]	[illegible]	[illegible]
Longford,	[illegible]	[illegible]	[illegible]	[illegible]	[illegible]	[illegible]	[illegible]	[illegible]	[illegible]	[illegible]	[illegible]	[illegible]
Louth,	[illegible]	[illegible]	[illegible]	[illegible]	[illegible]	[illegible]	[illegible]	[illegible]	[illegible]	[illegible]	[illegible]	[illegible]
Meath,	[illegible]	[illegible]	[illegible]	[illegible]	[illegible]	[illegible]	[illegible]	[illegible]	[illegible]	[illegible]	[illegible]	[illegible]
Queen's,	[illegible]	[illegible]	[illegible]	[illegible]	[illegible]	[illegible]	[illegible]	[illegible]	[illegible]	[illegible]	[illegible]	[illegible]
Westmeath,	[illegible]	[illegible]	[illegible]	[illegible]	[illegible]	[illegible]	[illegible]	[illegible]	[illegible]	[illegible]	[illegible]	[illegible]
Wexford,	[illegible]	[illegible]	[illegible]	[illegible]	[illegible]	[illegible]	[illegible]	[illegible]	[illegible]	[illegible]	[illegible]	[illegible]
Wicklow,	[illegible]	[illegible]	[illegible]	[illegible]	[illegible]	[illegible]	[illegible]	[illegible]	[illegible]	[illegible]	[illegible]	[illegible]
Total of Leinster,	[illegible]	[illegible]	[illegible]	[illegible]	[illegible]	[illegible]	[illegible]	[illegible]	[illegible]	[illegible]	[illegible]	[illegible]
MUNSTER.												
Clare,	[illegible]	[illegible]	[illegible]	[illegible]	[illegible]	[illegible]	[illegible]	[illegible]	[illegible]	[illegible]	[illegible]	[illegible]
Cork, E.R.,	[illegible]	[illegible]	[illegible]	[illegible]	[illegible]	[illegible]	[illegible]	[illegible]	[illegible]	[illegible]	[illegible]	[illegible]
Cork, W.R.,	[illegible]	[illegible]	[illegible]	[illegible]	[illegible]	[illegible]	[illegible]	[illegible]	[illegible]	[illegible]	[illegible]	[illegible]
Kerry,	[illegible]	[illegible]	[illegible]	[illegible]	[illegible]	[illegible]	[illegible]	[illegible]	[illegible]	[illegible]	[illegible]	[illegible]
Limerick,	[illegible]	[illegible]	[illegible]	[illegible]	[illegible]	[illegible]	[illegible]	[illegible]	[illegible]	[illegible]	[illegible]	[illegible]
Tipperary, N.R.,	[illegible]	[illegible]	[illegible]	[illegible]	[illegible]	[illegible]	[illegible]	[illegible]	[illegible]	[illegible]	[illegible]	[illegible]
Tipperary, S.R.,	[illegible]	[illegible]	[illegible]	[illegible]	[illegible]	[illegible]	[illegible]	[illegible]	[illegible]	[illegible]	[illegible]	[illegible]
Waterford,	[illegible]	[illegible]	[illegible]	[illegible]	[illegible]	[illegible]	[illegible]	[illegible]	[illegible]	[illegible]	[illegible]	[illegible]
Total of Munster,	[illegible]	[illegible]	[illegible]	[illegible]	[illegible]	[illegible]	[illegible]	[illegible]	[illegible]	[illegible]	[illegible]	[illegible]
ULSTER.												
Antrim,	[illegible]	[illegible]	[illegible]	[illegible]	[illegible]	[illegible]	[illegible]	[illegible]	[illegible]	[illegible]	[illegible]	[illegible]
Armagh,	[illegible]	[illegible]	[illegible]	[illegible]	[illegible]	[illegible]	[illegible]	[illegible]	[illegible]	[illegible]	[illegible]	[illegible]
Cavan,	[illegible]	[illegible]	[illegible]	[illegible]	[illegible]	[illegible]	[illegible]	[illegible]	[illegible]	[illegible]	[illegible]	[illegible]
Donegal,	[illegible]	[illegible]	[illegible]	[illegible]	[illegible]	[illegible]	[illegible]	[illegible]	[illegible]	[illegible]	[illegible]	[illegible]
Down,	[illegible]	[illegible]	[illegible]	[illegible]	[illegible]	[illegible]	[illegible]	[illegible]	[illegible]	[illegible]	[illegible]	[illegible]
Fermanagh,	[illegible]	[illegible]	[illegible]	[illegible]	[illegible]	[illegible]	[illegible]	[illegible]	[illegible]	[illegible]	[illegible]	[illegible]
Londonderry,	[illegible]	[illegible]	[illegible]	[illegible]	[illegible]	[illegible]	[illegible]	[illegible]	[illegible]	[illegible]	[illegible]	[illegible]
Monaghan,	[illegible]	[illegible]	[illegible]	[illegible]	[illegible]	[illegible]	[illegible]	[illegible]	[illegible]	[illegible]	[illegible]	[illegible]
Tyrone,	[illegible]	[illegible]	[illegible]	[illegible]	[illegible]	[illegible]	[illegible]	[illegible]	[illegible]	[illegible]	[illegible]	[illegible]
Total of Ulster,	[illegible]	[illegible]	[illegible]	[illegible]	[illegible]	[illegible]	[illegible]	[illegible]	[illegible]	[illegible]	[illegible]	[illegible]
CONNAUGHT.												
Galway,	[illegible]	[illegible]	[illegible]	[illegible]	[illegible]	[illegible]	[illegible]	[illegible]	[illegible]	[illegible]	[illegible]	[illegible]
Leitrim,	[illegible]	[illegible]	[illegible]	[illegible]	[illegible]	[illegible]	[illegible]	[illegible]	[illegible]	[illegible]	[illegible]	[illegible]
Mayo,	[illegible]	[illegible]	[illegible]	[illegible]	[illegible]	[illegible]	[illegible]	[illegible]	[illegible]	[illegible]	[illegible]	[illegible]
Roscommon,	[illegible]	[illegible]	[illegible]	[illegible]	[illegible]	[illegible]	[illegible]	[illegible]	[illegible]	[illegible]	[illegible]	[illegible]
Sligo,	[illegible]	[illegible]	[illegible]	[illegible]	[illegible]	[illegible]	[illegible]	[illegible]	[illegible]	[illegible]	[illegible]	[illegible]
Total of Connaught,	[illegible]	[illegible]	[illegible]	[illegible]	[illegible]	[illegible]	[illegible]	[illegible]	[illegible]	[illegible]	[illegible]	[illegible]
Total of Ireland,	[illegible]	[illegible]	[illegible]	[illegible]	[illegible]	[illegible]	[illegible]	[illegible]	[illegible]	[illegible]	[illegible]	[illegible]

* [illegible]

Number of Sires serving Mares in Ireland in the Year 1890.

Stallions. Thorough-bred. Bred in Ireland.	Stallions. Thorough-bred. Imported.	Stallions. Thorough-bred. Total.	Stallions. Agricultural. Bred in Ireland.	Stallions. Agricultural. Imported.	Stallions. Agricultural. Total.	All other Horses. Bred in Ireland.	All other Horses. Imported.	All other Horses. Total.	Total. Bred in Ireland.	Total. Imported.	Total. Total.	Counties and Provinces.
												LEINSTER.
[illegible]	[illegible]	[illegible]	[illegible]	[illegible]	[illegible]	[illegible]	[illegible]	[illegible]	[illegible]	[illegible]	[illegible]	Carlow.
[illegible]	[illegible]	[illegible]	[illegible]	[illegible]	[illegible]	[illegible]	[illegible]	[illegible]	[illegible]	[illegible]	[illegible]	Dublin.
[illegible]	[illegible]	[illegible]	[illegible]	[illegible]	[illegible]	[illegible]	[illegible]	[illegible]	[illegible]	[illegible]	[illegible]	Kildare.
[illegible]	[illegible]	[illegible]	[illegible]	[illegible]	[illegible]	[illegible]	[illegible]	[illegible]	[illegible]	[illegible]	[illegible]	Kilkenny.
[illegible]	[illegible]	[illegible]	[illegible]	[illegible]	[illegible]	[illegible]	[illegible]	[illegible]	[illegible]	[illegible]	[illegible]	King's.
[illegible]	[illegible]	[illegible]	[illegible]	[illegible]	[illegible]	[illegible]	[illegible]	[illegible]	[illegible]	[illegible]	[illegible]	Longford.
[illegible]	[illegible]	[illegible]	[illegible]	[illegible]	[illegible]	[illegible]	[illegible]	[illegible]	[illegible]	[illegible]	[illegible]	Louth.
[illegible]	[illegible]	[illegible]	[illegible]	[illegible]	[illegible]	[illegible]	[illegible]	[illegible]	[illegible]	[illegible]	[illegible]	Meath.
[illegible]	[illegible]	[illegible]	[illegible]	[illegible]	[illegible]	[illegible]	[illegible]	[illegible]	[illegible]	[illegible]	[illegible]	Queen's.
[illegible]	[illegible]	[illegible]	[illegible]	[illegible]	[illegible]	[illegible]	[illegible]	[illegible]	[illegible]	[illegible]	[illegible]	Westmeath.
[illegible]	[illegible]	[illegible]	[illegible]	[illegible]	[illegible]	[illegible]	[illegible]	[illegible]	[illegible]	[illegible]	[illegible]	Wexford.
[illegible]	[illegible]	[illegible]	[illegible]	[illegible]	[illegible]	[illegible]	[illegible]	[illegible]	[illegible]	[illegible]	[illegible]	Wicklow.
[illegible]	[illegible]	[illegible]	[illegible]	[illegible]	[illegible]	[illegible]	[illegible]	[illegible]	[illegible]	[illegible]	[illegible]	Total of Leinster.
												MUNSTER.
[illegible]	[illegible]	[illegible]	[illegible]	[illegible]	[illegible]	[illegible]	[illegible]	[illegible]	[illegible]	[illegible]	[illegible]	Clare.
[illegible]	[illegible]	[illegible]	[illegible]	[illegible]	[illegible]	[illegible]	[illegible]	[illegible]	[illegible]	[illegible]	[illegible]	Cork, E.R.
[illegible]	[illegible]	[illegible]	[illegible]	[illegible]	[illegible]	[illegible]	[illegible]	[illegible]	[illegible]	[illegible]	[illegible]	Cork, W.R.
[illegible]	[illegible]	[illegible]	[illegible]	[illegible]	[illegible]	[illegible]	[illegible]	[illegible]	[illegible]	[illegible]	[illegible]	Kerry.
[illegible]	[illegible]	[illegible]	[illegible]	[illegible]	[illegible]	[illegible]	[illegible]	[illegible]	[illegible]	[illegible]	[illegible]	Limerick.
[illegible]	[illegible]	[illegible]	[illegible]	[illegible]	[illegible]	[illegible]	[illegible]	[illegible]	[illegible]	[illegible]	[illegible]	Tipperary, N.R.
[illegible]	[illegible]	[illegible]	[illegible]	[illegible]	[illegible]	[illegible]	[illegible]	[illegible]	[illegible]	[illegible]	[illegible]	Tipperary, S.R.
[illegible]	[illegible]	[illegible]	[illegible]	[illegible]	[illegible]	[illegible]	[illegible]	[illegible]	[illegible]	[illegible]	[illegible]	Waterford.
[illegible]	[illegible]	[illegible]	[illegible]	[illegible]	[illegible]	[illegible]	[illegible]	[illegible]	[illegible]	[illegible]	[illegible]	Total of Munster.
												ULSTER.
[illegible]	[illegible]	[illegible]	[illegible]	[illegible]	[illegible]	[illegible]	[illegible]	[illegible]	[illegible]	[illegible]	[illegible]	Antrim.
[illegible]	[illegible]	[illegible]	[illegible]	[illegible]	[illegible]	[illegible]	[illegible]	[illegible]	[illegible]	[illegible]	[illegible]	Armagh.
[illegible]	[illegible]	[illegible]	[illegible]	[illegible]	[illegible]	[illegible]	[illegible]	[illegible]	[illegible]	[illegible]	[illegible]	Cavan.
[illegible]	[illegible]	[illegible]	[illegible]	[illegible]	[illegible]	[illegible]	[illegible]	[illegible]	[illegible]	[illegible]	[illegible]	Donegal.
[illegible]	[illegible]	[illegible]	[illegible]	[illegible]	[illegible]	[illegible]	[illegible]	[illegible]	[illegible]	[illegible]	[illegible]	Down.
[illegible]	[illegible]	[illegible]	[illegible]	[illegible]	[illegible]	[illegible]	[illegible]	[illegible]	[illegible]	[illegible]	[illegible]	Fermanagh.
[illegible]	[illegible]	[illegible]	[illegible]	[illegible]	[illegible]	[illegible]	[illegible]	[illegible]	[illegible]	[illegible]	[illegible]	Londonderry.
[illegible]	[illegible]	[illegible]	[illegible]	[illegible]	[illegible]	[illegible]	[illegible]	[illegible]	[illegible]	[illegible]	[illegible]	Monaghan.
[illegible]	[illegible]	[illegible]	[illegible]	[illegible]	[illegible]	[illegible]	[illegible]	[illegible]	[illegible]	[illegible]	[illegible]	Tyrone.
[illegible]	[illegible]	[illegible]	[illegible]	[illegible]	[illegible]	[illegible]	[illegible]	[illegible]	[illegible]	[illegible]	[illegible]	Total of Ulster.
												CONNAUGHT.
[illegible]	[illegible]	[illegible]	[illegible]	[illegible]	[illegible]	[illegible]	[illegible]	[illegible]	[illegible]	[illegible]	[illegible]	Galway.
[illegible]	[illegible]	[illegible]	[illegible]	[illegible]	[illegible]	[illegible]	[illegible]	[illegible]	[illegible]	[illegible]	[illegible]	Leitrim.
[illegible]	[illegible]	[illegible]	[illegible]	[illegible]	[illegible]	[illegible]	[illegible]	[illegible]	[illegible]	[illegible]	[illegible]	Mayo.
[illegible]	[illegible]	[illegible]	[illegible]	[illegible]	[illegible]	[illegible]	[illegible]	[illegible]	[illegible]	[illegible]	[illegible]	Roscommon.
[illegible]	[illegible]	[illegible]	[illegible]	[illegible]	[illegible]	[illegible]	[illegible]	[illegible]	[illegible]	[illegible]	[illegible]	Sligo.
[illegible]	[illegible]	[illegible]	[illegible]	[illegible]	[illegible]	[illegible]	[illegible]	[illegible]	[illegible]	[illegible]	[illegible]	Total of Connaught.
[illegible]	[illegible]	[illegible]	[illegible]	[illegible]	[illegible]	[illegible]	[illegible]	[illegible]	[illegible]	[illegible]	[illegible]	Total of Ireland.

[illegible]

TABLE B.—Showing, by Counties and Provinces, the number

COUNTIES AND PROVINCES.	[illegible]																	
LEINSTER.																		
Carlow,	[illegible]	[illegible]	[illegible]	[illegible]	[illegible]	[illegible]	[illegible]	[illegible]	[illegible]	[illegible]	[illegible]	[illegible]	[illegible]	[illegible]	[illegible]	[illegible]	[illegible]	[illegible]
Dublin,	[illegible]	[illegible]	[illegible]	[illegible]	[illegible]	[illegible]	[illegible]	[illegible]	[illegible]	[illegible]	[illegible]	[illegible]	[illegible]	[illegible]	[illegible]	[illegible]	[illegible]	[illegible]
Kildare,	[illegible]	[illegible]	[illegible]	[illegible]	[illegible]	[illegible]	[illegible]	[illegible]	[illegible]	[illegible]	[illegible]	[illegible]	[illegible]	[illegible]	[illegible]	[illegible]	[illegible]	[illegible]
Kilkenny,	[illegible]	[illegible]	[illegible]	[illegible]	[illegible]	[illegible]	[illegible]	[illegible]	[illegible]	[illegible]	[illegible]	[illegible]	[illegible]	[illegible]	[illegible]	[illegible]	[illegible]	[illegible]
King's,	[illegible]	[illegible]	[illegible]	[illegible]	[illegible]	[illegible]	[illegible]	[illegible]	[illegible]	[illegible]	[illegible]	[illegible]	[illegible]	[illegible]	[illegible]	[illegible]	[illegible]	[illegible]
Longford,	[illegible]	[illegible]	[illegible]	[illegible]	[illegible]	[illegible]	[illegible]	[illegible]	[illegible]	[illegible]	[illegible]	[illegible]	[illegible]	[illegible]	[illegible]	[illegible]	[illegible]	[illegible]
Louth,	[illegible]	[illegible]	[illegible]	[illegible]	[illegible]	[illegible]	[illegible]	[illegible]	[illegible]	[illegible]	[illegible]	[illegible]	[illegible]	[illegible]	[illegible]	[illegible]	[illegible]	[illegible]
Meath,	[illegible]	[illegible]	[illegible]	[illegible]	[illegible]	[illegible]	[illegible]	[illegible]	[illegible]	[illegible]	[illegible]	[illegible]	[illegible]	[illegible]	[illegible]	[illegible]	[illegible]	[illegible]
Queen's,	[illegible]	[illegible]	[illegible]	[illegible]	[illegible]	[illegible]	[illegible]	[illegible]	[illegible]	[illegible]	[illegible]	[illegible]	[illegible]	[illegible]	[illegible]	[illegible]	[illegible]	[illegible]
Westmeath,	[illegible]	[illegible]	[illegible]	[illegible]	[illegible]	[illegible]	[illegible]	[illegible]	[illegible]	[illegible]	[illegible]	[illegible]	[illegible]	[illegible]	[illegible]	[illegible]	[illegible]	[illegible]
Wexford,	[illegible]	[illegible]	[illegible]	[illegible]	[illegible]	[illegible]	[illegible]	[illegible]	[illegible]	[illegible]	[illegible]	[illegible]	[illegible]	[illegible]	[illegible]	[illegible]	[illegible]	[illegible]
Wicklow,	[illegible]	[illegible]	[illegible]	[illegible]	[illegible]	[illegible]	[illegible]	[illegible]	[illegible]	[illegible]	[illegible]	[illegible]	[illegible]	[illegible]	[illegible]	[illegible]	[illegible]	[illegible]
Total of Leinster,	[illegible]	[illegible]	[illegible]	[illegible]	[illegible]	[illegible]	[illegible]	[illegible]	[illegible]	[illegible]	[illegible]	[illegible]	[illegible]	[illegible]	[illegible]	[illegible]	[illegible]	[illegible]
MUNSTER.																		
Clare,	[illegible]	[illegible]	[illegible]	[illegible]	[illegible]	[illegible]	[illegible]	[illegible]	[illegible]	[illegible]	[illegible]	[illegible]	[illegible]	[illegible]	[illegible]	[illegible]	[illegible]	[illegible]
Cork, E.R.,	[illegible]	[illegible]	[illegible]	[illegible]	[illegible]	[illegible]	[illegible]	[illegible]	[illegible]	[illegible]	[illegible]	[illegible]	[illegible]	[illegible]	[illegible]	[illegible]	[illegible]	[illegible]
Cork, W.R.,	[illegible]	[illegible]	[illegible]	[illegible]	[illegible]	[illegible]	[illegible]	[illegible]	[illegible]	[illegible]	[illegible]	[illegible]	[illegible]	[illegible]	[illegible]	[illegible]	[illegible]	[illegible]
Kerry,	[illegible]	[illegible]	[illegible]	[illegible]	[illegible]	[illegible]	[illegible]	[illegible]	[illegible]	[illegible]	[illegible]	[illegible]	[illegible]	[illegible]	[illegible]	[illegible]	[illegible]	[illegible]
Limerick,	[illegible]	[illegible]	[illegible]	[illegible]	[illegible]	[illegible]	[illegible]	[illegible]	[illegible]	[illegible]	[illegible]	[illegible]	[illegible]	[illegible]	[illegible]	[illegible]	[illegible]	[illegible]
Tipperary, N.R.,	[illegible]	[illegible]	[illegible]	[illegible]	[illegible]	[illegible]	[illegible]	[illegible]	[illegible]	[illegible]	[illegible]	[illegible]	[illegible]	[illegible]	[illegible]	[illegible]	[illegible]	[illegible]
Tipperary, S.R.,	[illegible]	[illegible]	[illegible]	[illegible]	[illegible]	[illegible]	[illegible]	[illegible]	[illegible]	[illegible]	[illegible]	[illegible]	[illegible]	[illegible]	[illegible]	[illegible]	[illegible]	[illegible]
Waterford,	[illegible]	[illegible]	[illegible]	[illegible]	[illegible]	[illegible]	[illegible]	[illegible]	[illegible]	[illegible]	[illegible]	[illegible]	[illegible]	[illegible]	[illegible]	[illegible]	[illegible]	[illegible]
Total of Munster,	[illegible]	[illegible]	[illegible]	[illegible]	[illegible]	[illegible]	[illegible]	[illegible]	[illegible]	[illegible]	[illegible]	[illegible]	[illegible]	[illegible]	[illegible]	[illegible]	[illegible]	[illegible]
ULSTER.																		
Antrim,	[illegible]	[illegible]	[illegible]	[illegible]	[illegible]	[illegible]	[illegible]	[illegible]	[illegible]	[illegible]	[illegible]	[illegible]	[illegible]	[illegible]	[illegible]	[illegible]	[illegible]	[illegible]
Armagh,	[illegible]	[illegible]	[illegible]	[illegible]	[illegible]	[illegible]	[illegible]	[illegible]	[illegible]	[illegible]	[illegible]	[illegible]	[illegible]	[illegible]	[illegible]	[illegible]	[illegible]	[illegible]
Cavan,	[illegible]	[illegible]	[illegible]	[illegible]	[illegible]	[illegible]	[illegible]	[illegible]	[illegible]	[illegible]	[illegible]	[illegible]	[illegible]	[illegible]	[illegible]	[illegible]	[illegible]	[illegible]
Donegal,	[illegible]	[illegible]	[illegible]	[illegible]	[illegible]	[illegible]	[illegible]	[illegible]	[illegible]	[illegible]	[illegible]	[illegible]	[illegible]	[illegible]	[illegible]	[illegible]	[illegible]	[illegible]
Down,	[illegible]	[illegible]	[illegible]	[illegible]	[illegible]	[illegible]	[illegible]	[illegible]	[illegible]	[illegible]	[illegible]	[illegible]	[illegible]	[illegible]	[illegible]	[illegible]	[illegible]	[illegible]
Fermanagh,	[illegible]	[illegible]	[illegible]	[illegible]	[illegible]	[illegible]	[illegible]	[illegible]	[illegible]	[illegible]	[illegible]	[illegible]	[illegible]	[illegible]	[illegible]	[illegible]	[illegible]	[illegible]
Londonderry,	[illegible]	[illegible]	[illegible]	[illegible]	[illegible]	[illegible]	[illegible]	[illegible]	[illegible]	[illegible]	[illegible]	[illegible]	[illegible]	[illegible]	[illegible]	[illegible]	[illegible]	[illegible]
Monaghan,	[illegible]	[illegible]	[illegible]	[illegible]	[illegible]	[illegible]	[illegible]	[illegible]	[illegible]	[illegible]	[illegible]	[illegible]	[illegible]	[illegible]	[illegible]	[illegible]	[illegible]	[illegible]
Tyrone,	[illegible]	[illegible]	[illegible]	[illegible]	[illegible]	[illegible]	[illegible]	[illegible]	[illegible]	[illegible]	[illegible]	[illegible]	[illegible]	[illegible]	[illegible]	[illegible]	[illegible]	[illegible]
Total of Ulster,	[illegible]	[illegible]	[illegible]	[illegible]	[illegible]	[illegible]	[illegible]	[illegible]	[illegible]	[illegible]	[illegible]	[illegible]	[illegible]	[illegible]	[illegible]	[illegible]	[illegible]	[illegible]
CONNAUGHT.																		
Galway,	[illegible]	[illegible]	[illegible]	[illegible]	[illegible]	[illegible]	[illegible]	[illegible]	[illegible]	[illegible]	[illegible]	[illegible]	[illegible]	[illegible]	[illegible]	[illegible]	[illegible]	[illegible]
Leitrim,	[illegible]	[illegible]	[illegible]	[illegible]	[illegible]	[illegible]	[illegible]	[illegible]	[illegible]	[illegible]	[illegible]	[illegible]	[illegible]	[illegible]	[illegible]	[illegible]	[illegible]	[illegible]
Mayo,	[illegible]	[illegible]	[illegible]	[illegible]	[illegible]	[illegible]	[illegible]	[illegible]	[illegible]	[illegible]	[illegible]	[illegible]	[illegible]	[illegible]	[illegible]	[illegible]	[illegible]	[illegible]
Roscommon,	[illegible]	[illegible]	[illegible]	[illegible]	[illegible]	[illegible]	[illegible]	[illegible]	[illegible]	[illegible]	[illegible]	[illegible]	[illegible]	[illegible]	[illegible]	[illegible]	[illegible]	[illegible]
Sligo,	[illegible]	[illegible]	[illegible]	[illegible]	[illegible]	[illegible]	[illegible]	[illegible]	[illegible]	[illegible]	[illegible]	[illegible]	[illegible]	[illegible]	[illegible]	[illegible]	[illegible]	[illegible]
Total of Connaught,	[illegible]	[illegible]	[illegible]	[illegible]	[illegible]	[illegible]	[illegible]	[illegible]	[illegible]	[illegible]	[illegible]	[illegible]	[illegible]	[illegible]	[illegible]	[illegible]	[illegible]	[illegible]
Total of Ireland,	[illegible]	[illegible]	[illegible]	[illegible]	[illegible]	[illegible]	[illegible]	[illegible]	[illegible]	[illegible]	[illegible]	[illegible]	[illegible]	[illegible]	[illegible]	[illegible]	[illegible]	[illegible]

* [illegible]

of BULLS serving Cows in Ireland during the year 1880.

BULLS.									All Other Breeds.			Total.			COUNTIES AND PROVINCES.
[illegible]			[illegible]			[illegible]									
[illegible]	[illegible]	Total.	[illegible]	[illegible]	Total.	[illegible]	[illegible]	Total.	[illegible]	[illegible]	Total.	[illegible]	[illegible]	Total.	
															LEINSTER.
[illegible]	[illegible]	[illegible]	[illegible]	[illegible]	[illegible]	[illegible]	[illegible]	[illegible]	[illegible]	[illegible]	[illegible]	[illegible]	[illegible]	[illegible]	Carlow.
[illegible]	[illegible]	[illegible]	[illegible]	[illegible]	[illegible]	[illegible]	[illegible]	[illegible]	[illegible]	[illegible]	[illegible]	[illegible]	[illegible]	[illegible]	Dublin.
[illegible]	[illegible]	[illegible]	[illegible]	[illegible]	[illegible]	[illegible]	[illegible]	[illegible]	[illegible]	[illegible]	[illegible]	[illegible]	[illegible]	[illegible]	Kildare.
[illegible]	[illegible]	[illegible]	[illegible]	[illegible]	[illegible]	[illegible]	[illegible]	[illegible]	[illegible]	[illegible]	[illegible]	[illegible]	[illegible]	[illegible]	Kilkenny.
[illegible]	[illegible]	[illegible]	[illegible]	[illegible]	[illegible]	[illegible]	[illegible]	[illegible]	[illegible]	[illegible]	[illegible]	[illegible]	[illegible]	[illegible]	King's.
[illegible]	[illegible]	[illegible]	[illegible]	[illegible]	[illegible]	[illegible]	[illegible]	[illegible]	[illegible]	[illegible]	[illegible]	[illegible]	[illegible]	[illegible]	Longford.
[illegible]	[illegible]	[illegible]	[illegible]	[illegible]	[illegible]	[illegible]	[illegible]	[illegible]	[illegible]	[illegible]	[illegible]	[illegible]	[illegible]	[illegible]	Louth.
[illegible]	[illegible]	[illegible]	[illegible]	[illegible]	[illegible]	[illegible]	[illegible]	[illegible]	[illegible]	[illegible]	[illegible]	[illegible]	[illegible]	[illegible]	Meath.
[illegible]	[illegible]	[illegible]	[illegible]	[illegible]	[illegible]	[illegible]	[illegible]	[illegible]	[illegible]	[illegible]	[illegible]	[illegible]	[illegible]	[illegible]	Queen's.
[illegible]	[illegible]	[illegible]	[illegible]	[illegible]	[illegible]	[illegible]	[illegible]	[illegible]	[illegible]	[illegible]	[illegible]	[illegible]	[illegible]	[illegible]	Westmeath.
[illegible]	[illegible]	[illegible]	[illegible]	[illegible]	[illegible]	[illegible]	[illegible]	[illegible]	[illegible]	[illegible]	[illegible]	[illegible]	[illegible]	[illegible]	Wexford.
[illegible]	[illegible]	[illegible]	[illegible]	[illegible]	[illegible]	[illegible]	[illegible]	[illegible]	[illegible]	[illegible]	[illegible]	[illegible]	[illegible]	[illegible]	Wicklow.
[illegible]	[illegible]	[illegible]	[illegible]	[illegible]	[illegible]	[illegible]	[illegible]	[illegible]	[illegible]	[illegible]	[illegible]	[illegible]	[illegible]	[illegible]	Total of Leinster.
															MUNSTER.
[illegible]	[illegible]	[illegible]	[illegible]	[illegible]	[illegible]	[illegible]	[illegible]	[illegible]	[illegible]	[illegible]	[illegible]	[illegible]	[illegible]	[illegible]	Clare.
[illegible]	[illegible]	[illegible]	[illegible]	[illegible]	[illegible]	[illegible]	[illegible]	[illegible]	[illegible]	[illegible]	[illegible]	[illegible]	[illegible]	[illegible]	Cork, E.R.
[illegible]	[illegible]	[illegible]	[illegible]	[illegible]	[illegible]	[illegible]	[illegible]	[illegible]	[illegible]	[illegible]	[illegible]	[illegible]	[illegible]	[illegible]	Cork, W.R.
[illegible]	[illegible]	[illegible]	[illegible]	[illegible]	[illegible]	[illegible]	[illegible]	[illegible]	[illegible]	[illegible]	[illegible]	[illegible]	[illegible]	[illegible]	Kerry.
[illegible]	[illegible]	[illegible]	[illegible]	[illegible]	[illegible]	[illegible]	[illegible]	[illegible]	[illegible]	[illegible]	[illegible]	[illegible]	[illegible]	[illegible]	Limerick.
[illegible]	[illegible]	[illegible]	[illegible]	[illegible]	[illegible]	[illegible]	[illegible]	[illegible]	[illegible]	[illegible]	[illegible]	[illegible]	[illegible]	[illegible]	Tipperary, N.R.
[illegible]	[illegible]	[illegible]	[illegible]	[illegible]	[illegible]	[illegible]	[illegible]	[illegible]	[illegible]	[illegible]	[illegible]	[illegible]	[illegible]	[illegible]	Tipperary, S.R.
[illegible]	[illegible]	[illegible]	[illegible]	[illegible]	[illegible]	[illegible]	[illegible]	[illegible]	[illegible]	[illegible]	[illegible]	[illegible]	[illegible]	[illegible]	Waterford.
[illegible]	[illegible]	[illegible]	[illegible]	[illegible]	[illegible]	[illegible]	[illegible]	[illegible]	[illegible]	[illegible]	[illegible]	[illegible]	[illegible]	[illegible]	Total of Munster.
															ULSTER.
[illegible]	[illegible]	[illegible]	[illegible]	[illegible]	[illegible]	[illegible]	[illegible]	[illegible]	[illegible]	[illegible]	[illegible]	[illegible]	[illegible]	[illegible]	Antrim.
[illegible]	[illegible]	[illegible]	[illegible]	[illegible]	[illegible]	[illegible]	[illegible]	[illegible]	[illegible]	[illegible]	[illegible]	[illegible]	[illegible]	[illegible]	Armagh.
[illegible]	[illegible]	[illegible]	[illegible]	[illegible]	[illegible]	[illegible]	[illegible]	[illegible]	[illegible]	[illegible]	[illegible]	[illegible]	[illegible]	[illegible]	Cavan.
[illegible]	[illegible]	[illegible]	[illegible]	[illegible]	[illegible]	[illegible]	[illegible]	[illegible]	[illegible]	[illegible]	[illegible]	[illegible]	[illegible]	[illegible]	Donegal.
[illegible]	[illegible]	[illegible]	[illegible]	[illegible]	[illegible]	[illegible]	[illegible]	[illegible]	[illegible]	[illegible]	[illegible]	[illegible]	[illegible]	[illegible]	Down.
[illegible]	[illegible]	[illegible]	[illegible]	[illegible]	[illegible]	[illegible]	[illegible]	[illegible]	[illegible]	[illegible]	[illegible]	[illegible]	[illegible]	[illegible]	Fermanagh.
[illegible]	[illegible]	[illegible]	[illegible]	[illegible]	[illegible]	[illegible]	[illegible]	[illegible]	[illegible]	[illegible]	[illegible]	[illegible]	[illegible]	[illegible]	Londonderry.
[illegible]	[illegible]	[illegible]	[illegible]	[illegible]	[illegible]	[illegible]	[illegible]	[illegible]	[illegible]	[illegible]	[illegible]	[illegible]	[illegible]	[illegible]	Monaghan.
[illegible]	[illegible]	[illegible]	[illegible]	[illegible]	[illegible]	[illegible]	[illegible]	[illegible]	[illegible]	[illegible]	[illegible]	[illegible]	[illegible]	[illegible]	Tyrone.
[illegible]	[illegible]	[illegible]	[illegible]	[illegible]	[illegible]	[illegible]	[illegible]	[illegible]	[illegible]	[illegible]	[illegible]	[illegible]	[illegible]	[illegible]	Total of Ulster.
															CONNAUGHT.
[illegible]	[illegible]	[illegible]	[illegible]	[illegible]	[illegible]	[illegible]	[illegible]	[illegible]	[illegible]	[illegible]	[illegible]	[illegible]	[illegible]	[illegible]	Galway.
[illegible]	[illegible]	[illegible]	[illegible]	[illegible]	[illegible]	[illegible]	[illegible]	[illegible]	[illegible]	[illegible]	[illegible]	[illegible]	[illegible]	[illegible]	Leitrim.
[illegible]	[illegible]	[illegible]	[illegible]	[illegible]	[illegible]	[illegible]	[illegible]	[illegible]	[illegible]	[illegible]	[illegible]	[illegible]	[illegible]	[illegible]	Mayo.
[illegible]	[illegible]	[illegible]	[illegible]	[illegible]	[illegible]	[illegible]	[illegible]	[illegible]	[illegible]	[illegible]	[illegible]	[illegible]	[illegible]	[illegible]	Roscommon.
[illegible]	[illegible]	[illegible]	[illegible]	[illegible]	[illegible]	[illegible]	[illegible]	[illegible]	[illegible]	[illegible]	[illegible]	[illegible]	[illegible]	[illegible]	Sligo.
[illegible]	[illegible]	[illegible]	[illegible]	[illegible]	[illegible]	[illegible]	[illegible]	[illegible]	[illegible]	[illegible]	[illegible]	[illegible]	[illegible]	[illegible]	Total of Connaught.
[illegible]	[illegible]	[illegible]	[illegible]	[illegible]	[illegible]	[illegible]	[illegible]	[illegible]	[illegible]	[illegible]	[illegible]	[illegible]	[illegible]	[illegible]	Total of Ireland.

[illegible]

TABLE C.—Showing the Number of AGRICULTURAL MACHINES in Ireland in 1890, having for their object the diminution of Manual Labour, the power employed in working them, and the Total Number in the Years 1865, 1875, 1881, and 1886.

Names of Implements.	1890. Power Employed. Water.	Steam.	Horse.	Manual.	Total Number.	Total in 1865.	Total in 1875.	Total in 1881.	Total in 1886.
Bone Crushing Machines,	1	3	.	[illegible]	[illegible]	1	[illegible]	15	[illegible]
Churning Machines,	[illegible]	11	[illegible]	[illegible]	[illegible]	[illegible]	[illegible]	[illegible]	[illegible]
Furze Cutters,	[illegible]	.	[illegible]	[illegible]	[illegible]	967	[illegible]	[illegible]	[illegible]
Grubbers,	.	1	[illegible]	1	[illegible]	[illegible]	[illegible]	[illegible]	[illegible]
Harvesters (Steam),	.	1	.	.	1	[illegible]	1	1	.
Hay, Chaff, and Straw Cutters,	[illegible]	[illegible]	[illegible]	[illegible]	[illegible]	[illegible]	[illegible]	[illegible]	[illegible]
Hay Collectors and Rakes,	.	1	[illegible]	[illegible]	[illegible]	[illegible]	[illegible]	[illegible]	[illegible]
Haymaking Machines,	.	1	[illegible]	.	[illegible]	[illegible]	[illegible]	[illegible]	[illegible]
Hoes,	.	.	[illegible]	.	5	.	7	[illegible]	[illegible]
Land Rollers,	.	.	[illegible]	[illegible]	[illegible]	[illegible]	[illegible]	[illegible]	[illegible]
Manure Distributors,	.	.	[illegible]	.	[illegible]	[illegible]	[illegible]	[illegible]	.
Mowing Machines,	.	[illegible]	[illegible]	.	[illegible]	[illegible]	[illegible]	[illegible]	[illegible]
Mowing and Reaping Machines (Combined),	.	.	[illegible]	.	[illegible]	[illegible]			
Oat Crushers,	[illegible]	[illegible]	[illegible]	[illegible]	[illegible]	[illegible]	[illegible]	[illegible]	[illegible]
Oil Cake Breakers,	[illegible]	[illegible]	[illegible]	[illegible]	[illegible]	[illegible]	[illegible]	[illegible]	[illegible]
Ploughs (Steam),	.	[illegible]	.	.	[illegible]	[illegible]	[illegible]	[illegible]	.
Potato Diggers,	.	.	[illegible]	.	[illegible]	[illegible]	[illegible]	[illegible]	[illegible]
Reaping Machines,	.	1	[illegible]	.	[illegible]	[illegible]	[illegible]	[illegible]	[illegible]
Rock Pickers,	.	.	.	.	.	4	[illegible]	[illegible]	[illegible]
Root Pulpers,	[illegible]	[illegible]	[illegible]	[illegible]	[illegible]	[illegible]	[illegible]	[illegible]	[illegible]
Scufflers,	.	.	[illegible]	.	[illegible]	[illegible]	[illegible]	[illegible]	[illegible]
Threshing Machines,	[illegible]	[illegible]	[illegible]	[illegible]	[illegible]	[illegible]	[illegible]	[illegible]	[illegible]
Turnip, Corn, &c. Sowing Machines,	[illegible]	.	[illegible]	[illegible]	[illegible]	[illegible]	[illegible]	[illegible]	[illegible]
Turnip Slicers and Root Cutters,	[illegible]	1	[illegible]	[illegible]	[illegible]	[illegible]	[illegible]	[illegible]	[illegible]
Turnip Thinners and Sowers,	.	.	[illegible]	.	1	[illegible]	[illegible]	[illegible]	[illegible]
Winnowing Machines,	1	[illegible]	[illegible]	[illegible]	[illegible]	[illegible]	[illegible]	[illegible]	[illegible]
Total,	[illegible]	[illegible]	[illegible]	[illegible]	[illegible]	[illegible]	[illegible]	[illegible]	[illegible]

In addition to the above-named machines, the following were enumerated in the Returns for 1890, viz.:—100 churning and threshing machines; 54 reaping and binding machines; 37 cabbage-cutting machines; 37 mowing, tedding and raking machines; 27 milk separators; 23 threshing and winnowing machines; 8 grinding machines; 7 hay-pressing machines; 6 butter-making machines; 6 food-preparing machines; 5 corn gatherers; 5 cultivators; 3 mowing and raking machines; 3 corn-cleaning machines; 2 force pumps (in creameries); 2 hay lifts; 2 threshing, sawing, and hay-chopping machines; 1 binding machine; 1 butter breaker; 1 crushing machine; 1 crusher (grist mill); 1 corn-grinding machine; 1 hay-cutter and oat-crusher; 1 churning and winnowing machine; 1 churning and chaff-cutting machine; 1 elevator; 1 reaping and raking machine; 1 rumbler; 1 threshing, winnowing, and bagging machine; 1 threshing and sawing machine; 1 threshing, pulping, and hay-cutting machine; 1 threshing, grinding, pumping, and timber cutting machine; 1 threshing and oat-and-cake crushing machine; 1 threshing and grinding machine; 1 Silo machine; 1 salt crusher; 1 turnip raiser; 1 electric power threshing machine; 1 gas power threshing machine; 1 gas power pulping machine.

OBSERVATIONS

OF THE

DISTRICT INSPECTORS OF THE ROYAL IRISH CONSTABULARY AND OF THE SERGEANTS OF THE METROPOLITAN POLICE,

WHO ACTED AS SUPERINTENDENTS OF THE AGRICULTURAL STATISTICS;

IN REPLY TO A CIRCULAR DATED 20TH OCTOBER, 1890, ON THE PROBABLE CAUSE TO WHICH THE GOOD OR BAD YIELD OF THE VARIOUS CROPS IN EACH OF THEIR DISTRICTS MAY BE ATTRIBUTED.

PROVINCE OF LEINSTER.

PROVINCE OF LEINSTER.

CARLOW COUNTY. *Bagenalstown D.*—As far as my personal experience goes, and I have examined the crops very carefully in every part of this district, it is generally better than was at first expected, on the good land where the seed was sown early and not too well manured the crop has been good, in bad wet land the crop has been bad, it is not so much that the tuber is diseased in these places but that they are so small and only of use for feeding poultry and pigs. I believe the disease to be attributable to worn out seed that is bought by many of the small farmers, instead of importing good seed. To conclude, the crop has been better than was at first anticipated. *Carlow D.*—There was no injury by insects, &c., to crops in this district. The bad yield is caused by—I. Not making the planting earlier in the season. II. By putting in old seed again and again in the same land. III. By replanting the same crops in the same fields year after year.

DUBLIN COUNTY. *Balbriggan D.*—After careful inquiry I find that there has been no injury done to crops by insects, fungi, or weeds, injurious to farm crops in this district during the past season. *Glencullen D.*—The yield of the potato crop in this district has in comparison with other years been fairly good this year, and the probable cause of the disease may, in my opinion, be attributed to the wet season, and old seed. I believe it would be beneficial to change the seed more frequently. *College-street D.*—I beg to state that the yield of the various crops in my district for year 1890, was similar to previous years with two exceptions, viz.:—The potatoes were good except in one instance, i.e., the Deaf and Dumb Institution, Cabra, in that case the quarter of the crop was diseased and wholly unfit for use. In the other case the yield of beans and peas was not as good as in former years, principally owing to the wet season. *Dundrum D.*—The yield of the potato crop about Carrickmines, Cabinteely, Ballybrack, Shankill, was much better in regard to champions, white rocks, and kemps, than that in other portions of the district, the other kinds of potatoes are not grown there except flounders, for which the percentage is the same throughout. The great difference in yield is, in my opinion, very much due to the fact that comparatively little rain fell in that neighbourhood in proportion to the heavy rainfall elsewhere. There has been, so far as I can learn, no appreciable damage done to crops by insects, &c., save in one or two instances where the turnips seem to have suffered from something resembling, in one case a dry rot, and in another, by so stated, a kind of worm. The other crops generally seem good. *Kingstown D.*—From the inquiries made by the several enumerators in my district with regard to the potato crop of 1890, it appears to be upon the whole nearly up to the average of former years. There is about three-quarters of the crop sound, and the remainder, viz.:—a quarter partially diseased and small, owing principally to the wet season. *Lucan D.*—The general opinion all through this district is that the bad state of the potato crop has been caused by wet weather. I cannot find that any special injury has been caused by insects, fungi, or weeds. *Rathmines D.*—There has been a slight decrease in the produce of every kind of crop grown in this district except cabbage, which the farmers state is better than it has been for the three preceding years. The only crop in which there is a perceptible decrease is potatoes. The growers of this crop state that the only reason they can assign for this failure is that the blight came upon the potatoes this year earlier than in previous years owing to the dampness of the season. The farmers also state that they have not observed any injury to their potatoes from insects, fungi, or any other cause, except the blight.

KILDARE COUNTY. *Kildare D.*—All the crops have been interfered with by rain, especially potatoes, which are injured by blight. No special injury to crops from insects or fungi are reported. *Naas D.*—The low average yield of potatoes is entirely owing to the wet season, and not to the ravages of noxious insects, &c.; wherever new seed was planted in reasonably dry soil the yield was good; the only kind of potatoes grown to any extent are champions, kemps, and flounders. Other root crops are excellent, the corn crops were a fair average. *Robertstown D.*—In general, about a quarter crop was bad about here, and a quarter small. A potato called "blacksmiths" was sowed in a good many small gardens, and showed a very bad yield.

KILKENNY COUNTY. *Callan D.*—The crops in this district were very good this season, with the exception of the potato crop, which was seriously injured by the blight. Potatoes set in March remained a good crop in fresh land, as they escaped the heavy rains. Potatoes set in late April and May were seriously affected by the blight. The farmers here do not consider that their crops were injured by insects or fungi to any estimated degree. *Castlecomer D.*—The probable cause of partial failure in the various crops can solely be attributed to the wet and very inclement weather during the late spring, and throughout the whole summer. This affected all general crops as well as the potato crop. With regard to insects I cannot discover that they have done more injury to crops during this year than at any previous time, or probably not so much. *Kilkenny D.*—The wetness of the middle months of summer, caused potatoes on wet low-lying and undrained land to be partially diseased and in-

PROVINCE OF LEINSTER.

lurios. A good sign at the present time, however, is that the price is slightly falling, an indication that scarcity is not apprehended. In the tabular form of percentages of disease of the potato crop, the superiority of the champion variety is not impaired by its comparison with the Scotch, as the former is the main crop of the country and is not dug till the autumn, while the latter is grown to a comparatively small extent for consumption in July and August, and these were dug (except the small quantity kept for seed) before the disease appeared to any extent. *Johnstown D.*—The yield of crops in this district is as follows:—Wheat which is not sown to any great extent in district gave a bad yield owing to the wet season and land not being suitable for it. Barley also gave a poor yield which is attributed to the very wet season. Oats was a fair average crop, and farmers appear satisfied with the yield; they say the moisture in the beginning of the season is the cause—moist season being, it seems, unfavourable for wheat and barley, but favourable for oats. Mangolds and turnips are also good crops, which is attributed to the moist season. Hay has not given as good yield as previous years, the season being too dry and parched in the beginning. Potatoes, on the whole, are a two-thirds crop, and such are of a small size generally. The season being wet and generally unfavourable, I cannot offer any remark as to insects and their ravages. *Pallbown D.*—The yield of the various crops in my district this year has been good, except potatoes, which have partially failed, the crop being only about two-thirds of the average. This partial failure seems attributable to an unusually early appearance of disease before the tubers in late sown crops were properly formed; the disease spread during the cold wet weather in July and August, but subsequent seasonable weather greatly checked its progress. Champions and Scotch are the description of potatoes principally grown, and they appear to have been affected by disease to about the same extent. Cereals promised very well until injured by the excessive rainfall in August; fine weather fortunately set in soon after the harvest commenced before very much damage had been done, so that after all an average crop was realised. Hay was an abundant crop, but much of it has been badly saved in consequence of unfavourable weather. The season has been favourable for turnips and mangolds, the yield of these crops being above the average. I find that no material injury has been done to the crops by insects or fungi, although in certain cases wire-worms have done a certain amount of mischief to potatoes. *Thomastown D.*—It is unnecessary to go into detail regarding the causes of potato failure. With the exception of the failure in that crop the others may be characterised as good. Oats especially so and wheat and barley average. Turnips and mangolds never better. Hay is plentiful, but a good deal of it indifferently saved.

KING'S COUNTY. *Edenderry D.*—Without any apparent reason the potato crops vary tremendously. On one farm you will find hardly any disease, and on the very next farm all are diseased, and on another though not diseased, they are not larger than marbles. I would say that taking the whole district into account about one-third are sound, one-third partially diseased, and one-third quite gone. All the other crops are good. Owing to the wet season a quantity of hay was very badly saved. *Portarlington D.*—The grain and root crops in this district were very good crops. With the exception of the potato crop the yield has been considered satisfactory. Hay was good in uplands, but that grown on lowlands and old meadow lands was light. The frosts in May checked the growth of potatoes and left them no strength to resist the attack of blight which came early in August. I cannot learn that any special injury has resulted from insects, &c. The book supplied will be of great service next year in guiding the inquiries of the enumerators so that fuller information may be given to the statistical department as to such injuries. *Parsonstown D.*—The wet season, and want of heat in months of July and August of this year was to a great measure the cause of the bad yield. *Tullamore D.*—Owing to the incessant rains of the past three months, the potato crop is not up to the average, although there is a fair percentage of sound tubers, particularly in the sorts that came in early. I attribute much of the failure to want of proper cultivation, which in innumerable farms is prejudicial to a healthy good crop.

LONGFORD COUNTY. *Ballymahon D.*—The crops in this district were generally up to the average except the potato crop, which has suffered considerably from the wet season, and I believe also from want of change of seed. There has not been any special injury to crops observed to have been done by noxious insects or fungi. Weeds generally are injurious to crops of all kinds, and have done some injury in this district, but farmers, as a rule, will not attend to their eradication. *Granard D.*—The partial failure in the potato crop is attributed to the wetness of the early part of the season. Not much damage has been done to the crops by fungi or insects, but considerable tracts are overrun with weeds. *Longford D.*—It is hardly necessary to observe that the bad yield of the potato crop is due to the "blight," and the persistent wet weather. The good yield of oats is attributed to the genial spring. In one part of the district (Lanesboro'), it is stated that the cabbage crop is not good owing to the ravages of grubs.

LOUTH COUNTY. *Ardee D.*—The partial disease in the potato crop in this district is altogether attributed to the inclemency of the weather last summer. *Collon D.*—The potato crop here has been only fair. In every case where potatoes were planted early, with change of seed, and in fresh ground they withstood the blight. The planting early appears to have been the most certain preventive as the farmers say that when such a course was pursued the potato was too strong on the arrival of blight to be affected by it. In most cases however the disease, they say, arrived a fortnight or three weeks before the potato was fit to resist the attack. The Skerry blue potato appears to have been the hardiest of the lot. I find that when the individual potatoes of the crop have been small a larger percentage have been sound than when they were large, and in these cases I fancy not much manure was used which might result in the potato not being too much forced at the commencement of its growth and being consequently strong to resist disease. I cannot find that any observation of insects or fungi has been made save the attack of the white slug on the stalks. *Drogheda D.*—Hay, oats, turnips and mangolds have been good owing to the continued moisture in the early part of the season which favoured the growth of young plants; the moisture which favoured these crops has been injurious to potatoes, particularly in low-lying or heavy lands, which require a hot season. Inquiries have been made by the several enumerators in this district as to the ravages of noxious insects on crops, and they report that cabbage has slightly suffered from caterpillars, no other crop has suffered from insects. *Dundalk D.*—The good yield of the various crops in this district for present year may be attributed to good cultivation, and tolerably good weather.

MEATH COUNTY. *Ashbey D.*—The potato crop in this district is generally a very poor one, owing to the early appearance of disease, caused by (1) wet weather, (2) the prevailing habit of growing the crop in worn out soil, (3) using as seed, chiefly potatoes grown in the same land. The grain crops were much above the average, being not so much injured by wet weather. Turnips and mangold are also good for same reason, and hay was a very abundant crop. So far as I have been able to ascertain no special damage has been done to the crops in this district by insects or fungi during this season. *Dunshaughlin D.*—The potato crop would have been very good, had it not been for the heavy frost on the 18th May which burned down the stalks, then in the latter end of July the distemper got hold on the crops before it had come to maturity. This, combined with the constant damp weather during August and part of September, is believed to be the cause of the failure, particularly in heavy land. I beg to add that as far as I can learn none of the potato crop is entirely lost, as the people used all that was bad for feeding their pigs, &c. *Kells D.*—The good yield of hay, oats and turnips in this district is attributed to the good season which favoured the soil, and the bad yield of the potato crop, to the early setting in of blight and disease. As far as I could ascertain, the crops in this district suffered no special injury from insects, or fungi, during past season. *Navan D.*—Potatoes are a limited crop in this locality and the only sort grown are champions, except a very inconsiderable quantity of early potatoes which were consumed before the blight appeared. The injury to the crop is attributed to the dampness of the season and the early appearance of the blight. The people have not the slightest idea of injury from insects or fungi, except that they believe a hard frosty winter does kill insects in the ground. *Slane D.*—I have not been able to obtain any information relative to special injury to crops in this district for past season from insects or fungi. *Trim D.*—The failure (partial) in the potato crop is principally due in the early sorts to prevalence of heavy frosts in May last, and in the later sorts to continuous rain. From inquiry I cannot however discover that any material damage was caused either by noxious insects or weeds.

Queen's County. *Abbeyleix D.*—The principal crop grown in this district is champion potatoes, about 80 per cent. of the whole. With the exception of the potato crop, which has failed to the extent of about one-third, all the others have done exceedingly well, root crops especially. Hay and straw are also abundant. *Ballylinan D.*—There was a good yield of all the crops in this district, except potatoes. Owing to the wet season and poverty of some of the land, this crop has not been so good a yield as in former years. I think this bad yield may also be attributable to a want of change of seed by the farmers. *Maryborough D.*—I have not heard of any insects injuring the crops in this district, but I observe that farmers are very careless regarding the weeding of their crops. Weeds are most injurious to all kinds of crops. They absorb that which should go to nourish the roots, and thereby impoverish both present and future crops. Potatoes fail more rapidly in dirty wet land than they do in dry clean land. Some farmers have not sufficient help to enable them to keep their crop thoroughly weeded, and perhaps are unable to pay labourers; others are careless, and do not appreciate the value of such work. I fear this state of things is likely to continue, as most people like to go on as usual without any change for the better. *Mountrath D.*—Hay has been a good crop so far as yield, but quality, especially old meadow hay, is below average, owing to the very wet weather which prevailed during July last. First-crop hay in many cases was saved during comparatively dry weather. Oats is well up to average in yield, but quality is not so good as other years, which is entirely attributable to wet season, and same remark applies with greater force to barley. Turnips are an average crop. Mangolds in many cases ran to seed, owing to wet season. Failure of potato crop is attributable to the very wet season, and in many cases matters have been made worse by the bad system of cultivation adopted by many of the smaller farmers. Potatoes sown on boggy or heavy and badly drained land have naturally suffered most. Potatoes sown comparatively early on well-drained ground and assisted by the application of artificial manures, appear to have done best. The cold and wet season appears to have been adverse to the existence of insect pests and fungi, excepting, of course, potato blight.

Westmeath County. *Castlepollard D.*—The failure of the crop is due to the extreme wetness of the season, due to the early attack of the blight, the tubers not being sufficiently developed to withstand it. There has been no damage done by noxious insects, nor any attributable to fungi or weeds. In the hilly districts the potatoes were not so much affected by the extreme damp, and were sufficiently developed to withstand the blight. *Delvin D.*—All the crops this year were fairly good, with the exception of potatoes, which have been a partial failure (25 to 50 per cent. of entire crop being bad), owing to blight, probably being caused by the continuous wet weather in the early part of the season. *Kilbeggan D.*—Very few potatoes are grown in this district except champions and flounders. The good yield of root crops and cereals is due to the plentiful rains. These crops were, however, slightly injured by the rain at harvest time. The potato failure is due to:—(1.) Early frosts. (2.) Wet season. (3.) In a few instances growth of fungi. (4.) Growth of weeds, after the blight had set in. (5.) In a few cases late planting. (6.) Only applies to boggy land and moorland. *Moate D.*—As is well known, the potato crop has been a bad one this season, not half so good as the average. This appears due, firstly, to the early frosts which cut away the stalks, and, secondly, to the amount of weeds which smothered the growth of the young potatoes. This large amount of weeds is to a great extent, no doubt, due to the wet season. When the weeds are cut, compared they naturally harbour insects which injure the young potatoes. I am informed that the same remarks also apply to other crops, such as oats. The wet season has naturally favoured such crops as cabbages. *Mullingar D.*—The crops generally, with the exception of the potatoes, have been good in this district. The failure of the potatoes is ascribed to the early blight brought on by the wet season. As regards ravages by noxious insects, in some portions of the district the turnip crop suffered from a maggot resembling that found in sheep. It is the first time it has appeared in this district, I am informed. I presume this must be the grub of the root fly described in the "Special Report" you have been kind enough to send me. The damages to the crop, however, have not been general nor extensive. The land is pretty good generally, and that under tillage is well farmed, and there does not appear to have been any damage of sufficient extent to be noticed as caused by insects or fungi. I am not aware of what is the exact nature of the potato blight, but it seems to be caused by sudden changes of temperature, and the weakly plants succumb, their weakness having originated in rapid growth during damp weather, causing fungus on the tuber when the leaves have been destroyed by blight.

Wexford County. *Enniscorthy D.*—The bad yield of potatoes this year was owing to the wetness of the season. The blight set in very early and stopped the growth of the tubers before they came to maturity. The other crops were about an average in this district; quality of grain not up to average in consequence of wet season; mangolds and turnips an excellent crop. *New Ross D.*—The tubers are more or less wet and sodden when cooked. Were it not for the dry sandy nature of the soil in this district, along with careful tillage, the crop would be far worse than it is. It is unnecessary to say that the heavy rains in the early part of the season, followed by a visitation of fungus, was the cause of the partial failure of the crop. All the other crops are well up to the average of former years, and no special injury was caused by the ravages of insects. *Tipperary D.*—The potato crop this year is about onehalf that of last year in this district, and is of inferior quality. The crop has not been much affected by disease. The blight, which set in early in July, is the cause of the small crop. *Wexford D.*—I regret I have not information which would enable me to give a useful report on insects and fungi injurious to crops. I beg to acknowledge receipt of the very interesting "Special Report" on insects, fungi and weeds injurious to farm crops. If generally known and the advice given acted on, it should be of great use to the farming class, as a general rule they appear to pay no attention whatever to clearing their lands of weeds.

Wicklow County. *Arklow D.*—The cause of the bad yield is attributed to the want of heat in June and the wet weather in subsequent months. *Bray D.*—The crops in general in this district have been good. The potatoes a fair crop, but a small proportion diseased, owing to a continuance of wet weather, just when fine, dry, warm weather was required to ripen them. No observations to make regarding insects, fungi, &c. *Dunlavin D.*—The exceptionally bad yield of the potato crop in this district this year is attributable to the wet season, all other crops are as good as they have been for years past. *Wicklow D.*—The general opinion of the farmers is that the diseased percentage of the crop was caused entirely by the very wet season, and want of new seed. Where new seed was used it was found that there was no disease. Some farmers consider that the description of manure used had something to do in producing disease on certain farms, where, for instance, heavy wet manure was put on the land. It is not considered that insects or fungi injured crops in this part of the country.

PROVINCE OF MUNSTER.

Clare County. *Ballyvaghan D.*—I am quite unable to give the report called for as to fungi or insects, and I have no means of getting information. The principal causes of the failure of the potato crop were the very wet weather and the fact that the produce from the same seed has been employed too often. *Ennis D.*—There is a class of potatoes which, though very little sown, yet, where sown, seems to have suffered less than other kinds. I mean the "Leather Coats." Most of this district is of light dry soil, and will account for the percentage being fairly good; in some parts the potatoes are excellent; in boggy, mountainous land the crop is the reverse. It is a matter of notoriety that excessive rain at the time when the tubers ought to be swelling caused the failure in the potato crop. At the time of ripening some fine weather just saved the oat crop, &c., of which no great quantity is sown. A fine summer gave the farmers ample opportunity of saving and carrying excellent crops of hay. The root crops are distinctly good, the saturated land being beneficial to them. *Ennistimon D.*—The general potato crop sown in this district was the champion, which seems to be run out, as the yield was bad and the quality very inferior. The Scotch Down did best and kept best, and is altogether the best food. I, in a great measure, attribute the disease and bad yield of the potato crop to shop manures of an inferior quality, bad drainage, and worse tillage. The inattention to weeding leaves ample covering and encouragement to breed the various kinds of insects injurious to the crop, and prevents the free air from nourishing and strengthening the plant. In this district such a thing as weeding is almost unknown. *Kildysart D.*—I. The potato crop is extremely varied, both as to quality and yield. Where new seed was sown early, the quality is excellent and the return average. On the other hand, wherever the crop was sown late, the return is much below the average in quantity, and the quality ranges from indifferent to bad, according to the nature and situation of the land. In many mountainous localities, where mists prevailed even when rain was not falling, the return is practically nil. On the whole, the yield of sound potatoes is only about half the crop, and the quality of these is, as a general rule, much inferior to the crops of former years, the extreme and constant wet having rendered the tubers soft, wet, and soapy. II. Hay was an abundant crop, and up to the average in quality; but much difficulty was experienced in saving any but early cuttings. III. Cereals (chiefly oats) were never better, as a rule, but they have suffered much in saving. IV. Green crops are good as a whole. I cannot trace any special injury from insects or fungi. *Kilrush D.*—As regards the potato crop, which is undoubtedly a poor one this year, the percentage of diseased potatoes is small, but the potatoes which are sound are not good; they are soft and soapy. It seems to me that the growth of the potatoes stopped and they never matured properly; they are small in size as well as deficient in yield. The deficiency in quantity was not so great as was anticipated. I estimate the average at sixty per cent. of the usual crop. Some farmers anticipate that the potatoes will not keep, and only time can prove that question. The earlier potatoes were a very good crop, being mostly ready for digging when the blight came on. In some places imported seed has produced no better crop than the champions grown from old seed, in old land; but in almost all cases new potato ground has done better than old. *Sixmilebridge D.*—The various crops in this district are fully up to the average of past years, except the potato, which is very little more than one-third an average crop. I attribute the failure of the potato crop this year to the cold wet summer which we have had, combined with the fact that the kinds of potatoes sown are too long in use in the district. *Tulla D.*—The bad wet weather coming before the potato crop was matured is the cause of the bad yield in that crop, which in many portions of the district has been very late in being sown, especially in the mountainous and poorer lands in the district. So far as can be ascertained, the disease, this year, has not been attributed to noxious insects or fungi. The yield of the several other crops has been a fair average, though a good deal of heavy oat crops have been injured by getting lodged from the heavy rains. The small percentage in the [illegible] of diseased potatoes is accounted for by their being dug earlier in the year for use. This description is only sown in small quantities.

Cork County, E.R. *Ballincollig D.*—The potato crop in portions of this district was a fair average one, while in other parts it was not more than a third; as a rule those which were sown early in warm sandy soils escaped the effects of the blight to a great extent, the tubers being nearly matured; while those sown late in cold clayey soils were not sufficiently advanced before the wet came on. The only insect which has, so far as is known, done any injury to the potato crop, is the wire worm. The farmers here do not appear to watch with any interest the injury caused to their crops by insects, &c., and are not able to give any information of value on the subject. But if they each had a copy of your valuable book they might awaken to the importance of the subject. *Charleville*

D.—The failure of the tuber crop is due to the wet cold season which prevented the potatoes maturing before the blight came on them. The blight appeared earlier than usual by several weeks. *Cork, North, D.*—I attribute the bad yield of the potato crop to the very unfavourable weather in the early part of the season. *Cork, South, D.*—The potato crop in this district shows a fair average—(1.) The land is dry and well tilled. (2.) A good many market gardeners reside in the district and they had them dug out for the market before the disease set in. *Fermoy D.*—The bad yield of potatoes was due to the very wet weather at a time when the greater part of the crop was most liable to injury from that cause, to the greater part of the crop having been sown late, and to its having been mainly sown in "beds," rather than in drills. Potatoes sown in March and those sown in drills stood best. Potatoes grown from seed imported direct from Scotland and not got from local seedsmen (as imported seed) did well. The defective yield of grain crops was due to the wet weather preventing the ear filling properly, so that, when ground, the grain gives an unusually low return of meal, &c. There was no special injury to crops from insects or fungi. Turnips were in some cases slightly injured by wire-worm, and potatoes were injured by fungi, but I think rather less than usual. *Kanturk D.*—I attribute the potato failure in this district to the excessive rainfall during the past summer. Up to the middle of July the crop was very promising, but the continuous rain caused the blight. *Kinsale D.*—I consider the bad yield of the potato crop this year is entirely due to the excessive fall of rain in the early part of the season, and also to the lateness in putting in the seed. Wherever the crop was sown anyway early there is a fair and average crop. I also consider the seed planted should be changed oftener than it is. *Mallow D.*—I do not think that there is any reason to believe that insects, fungi, &c., have had any influence on the crop but that the bad weather had. *Middleton D.*—I cannot say that any crop in this district has during past season suffered in anyway from the effects of ravages of noxious insects, &c. *Mitchelstown D.*—But for the failure of the potato crop the harvest this year would have been an abundant one. The yield of all green crops has been particularly good, as the wet season which told so much against the potato has been in their favour; the wet summer contributing to their growth and the fairly good harvest season enabling them to come to maturity. Flounders appear to have done better than champions, but this is because the former were dug out early. The champion seems to have been too long in use and new seed seems now necessary. Those farmers who put in their seed early have had in limestone land fair crops, but the blight did great harm to crops set late and in soft boggy land. It is not considered that insects did any harm to the crop—the failure being attributed to the blight entirely. *Newmarket D.*—I find that in a few cases where the champions were planted in March the yield has been a fair average. This district being high and damp the farmers do not plant early. I have heard no complaints as to injury by insects. This may be accounted for by the use of lime in this part of the country, in addition to manure. *Queenstown D.*—As far as I have been able to ascertain from inquiry and observation the crops of this district, with exception of the potato, are good; the corn and green crops and hay, I believe, exceed the average yield. I have heard in some places that the oat crop received damage by being lodged. The hay crop is large, but in quality it has suffered from excessive rain and the low temperature of the summer, and it was considerably damaged by rain while being saved. I have read the Special Report on "Insects, fungi, and weeds injurious to crops." The farmers here invariably say that their crops have not been damaged by insects, or fungi, and I believe no special damage has been caused by them, except the potato blight, which appears to be a fungus. The turnips and mangolds appear to have sustained exceptionally little damage this year from attacks of insects. I think the general causes of the inferior potato crops this year, are firstly that there was little heat in early part of year, which retarded the growth of the tubers, and then the blight came early and stopped the growth of the tubers even where it did not actually reach the tubers. I find in many instances that after the blight attacked and withered the potato stalk, the farmers let the weeds grow, and consequently owing to the wetness of the season a luxuriant crop of weeds was the result, which must have caused considerable damage. The potato crop varies very much in different parts of this district, and in the extra inland portions it is nearly an average crop, and of good quality, and owing to the high prices obtainable its value is, I believe, above the average. In the localities of Monkstown, Passage West and Crosshaven, the yield appears to be 50 per cent. under the average, and the tubers of inferior quality generally. Some good farmers have good crops in these localities. *Youghal D.*—The cause of the bad crop of potatoes this year is due to the blight which fell upon them unusually early, and also the wet season which rendered the crop very bad near the sea coast and in mountainous districts.

CORK COUNTY, W.R. *Bandon D.*—The cause of the bad potato crop here is believed to be in consequence of the wet season, and the blight attacking the stalks so early in the season. *Bantry D.*—The good yield of Snowdrops (which are not a good keeping variety) is due to the fact that being an early potato, the crop was dug out before the blight began to affect the quality. Practically, the entire potato crop in this locality consists of champions. As regards injury to the crops from insects or fungi, the enumerator at Kilcrohane reports that wheat has suffered to the amount of one-fourth from insects and fungi; the enumerator at Ouvane reports that fungi have in many cases caused the partial failure of mangold wurzel and turnips, and the enumerator at Kealkil reports similar loss from fungi. The failure of the potato crop this year may be attributed to the effects of excessive rain. *Castletown Bere D.*—The bad yield this year of the various crops in this district has been due entirely to the bad weather that has prevailed during the summer and autumn. *Clonakilty D.*—The partial failure of the potato crop in this district is attributed to the fogs during the months of June and July. The deterioration in grain crops is attributable to the same cause and the wetness of the summer months. This moisture was an advantage to the root crops, which were good. The farmers do not attribute the failure of the crops to insects, fungi, &c., of which they appear to have no knowledge. As a rule, the farmers are very neglectful of the growth of weeds which they allow to overrun their farms—particularly the potato fields. *Dunmanway D.*—I cannot at present give an opinion as to the probable effect on the potato crop by the ravages of any particular insect, but I have myself personally inspected some of the diseased potatoes, and I perceived that in some cases there was no smell from them as if they had been rotten, they had not at all the same smell as the diseased potato of 1880, and I believe that the blight fell on them in a different way this year than in other years, and it may not be at all unlikely that the great quantity of rain which fell in the months of June, July, and August, may have in certain soils been favourable to the growth of a certain insect which found its way to the potato. *Macroom D.*—The potatoes are small and generally up to the present sound. The people complain that the tubers never came to proper maturity, this may be attributed to the wet season we had during the early growth of the potato, and the fact that the blight set in so early, causing the stalks to decay. The weeds then diminished and the people, thinking that the crop was utterly lost (from the outcry made by some persons), made no effort to clear them away. I find that light, high, sandy soil, where the crops were put in early and well manured and limed, has given the best yield, but in wet heavy soil or higher mountainy farms, even though limed, the crop did not do so well as in the former case. *Millstreet D.*—In my opinion the failure—partial—of the potato is due to the bad season and to the fact of the seed not being changed. *Skibbereen D.*—With the exception of the potato crop, the crops in this district have been very fair, but are slightly below the average in most cases. As regards the potatoes they have now nearly all been dug, and the result has been about one-third of the usual crop, of these little more than one-half were sound. The failure of the crop is generally attributed in the first instance to late planting, and secondly to the unusually early appearance of the blight which set in before the growth was strong enough to resist it. The blight itself is believed here to be greatly due to the heavy sea fogs which were very prevalent in the early part of the season, and the wet weather and want of heat prevented subsequent growth. Inferior seed was also one of the causes of the failure, combined in many instances with a worn-out soil. Champions and flounders are the principal descriptions grown. The other kinds are only grown in small quantities. No special injury has been caused by insects or fungi.

KERRY COUNTY. *Cahersiveen D.*—In my opinion the failure of the potato crop this year may chiefly be attributed to the very wet season. I think it would be a great improvement if the farmers could be induced to import fresh seed every second or third year, and till fresh lands in place of tilling the same ground for several years after each other. *Castleisland D.*—The potato crop is a very bad one in this district, and this applies to all varieties sown; of course, the chief cause for this has been the unusually wet season. I am not in a position to enter into particulars regarding the injury done by insects, fungi, &c., but I can safely say, that I often wonder how potatoes grow at all here owing to the way they are treated. They are usually planted in the worst kind of land, boggy and swampy, badly manured, badly attended to during growth, and seldom or never weeded. The most hopeless state of ignorance prevails as to the cultivation of potatoes. *Dingle D.*—The loss in the potato crop consisted more of wet soapy potatoes than of those actually diseased. Those diseased suffered from the usual fungus, no others are noticeable. *Kenmare D.*—The bad yield of the potato crop is due to the blight having set in early owing to the constant wet weather. The hay is a good crop, but in some instances badly saved. The oat crop, very little of which is sown by the farmers in this district, is fair. Turnips are an average crop and doing fairly well. No complaints have been made of any injury done to the various crops in this district by noxious insects. *Killarney D.*—As far as I can ascertain insects have done no harm to crops in this district. As regards weeds, I believe that a certain amount of injury has been done by them to crops in this district, as the people are not at all careful to weed their land, and the crops become choked up with weeds. Of course the principal cause of the failure of the potato crop was the very wet season. *Killorglin D.*—The bad yield this year was occasioned by the wet season which brought on the blight early. The early sowing yielded a good crop, but the late sowing, say in April and May, yielded a bad crop. The early sowing had a good growth made before the blight made its attack. The potato crop did not suffer from worms, fungi, or any other cause in this district, but solely from the cause mentioned. *Listowel D.*—The bad yield of crops in this district may be attributed to the wetness of the season, and in the case of potatoes, to the wetness of the season, not changing the seed more frequently, and not cleaning the land of decaying potato stalks and weeds. *Tralee D.*—The bad yield in this district may be attributed to late planting, wet spring, and blight setting in before tubers had matured. The amount of weeds permitted to exist in the potato crop in this district is extremely detrimental, excluding light and air and retaining moisture. Noxious insects and fungi are not believed to have had much effect upon the bad yield this year, and certainly nothing comparatively with the causes as above stated.

LIMERICK COUNTY.—*Abbeyfeale D.*—The principal cause of the failure was the early visitation of the blight before the potatoes could come to maturity, the natural wet description of the land in this district and the continual rainy weather during the season. Champions are the only description of potatoes principally grown, all other kinds are only grown in isolated small patches and are dug out early, which accounts for the high percentage of produce, with the exception of white rocks which have done very badly. *Adare D.*—The potato crop has now been dug out in this district, and notwithstanding the bad year generally for that crop, in this district it has been quite up to the average or at least very nearly so. I chiefly attribute this to the fact that the farmers of this district, are as a rule good careful tillers, and are better off as a rule than in other districts. No special injury was caused to crops from insects or the growth of fungi. *Bruff D.*—There is not much tillage in this district. The land in general is rich and the greater portion is in grass. The oats and wheat were good crops but suffered somewhat by heavy rains. Turnips and mangolds were good crops. Potatoes yielded badly. In general they were planted late, the wet season affected them prejudicially, there was an absence of warm ripening weather, and the crop was much overgrown with weeds. When disease set in the potatoes were not fully matured to resist the effects of the disease and hence large quantities became injured. Flounders are a sort that came in early and were largely used before they could be affected. I believe some of the poor people cut small potatoes as seed, which I believe is not a good thing to do. I cannot learn that injury was done by insects, but I think it is to be regretted that the people do not weed their potato crop better than they do. There is a large quantity of hay in the district, some of it not in good condition from the heavy rains. *Kilfinane D.*—I received a copy of your *Special Report* on insects, fungi, and weeds, which, if generally known and acted on by the farmers, would prove a great benefit to them. I cannot really state the amount of damage done by these pests, but it certainly is very considerable. *Newcastle D.*—With the exception of the potato crop all crops have turned out favourably this season. Hay and oats were fair average crops, and have on the whole been well saved. The yield of turnips and other green crops is above average. Potatoes were a smaller crop than for some years previously. In the mountain parts and wet boggy land an average of more than one-fourth were black and unfit for use. Potatoes set late in the season were soft and worthless, but the failure of the crop is not nearly so general as it is represented. The crops in this district have not been injured by insects &c., to any appreciable extent. *Limerick D.*—The champions, Scotch downs, and flounders are the principal potato crop grown in this district this year, the bad yield of which is due to the wet season and the blight coming earlier, and before the crop was sufficiently grown to resist the disease to any great extent. I find only one man in the district grew lumper seeds. This crop appears to have turned out fairly well. The Scotch downs is a hardy potato, and not so liable to disease as champions or flounders. I cannot find that any special injury has been done by insects or fungi to the crops during the past season. *Fox Valley D.*—Dairy business is the chief industry in this district. The crops grown here—corn, potatoes, and turnips, are cultivated to a limited extent only. Oats are up to the average in quantity, but the quality, owing to the wetness of the season, is inferior to that of other years. Potatoes have suffered from the blight, and such as have escaped are below the average in size and quality because of excessive moisture and the absence of heat. Turnips are above the average, as is also hay, but the latter has suffered in quality from the constant rain. *Rathkeale D.*—The bad yield of the various crops in this district may be attributed to the unusually wet weather during the summer months, and also to a lesser extent to late planting. There has been no injury to crops by insects or fungi during the past season.

TIPPERARY COUNTY, N.R. *Borrisokane D.*—With the exception of potatoes, all the crops in this district were good. The bad yield in the potato crop was caused by the blight setting in so early this year. No special injury has been done to crops by insects. *Nenagh D.*—All farmers about here agree in attributing the partial failure of the potato crop to the heavy rains of July and August, and the setting in of the blight before the tubers had done growing. Some also attribute it partially to weak seed. No crops suffered this year from insects, or fungi, or weeds. Turnips, which in dry seasons suffer from the fly, escaped this year owing to the rains. *Newport D.*—The bad yield of the potato crop in this district is due to the very wet season. I have heard no complaints of injury done by insects or fungi. *Roscrea D.*—The bad year in this locality is attributed to the wet season preceded by frosts, and the fact that the present champion seed is considered worn out. No reports have been received with reference to insects and fungi from constabulary. I need hardly add that there are plenty of weeds injurious to crops. *Templemore D.*—From inquiry made and observation, I attribute the bad yield of the potato crop to sowing the same seed year after year in the same soil; and the disease called blight set in early this year in consequence of the wet season. I consider the yield of the other various crops a good average, the season being favourable for them. *Thurles D.*—So far as I can learn there have been no ravages from noxious insects or fungi in this district. The wet season caused a large crop of weeds, and the moisture caused the increase in the blight.

TIPPERARY COUNTY, S.R. *Cahir D.*—The cause of the bad yield in the potato crop is attributed to the early blight, and wet summer. All other crops were good, and no injury was caused from insects or fungi during the past season. *Carrick-on-Suir D.*—It is believed that the principal cause of the potato blight was the wet year. The crop of Scotch Downs showed a better percentage of sound potatoes, chiefly owing to the fact that it was sown earlier. At this period it is difficult to trace what injury may have been done by insects or fungi. *Cashel D.*—The large percentage of champions lost by disease was owing to continuous rain during July and August. The Regents, being an early crop, did not suffer so much. *Clonmel D.*—Owing to the moist growing weather, with occasional gleams of sunshine, experienced early in the season, there was in the potato crop a most extraordinary growth of haulm, and little development of tuber, which in the majority of instances matured badly owing to the continued rain, and want of ripening weather, hence the crop generally was deficient in quantity and quality. In many places, however, I noticed that the luxuriant growth of weeds was allowed to remain on the drills, and these effectually prevented the crop getting any sun or air, and this negligence on the part of the farmers further militated against the crop. *Dundrum D.*—The potato crop was injured by the very wet summer. It is about two-third an average crop. In the low lands and boggy mountainous parts of the district the crop was half average, or under the other parts, good in some places. Hay well above average, most of it well saved. Corn excellent, well above average. Bere heavy grain, good quality. Stalk over six feet in many places. Turnips large and sound. All crops excellent, but potatoes. The wet followed by sunshine saved the corn. From my present inquiries and observation, I am unable to make any special injuries resulting from insects or fungi. I shall examine the contents of the book received, and after further inquiry submit report. *Killenaule D.*—The only cause I know of for the partial failure of the potato crop is the blight, which has rendered about one-third, and more in some parts, of the crop unfit for food. Recent heavy rain also had an injurious effect on the potatoes. *Tipperary D.*—Champions form the principal crop of potatoes planted. White rocks and Regents have not been grown generally, but in small patches near dwelling houses. This is not an agricultural country—it is more adapted for pasture. The potato crop has, in part, failed here in consequence of the damp summer, and the moist nature of the land.

PROVINCE OF MUNSTER.

WATERFORD COUNTY. *Cappoquin D.*—The bad yield of potatoes is attributable solely to the cold wet season. The yield of all other crops is good, as there was not too much rain—corn, though good, has not so much weight as other years, owing to the cold. *Dungarvan D.*—The bad yield of the potato crop is due to the blight, and an unusually wet summer. There was a very fair return of all other crops. There was some slight injury done to the oat crop by the wire worm, which appears to be the only damage done by insects in this district. *Portlaw D.*—The bad yield of the late potatoes was due to the wetness of the summer and autumn. Those lands which were planted and dug early want a better crop, as the spring and early summer were more favourable. *Waterford D.*—Owing to the wet weather at the end of summer, there has been a great amount of disease this season. The Regents were all dug out early, hence the smaller percentage of loss.

PROVINCE OF ULSTER.

PROVINCE OF ULSTER.

ANTRIM COUNTY. *Antrim D.*—There has been a very fair yield of crops except potatoes in this district, and there was no special injury caused by insects or fungi. *Ballymena D.*—So far as this district is concerned, the potato crop may be considered a fair yield, but owing to continuous wet weather, fully one-third of the crop has suffered from disease, and this has especially been the case where the crop occupied low-lying ground. Hay was an abundant crop, but considerable difficulty was experienced in saving it, and much of it has been injured owing to rain. Oats was a very good crop, with a very fair yield of straw. It would have been much better, but like every other crop, suffered much for want of warm ripening weather, and about the time it was being cut, the weather cleared up for a short time only to break again as the corn was in stooks. Fortunately this crop suffered little from high winds. Turnips and other root crops are fully up to the average. Flax was an excellent crop, and suffered little from the wet weather, besides the yield being much over the average. Little wheat is sown in this district. I have not heard of any harm done by insects or fungi during the past season. In common with many parts of Ireland, sufficient trouble is not taken to eradicate weeds. *Ballymoney D.*—It would appear that on an average more than one-half of the crop is rotted. The "Flounders" were dug out early, which is the cause of their having suffered so little. The failure of the crop generally is due here to the wet season, and also largely to the want of fresh seed. I do not think that insects or fungi have caused any appreciable damage. *Belfast, North, D.*—I have endeavoured to ascertain from reliable sources the probable cause why the produce of crops this season is less than last year. The farmers in this district attribute the failure to a continuously wet and unseasonably cold summer, and the early appearance of blight; and believe that no injury was traceable either to noxious insects or fungi. *Belfast, South, D.*—The yield in this district is good, above the average, as a moist season is best suited to the soil. No special injury from insects or fungi. *Carrickfergus D.*—There is an abundant harvest of corn and hay in this district—which extends forty-five miles along the coast, from Belfast to Garron Tower, beyond Glenarm—and about ten miles inland to Ballyclare, &c. Green crops (turnips and mangolds) promise well. As regards potatoes, the early sorts, cruffles and [illegible], suffered from the cold and damp of spring and summer, and from the use of old seed. The dry weather in autumn checked the progress of fungoid evils, and saved the general crop, which is an average in quantity and quality. The more enlightened farmers have for some years been burning the decayed potato stalks and weeds with advantage, and they find that money spent in drainage and change of seed pays well. Farmers do not fully appreciate their friends, the birds of the air, which battle the destructive insects. Among the most useful air scavengers is the swallow—owing to the cold spring, his visit was limited in time and numbers—the latter was very apparent, particularly at his roll-call parade on telegraph wires, &c., before leaving for winter quarters. *Lisburn D.*—The only information I can afford regarding the disease in the various kinds of potatoes is attributable to the exceedingly bad weather which the county experienced during the spring and summer of this year. I have not heard of any particular complaints regarding insects or fungi. The other crops were all satisfactory.

ARMAGH COUNTY. *Armagh D.*—The yield of the various kinds of potatoes was about the same; the losses from disease were almost altogether confined to the northern portion of this district. The blight was due to the wet season and heavy character of the soil. I have received your book on the subject of insects, fungi, and weeds. There has been no injury to crops from fungi or weeds. In one portion of the district about five per cent. of the turnip crop was injured by the blue fly, and in the same locality about a similar percentage of the cabbage crop was damaged by the caterpillar. In another part of this district the oat crop was slightly injured by an insect locally known as the grub. *Lurgan D.*—The cause of the good yield of potatoes in this locality may be attributed to the frequent change of seed, a considerable quantity being imported from Scotland. *Newry D.*—In this district of the county Armagh the yield (average) of all kinds of potatoes was fair this season, but so much rain in the autumn caused much more of the potatoes to decay than otherwise would have been the case had the season been dry up to digging. In some cases heavy manuring caused early potatoes to decay to a heavy extent, but in that respect there was little difference from former seasons. *Portadown D.*—The reason that the potatoes in this district have been so good is, the land is generally dry and hilly, and the potatoes are planted early, and, in addition, the people allow no weeds to grow in the drills or ridges. Seed is frequently changed, and the people pay the greatest attention to them during their growth. At present the best champions in Portadown market are sold from 3s. 6d. to 3s. 4d. per cwt., Magnums are somewhat dearer. The potatoes are very dry and mealy; I have never seen better. The crop of potatoes has not been so good in this part of the country for many years. We have had a dry season here. Last year we had floods very early in the harvest, but this year the weather has been here delightful.

CAVAN COUNTY. *Bailieborough D.*—Every crop this season has been reported fair, save the potato, the failure of which is attributed to the wet season, and partly to the early frost which came in spring. The blight was much more serious in its effects whenever the old native seed was used. On patches where the seed imported from Scotland was planted the crop is good and not much diseased. The hay and oat crop was very heavy, but somewhat damaged in the saving, owing to the rains. Flax was a heavy crop, but fetched low prices. Turnips have not come up to the yield which was expected, but they are fair. *Ballyjamesduff D.*—Oats a very good crop, but owing to wet weather about one-fourth was more or less damaged. Wheat very little sown in district, any that was was good. Hay plentiful and pretty well saved. Some late meadows were injured by the rain, but not to any great extent. Turf scarce and not well saved, owing to wet weather. Turnips and mangolds good crop everywhere. No insects or weeds interfered with the crops in this district, as far as I can find out. The failure in the potato crop is entirely owing to wet weather and early appearance of the blight this season. Early sown potatoes did very well, but in those sown late the tubers were scarcely formed when the blight set in. *Cavan D.*—The bad yield of the potato crop this year is due to blight, caused by the constant rains. Large quantities of the tuber have been destroyed by worms. This too is attributed to the wetness of the season. So far as can be ascertained, no injury has been done to the crop by insects. *Killeshandra D.*—The only crop in my district which was a partial failure, owing to the constant wet weather, was the potato crop. The remainder show a fair average yield. No special injury has been done to crops in my district by insects or fungi. *Swanlinbar D.*—The potato crop in this district has been much below the average. In fact, in parts of the district it may almost be said to be a total failure. The principal causes which have produced this are as follows:—I. Late planting, followed by a wet autumn. The blight took hold of the stalks of tubers before they were matured. II. A bad system of tillage and seeding; planting in old ground with same seed; generally the smallest potatoes are reserved for seed. III. Insects and weeds. These, however, only to a minor extent. Wheat has been a very fair crop, but is little crop here. Oats have been fully up to average. Hay has been a fair crop. Turnips a very fair crop. These may be said to be the only crops grown in the district.

DONEGAL COUNTY. *Ballyshannon D.*—The partial failure of the potato crop is due to the wet season experienced inducing blight. Hay crop is abundant, but badly saved. The wet weather also affected grain crops and prevented them being over the average, though there was a splendid promise at one time. The green crops are very good and flax average. The farmers do not complain of ravages by insects or fungi. *Buncrana D.*—There has been no special injury to the crops in this district from insects, fungi, or weeds. The bad yield of the potato crop is attributed to the appearance of frost shortly after the potatoes were planted, which had the effect of checking the growth of the tubers. The continued wet weather is looked upon as having been the cause of the disease. *Dunfanaghy D.*—I think it should be taken into consideration that in nearly all cases the tubers in this are much below the average. *Dunglow D.*—The only crops grown to any extent are potatoes, oats, rye, and turnips. With regard to the potato crop, the cause of the bad yield this year is due to the disease known as "Potato blight," while I cannot give any opinion as to the direct cause of this disease, I believe it was favoured in its ravages in this district this year by want of change of seed. The crop not having been planted early enough. The soil in which it was planted being in most cases too long under tillage, and lastly, exposure to the sun. The oat crop seems to be good or bad according to the manure and the ground in which grown. Same remarks apply to rye and turnips as to oats. With regard to the ravages of insects, fungi, and weeds, I think that the people are not sufficiently educated to know much about the first two named, but there is no doubt that weeds have in this locality been a great cause of injury to the potato crop. *Letterkenny D.*—The principal cause to which the failure of the potato crop is to be attributed in this district is the too frequent cropping of the same kind of seed, without changing, which so weakens it as to cause the crop to be in course of time deficient both in quantity and quality. To the foregoing may be added a wet, and therefore, unfavourable season, when the seed for reasons already given is an easy victim to blight. The other crops grown in the district are fairly good crops, and as such require no remarks at present. *Moville D.*—I beg to state the early crop of potatoes were somewhat affected by the blight, but to no great extent in comparison with other districts. The continued wet weather was in a great measure the cause of the bad yield in this district. All through the district the ground is either a high mountainous or very low-lying wet region, the poor soil in the mountainous portion, and the wet in low-lying, tended to reduce the yield. *Raphoe D.*—I beg to observe that the principal crops in this district are hay, oats, flax, potatoes, and turnips; all these principal crops are good in this neighbourhood. There was considerable difficulty in getting the oat crop saved owing to the wet season. Potatoes are a fair good crop, except in some part of the mountain lands where the spring was late they did not come to maturity. Turnips appear an excellent crop. Cabbage and other green crops are also good. Farming is generally carefully attended to in this district, and the crops have suffered in no exceptional way except from the wet season. *Rathmelton D.*—The bad yield of the potatoes in the present year is, of course, mainly attributable to the blight which set in early; also, it is said, to the frequent continuation of old seed, instead of changing it occasionally. The constant rains of the autumn were also very unfavourable after the blight had set in. I have not heard of any ravages by insects in this locality. Likely too near sea-coast for such.

DOWN COUNTY. *Downpatrick D.*—I beg to inform you that the potato crop in this district is nearly up to usual average. The cause of any failure is owing to the blight. Kemps, Scotch downs and flounders, being early sorts, were scarcely affected. [illegible] and magnums were not affected. With regard to champions—in light land, winter manured, the crop was light and very slightly diseased. In heavy land, lightly manured, the crop was beyond the average and not much affected; while in some sort of land, well manured, the crop was very large but badly affected. *Newtownards D.*—In general, the potato crop is an average one. The blight existing is attributed to a wet season, use of small seed, not sufficiently frequently changed, and use of manure not sufficiently decomposed. Champions are regarded as "run out," magnum bonums, a comparatively new potato, give very good returns. Skerry blues give a very good return. The [illegible] and Brown raised from seedlings (crabs) a few years ago by Mr. James Watson, steward to General Nugent, of Portaferry, are looked on with great favour, yielding ten to twelve tons per acre. Croftons—unless planted very early, are delicate, and don't resist disease well. All other crops are excellent. No special loss due to insects or fungi is reported. *Ballynahinch D.*—The weather is accountable for the variations in average yield of the various crops—modified in certain cases by special circumstances, such as nature of ground and system of cultivation. No complaints as to insects have reached me from any quarter.

PROVINCE OF ULSTER.

FERMANAGH COUNTY. *Derrygonnelly D.*—This district is mainly a grazing one. The only crops grown, and these in small quantities, are potatoes, turnips, corn and wheat. The three latter crops have been of average excellence, and require no particular comment. The potato crop has been a comparative failure. The causes were, in my opinion, heavy rains in June and July, the practice of planting potatoes for several consecutive years in the same ground, and using the same seed year after year. I am not in a position to offer any observations as to any special injury done to the crops in this district by insects or fungi. *Enniskillen D.*—To some extent Skerry blue potatoes have been injured by insects, and to a less extent "Scotch downs" and "white rocks." Champions or other sorts have not, so far as I can find, been injured by insects, and whether the injury reported has been by any special insect has not been ascertained. *Kesh D.*—From information received from various sources, I find, as regards this district, the grain crops, viz., wheat, oats, barley and rye, yield a good supply, as do also turnips, mangolds, and flax. This is attributed to their having been sown in dry weather and the almost continual wet season which seemed beneficial, rather than retarded, these different kinds, the country being somewhat hilly. The failure of the potato crop is, on the other hand, owing to the same cause, added to the blight having set in early in July before the stalks had come to maturity. This sort of crop is not sown here until April and even beginning of May, the soil being of a cold heavy nature. *Lisnaskea D.*—I am not aware that noxious insects had anything to do with the failure of the potato crop.

LONDONDERRY COUNTY. *Coleraine D.*—The yield of all crops in this locality has been good, which is attributed to the season being favourable. However, the wet weather affected the potatoes considerably. *Limavady D.*—The potato crop in this district has been up to a fair average, about one-third of the crop being lost. In this district potatoes are planted early, and the land is exceptionally good throughout the greater part of it. Skerry blues have been marvellously successful, and next to them come Scotch downs, Irish whites, white rocks, and magnum bonums. Turnips and mangolds have been a splendid crop this year, and do not appear to have suffered from the ravages of insects or from fungi. Cereals have also been good, but the hay crop was a little short owing to the dry, hard weather in May. On the whole, the year's yield for all crops has been good. *Londonderry D.*—The sole causes of the potatoes being injured or destroyed in this district, are the heavy rains in June and July, and the blight having set in before the tubers had matured. *Magherafelt D.*—The grain crop in this extensive district has been up to, if not above, the average. Flax has been up to average, and in many cases farmers have told me that they very seldom have had so abundant a crop. Green crops are as good as heretofore. Hay was also a good crop this season. The potatoes have done better, when being stored, than the farmers anticipated. A very curious circumstance is that "Skerries," or, as some call them, "Irish Rocks," have almost entirely escaped the disease. All round, where fresh seed was used, and in new gravelly land, the potato crop in this district is fairly good. However, this district cannot be taken as even an average in comparison with other parts of Ireland—the soil is rich and farmers very cute.

MONAGHAN COUNTY. *Carrickmacross D.*—So far as I have been able to ascertain, the bad yield of potatoes this year is attributed to the blight appearing so early in the season, before the potatoes were sufficiently matured. *Clones D.*—I can assign no cause for the bad yield of the potato crop. *Monaghan D.*—The yield of the potato crop in this district for the present year falls short of the produce of last year, this is the case especially in lowlying lands, where the disease has done most injury, on account of the humidity of the season. Although the wet season was injurious to the potato crop, it was beneficial to other crops, namely, corn, hay and flax, particularly on uplands, where these crops are much above the average. No special injury has been done to crops in this district by insects or fungi.

TYRONE COUNTY. *Aughnacloy D.*—In this district there are two widely separated classes of farmers, viz., those on the mountain slopes, where the land is light and the people poor, and in these localities potatoes suffered from late planting and disease consequent on climatic conditions. In the greater part of the district good land and high farming prevail, and the potato crop resisted the ravages of the disease wonderfully. In the neighbourhood of Caledon the farmers say that the sound potatoes are an average crop. As to cereals and grass, as well as other root crops, the season was favourable, and yield good. Many years ago it was suggested to me that the blackberry carried the disease from year to year though it did not suffer from it. I have noticed that red spots on the leaves are more prevalent in years of potato disease. Microscopists might investigate these red spots profitably. As the disease appears equally on freshly-broken old meadow, where the seeds has been carefully selected, I am inclined to think it is mainly carried in the atmosphere. *Cookstown D.*—The potato crop in this district is on the whole a fair one. Skerry blues are the best yield. The cause of the failure of the crop is the wet season, and bad land in some districts. *Dungannon D.*—The cereal crops in this district are up to the average of former years. The partial failure of the potato crop is due to the continued wet season combined in many instances with defective drainage and bad cultivation. All the other root crops are up to the average of former years. No damage has been done by insects or fungi in this district during the past season, so far as can be ascertained. *Newtownstewart D.*—The only cause which I can ascertain accounting for the bad yield of the potato crop in this district, is the continuous wet weather. *Omagh D.*—1st. The cause attributed to the good yield of oats and turnips this year is the moderate rain and continuous dampness during the summer, which had the effect of keeping the oat crop, &c., growing all the time, and made it grow a heavy good crop on high-lying land, which otherwise would not have been the case. 2nd. The cause attributed to the bad yield of the potato crop was the rain and continuous dampness during the summer, which had the effect of keeping the crop growing in tops at the time the tubers should be maturing, and then the blight commencing on them before the tubers had come to maturity and therefore stopped the growth. *Strabane D.*—Champions are decidedly the best class of potato, the others which show a higher percentage have been grown in much smaller quantities, and on specially prepared ground. The crop as a whole was good in the dry lands, but in low-lying wet land one-third were damaged, the wet season being considered the cause.

PROVINCE OF CONNAUGHT.

GALWAY COUNTY. *Athenry D.*—The bad yield of the potato crop is attributed to the excessive moisture of last summer. The yield would have been far worse were it not that the soil in the greater portion of this district is very favourable to the growth of potatoes. It is in general a light gravelly soil, resting on limestone. *Ballinasloe D.*—The general bad yield of the various crops in this district may be attributed, especially in the case of the potato crop, to the dampness of the past season, and to the fact of the blight having made its appearance three or four weeks earlier than in former seasons and before the potato crop had time to come to maturity. It is estimated to be about one-half what a favourable year would yield of potatoes. Turnips are light in yield, which is also attributed to the dampness. The farmers are satisfied with the yield of hay and corn, and say it is as good if not better than last year. There has been very little, if any, injury done to crops in this district from insects or fungi during the past season. *Clifden D.*—The principal cause of the failure of the potato crop in this district is owing to late sowing, early blight this year, continuous wet, and failing to change the seed. *Glenamaddy D.*—The cause of the comparative failure of the potato crop in this district this year, is due, primarily, to the very wet season. I have heard of no complaints as to the action of noxious insects, &c., on the crop, but doubtless they too had something to do with the failure. *Dunmore D.*—As regards the "Railways," they are a very late crop, and they escaped the blight, but they are not fit for human food, being little removed from the turnip, and are only used here for cattle. *Galway D.*—It may now be safely stated that nearly one-half the potato crop will be unfit for food in this district. Ravages from fungi, or insects, &c., have not been observed in this district during the past season. The bad yield of the potato crop may be attributed, generally, to the wet season, late sowing, and early blight. The want of change of seed has also contributed to the cause of the bad yield. Where the crop has been good it may be attributed to good, dry uplands, and early sowing. All grain crops are up to the average of former years. Wheat and oats have suffered to some extent from the continued wet weather, and the yield, in some instances, is not up to the average. Hay has also suffered slightly from the wet weather. Turnips, mangold wurzel, and other green crops are up to the average of past years. *Gort D.*—It appears to be the general opinion of farmers in this locality that the peculiarly wet summer and spring has been the cause alike of the good yield in such crops as are good, and of the bad yield in such as are not up to the average. The damage done by noxious insects and fungi appears to have been small about here. *Moylough D.*—Fungi were very injurious to the potato crop in this district during the past season. *Loughrea D.*—I believe the bad yield of the potato in this district is chiefly attributable to late sowing, the bulbs being unable to come to maturity before being affected with the blight. The undrained state of the land in the mountain districts also materially affects the crops, as by the presence of stagnant water the plants are unable to have a healthy growth. *Portumna D.*—With reference to the failure of potato crop this season, I believe the cause is attributable to the use of the same seed for years in succession. *Dunmore D.*—The chief cause to which the bad yield of crops all round may be attributed is the long-continued rains of the summer months from which everything suffered more or less. I have not heard any complaints regarding the ravages of noxious insects, &c., this season. *Spiddle D.* The cause of the bad yield in the potato crop this year was due to the late sowing, as well as the continual rain in the summer months, the blight attacking them very early. It is believed, too, that the champions are dying out, having been used now over ten years in the same land. *Tuam D.*—The bad yield of potatoes this year may be attributed to the blight having set in so early. Champions being of a soft texture, suffered severely; and this seed is getting worn out. Early potatoes, such as flounders and kemps, were nearly ripe before the blight set in, and consequently did not suffer so severely. Green crops, turnips, mangolds, &c., were very good, the moist weather favouring them. Hay was a fair crop, but as wet weather prevailed during the time it was being saved, a considerable portion of it was damaged. Oats very fair; but for the excessive rain it would have been a much heavier crop. *Woodford D.*—With the exception of the potato crop all crops are good in this locality. The hay crop is somewhat lighter than last year, which is probably due to the cold spring and summer. The wet was very favourable to the turnip crop, and the oat crop was also very good. Potatoes in wet boggy soil suffered greatly from frost in May. There is a good deal of the ordinary potato disease, but in some fields the crop is nearly as good as usual. Potatoes set in drills have decidedly come off best. I have heard no complaints as to ravages made by insects, &c.

LEITRIM COUNTY. *Ballinamore D.*—I believe the continual rain is the main cause of the blight. Mr. Lawder, J.P., D.L., informs me that it is also due to not changing the seed often enough. He has imported the Reading Heroes which are doing well. *Carrick-on-Shannon D.*—I consider the bad yield in the potato crop due to the wet season, and the disease setting in so early this year. I believe the potatoes should be set earlier than the months of April and May, and that the people should not set all in low-lying land, and they should frequently change the seed. *Dromahaire D.*—The diminution in the crop this year is due to the incessant rains and the subsequent blight, which set in before the potatoes had arrived at maturity. *Manorhamilton D.*—The bad yield in the various crops in this district is attributed to the very wet season, and the nature of the soil being wet and boggy. The crop is not put in in time, owing to the lands being too wet for the want of draining. This applies to all kind of crops. This year the crop was late, and a frost in the latter end of May injured the potato crop to a very great extent. I saw, myself, several fields of potatoes that looked well, and promised to be a good crop, all blackened, the leaves all withered, and the stalks lying. This put back the growth considerably, and I have been informed that the disease then setting in before the tubers were matured left the crop worth very little indeed. The oat crop is bad, owing to the wet season, and the corn is very inferior, ill matured, and not fit for feeding purposes. I cannot procure any good oats. The hay is a fair crop, but badly saved, from the same cause—the wet season. I have received no reports as to the ravages of noxious insects. The farmers permit weeds of all kinds to grow with the crops which smothers and destroys the crop which was most remarkable this year; and when asked the cause, the reply was usually given, "The crop was not worth cleaning." *Mohill D.*—The wet season is chiefly the cause of the bad yield, together with late frost. I hope the "Special Report on Insects, Fungi, and Weeds injurious to Farm Crops," will be interesting, but I have no observations to offer on the subject.

MAYO COUNTY. *Ballaghaderreen D.*—So far as I can learn the potato crop in this district is far below the average of an ordinary successful year, and no special reason can be attributed for this by local farmers beyond a general statement of the existence of a "blight" in the early part of the year, the ill effects of which were subsequently increased by lack of heat and excessive moisture. Champions are chiefly grown in this district. *Ballina D.*—Except potatoes, the general yield of crops in this district has been up to a fair average. The potato crop is considerably below that of former years, owing in a great measure to a severe frost in latter end of June, the unusually cold wet season we have had this year, and the early appearance of the blight which was more severe than for some time past. Bad cultivation and neglect to remove weeds, &c., no doubt added to the unsatisfactory state of things in this respect. Champions are the principal crop grown in this district, the others being only to a small extent. *Ballinrobe D.*—The potato crop was injured by the wet weather and the blight, which appeared before the tubers had come to maturity, and consequently caused more damage. The seed used was unfit for the purpose, no fresh seed having been provided, and the smallest potatoes were planted or pieces cut from large ones were used instead. All the corn crops very good, as the wet weather suited the dry limestone land in which these crops were principally planted, with the exception of the wheat crop. The wet weather prevented the grain from growing to the usual size. Very little damage was done to any crops by insects, and I cannot name any particular insect that caused any injury. I noticed that the people were very dilatory in cutting down their crops. I saw many fields of perfectly ripe wheat, oats, &c., remaining uncut for a fortnight or three weeks. Although the weather on several days was fine the work was not done, and storms and rain during the time the corn remained uncut must have done great harm. The wet weather caused a great growth of weeds which injured the potato crop to some extent. *Belmullet D.*—The people of this district attribute the bad yield of potatoes to frost in June, followed by the blight. There was no appearance of insects or fungi during the past season. The other crops yielded a fair average return. *Castlebar D.*—The partial failure of the potato crop only calls for any remark. The yield in other crops is a fair average. There were frosts in May and early in June, which burned the young potato stalks, which put back the growth very much. A good warm harvest would have made up for this, but instead, the season was cold and wet, and the tubers were not nearly matured when the blight set in with great severity. No injury was observed from insects or fungi, but small worms, in the clay, have damaged, in some places, the portion of the crop which is safe. *Claremorris D.*—Champions and flounders are chiefly grown; [illegible] not extensively, and white rocks very little. It does not appear that any injury has been caused by insects or fungi, but in many fields weeds are allowed to grow unchecked. In my opinion the chief causes of the poor yield are, poorness of the soil, susceptibility to disease of worn out seed, and the wet weather bringing on disease when the potatoes were far from maturity. Even those which escaped disease are [illegible] and small. *Swinford D.*—I believe the failure of the potato crop this year is mainly due to the want of fresh seed, constant wet season, and sowing the same crop so often on the same land. I have heard of no complaints of any insects attacking the crop. *Westport D.*—The only cereals grown in this district—oats, and very small quantities of wheat and rye—yielded an average crop this year. Turnips and mangel wurzel have also yielded a good average, but the potato crop is much below that of

M

former years, and about half was unfit for human food. This is attributed to a frost which set in early in June, when the stalks were young and tender; an almost continuous wet season, and the blight having made its appearance before the tubers were fully matured. There was no special injury caused to any of the crops by insects or fungi.

ROSCOMMON COUNTY. *Athlone D.*—I am of opinion that the potato crop of this district and indeed of the country generally is very much injured each season by the almost unchecked growth of weeds. *Boyle D.*—The only cause for the failure of the potato crop in this district is the blight which set in very early in the season. *Roscommon D.*—Late frosts, when the main crop of potatoes were just over ground, and a wet summer made them a very bad crop. At same time the wet gave good meadows and plenty of straw and brought on green crops. There was very favourable weather for harvesting white crops which are quite up to average; that same weather however put a stop to growth of green crops which will not be so heavy as expected. *Strokestown D.*—The principal crops grown in this district are hay, oats, turnips, and potatoes—all are average except turnips and potatoes. The turnip was a good crop, the damp season being favourable to it. The potato was a bad crop, owing to the frost in the early part of the year, and the appearance of the blight unusually early in the harvest. In the early part of this year insects did some injury to turnips and the caterpillars to cabbages, but not to such an extent as in previous years.

SLIGO COUNTY. *Ballymote D.*—The wheat crop in this district was up to the average of the former years. The oat crop is good in yield and quality, and is also up to the average of the past few years, and in some localities the yield is better this year. This is accounted for by the damp weather in July last, supplying more than sufficient moisture, the ground being thus warm, causing an abundant growth. This damp weather, while causing hay and oats to improve, had quite an opposite effect on the potato crop, bringing on the blight before the crop was ripe. On good dry soil, where the seed was sown early, the potato crop is fair, but in low lying and badly tilled land the crop is hardly worth digging. The potato crop was injured in this district by worms, but this was confined to a very small area, and I believe the presence of these worms may be [illegible] to the particular kind of soil in the locality. *Collooney D.*—The potato crop has been a partial failure in this district this season, owing partly to May frosts, and partly to the early appearance of the blight, due to wetness of the season. All other crops have been up to average, turnips and mangold being particularly good. There are no complaints of the ravages of insects. *Easky D.*—All the crops cultivated in this district this year are, generally speaking, a good average crop, except the potato—viz. [illegible], wheat, barley, rye, turnips, mangolds, hay, &c. In the greater portion of the district the land is good and bordering the sea, hence the wet season had not so injurious effect as in other places. The potato crop too has been good in some parts of the district. The description of potato cultivated is generally "champions" and "[illegible]." There are very little of any other kind. I find there are but few complaints as regards insects. I have distributed the "Special report on insects, &c." to the several stations, and doubtless it will do much good. *Sligo D.*—There has been no special injury to crops in my district by insects or fungi during the past season. The falling off in yield of the various crops can be attributed to no cause, save the "early blight" and "wet season." *Tobercurry D.*—The early seed appears to have done best. The potato crop was checked in growth by frost in May, after which there was a considerable growth of stalk owing to rain in June and July. A great growth of weeds was also caused, but little development of the tubers until the blight came, hence the poor yield. The ground covered by weeds retained the wet and prevented the ripening of the tuber, as the heat, so necessary to the potato, was unable to reach it. Generally, the cultivation of the potato crop is very late here; the ground is not sufficiently prepared or cleaned of weeds; and the champion is too late in reaching maturity, being thereby open to blight attack later in the season than any other seed. The other crops have been fairly good. Oats, the principal grain crop, suffered a little in bog land from [illegible]. There have been no complaints of insects or fungi, nor have I observed any injury to crops by them myself this year. I have looked through Mr. [illegible]'s report, and I am of opinion that every farmer should have a copy of it.

APPENDIX.

SILOS AND ENSILAGE.

SILOS AND

The following statements have been received from persons who have made Ensilage in Ireland in 188[illegible]

PROVINCE OF

[illegible]	Dimensions of Silos—Length, Breadth, Depth.	Materials of Silos.			[illegible]	[illegible]	[illegible]
		Walls.	Floor.	Roof.			
[illegible]	—	—	—	—	—	—	[illegible]
[illegible]	—	—	—	—	—	—	—
[illegible]	—	—	—	—	—	—	[illegible]
[illegible]	—	—	—	—	—	—	[illegible]
[illegible]	—	—	—	—	—	—	[illegible]
[illegible]	[illegible]	Concrete,	Concrete,	Wood, [illegible]	[illegible]	Partly below surface.	No.
[illegible]	[illegible]	—	—	—	[illegible]	Above surface.	Yes. [illegible]
[illegible]	[illegible]	Brick,	Cement,	Do.,	[illegible]	Above surface.	Yes. [illegible]
	[illegible]	—	—	—	Do.	Do.	

ENSILAGE.

[illegible]	[illegible]	[illegible]	Corrugated iron	Not drained	[illegible]	—
—	—	—	—	—	—	[illegible]
—	—	—	—	—	—	[illegible]
[illegible]	[illegible]	[illegible]	[illegible]	Drained	[illegible]	[illegible]
[illegible]	[illegible]	Do.	[illegible]	Not drained	[illegible]	
[illegible]	Do.	Do.	Do.	Do.	Do.	
[illegible]	[illegible]	[illegible]	Corrugated iron	Do.	Above	Yes, in a [illegible]
[illegible]	[illegible]	[illegible]	[illegible]	Yes	[illegible]	Do.
—	[illegible]	The Field	Clay	[illegible]	[illegible]	Yes, [illegible]
—	[illegible]	Field	[illegible]	[illegible]	[illegible]	[illegible]
—	—	[illegible]	[illegible]	—	On the [illegible]	[illegible]
—	—	Do.	Do.	—	Do.	

LEINSTER—continued.

[illegible]	[illegible]	Temperature.		[illegible]	[illegible]
		[illegible]	[illegible]		
[illegible]	[illegible]	—	—	[illegible]	[illegible]
[illegible]	[illegible]	—	—	[illegible]	[illegible]
[illegible]	[illegible]	[illegible]		[illegible]	[illegible]
[illegible]	[illegible]	[illegible]	[illegible]	[illegible]	[illegible]
[illegible]	[illegible]	Not taken.		[illegible]	[illegible]
[illegible]	[illegible]	Not taken.		[illegible]	[illegible]
[illegible]	[illegible]	[illegible]	[illegible]	[illegible]	[illegible]
[illegible]	[illegible]	[illegible]		[illegible]	[illegible]

—	—	—	—
—	—	—	—
—	—	—	—
—	—	—	—
—	—	—	—
—	—	—	—
—	—	—	—
Stone and Iron, [illegible]	Concrete, . .	Corrugated iron,	Do. . .
Wood, . . .	Rubble . .	Wood, . . .	Do. . .
None, . . .	None, . . .	Can be [illegible] [illegible] [illegible]	Not, . .

LEINSTER—continued.

[illegible]	[illegible]	[illegible]		[illegible]	[illegible]	[illegible]
		[illegible]	[illegible]			
[illegible]	[illegible]	[illegible]		—	[illegible]	[illegible]
[illegible]	[illegible]	[illegible]		[illegible]	[illegible]	One stock is not yet opened.
[illegible]	[illegible]	[illegible]		[illegible]	[illegible]	[illegible]
—	—	[illegible]		—	[illegible]	[illegible]
[illegible]	[illegible]	[illegible]		[illegible]	[illegible]	[illegible]
[illegible]	[illegible]	[illegible]	[illegible]	[illegible]	[illegible]	[illegible]
—	—	—	—	—	—	[illegible]
—	[illegible]	—	—	[illegible]	[illegible]	[illegible]
[illegible]	[illegible]	[illegible]		[illegible]	[illegible]	[illegible]
[illegible]	[illegible]	[illegible]		[illegible]	[illegible]	[illegible]

Mortar,	Board.	Do.
Clay,	Galvanized iron and wood frame.	Do.
Do.	Do.	Do.
Do.	Do.	Do.
Earth,	Government camp,	Do.
—	—	—
—	—	—
—	—	—
—	—	—
—	—	—

LEINSTER—continued.

[illegible]	[illegible]	Temperature.		[illegible]	[illegible]
		[illegible]	[illegible]		
[illegible]	[illegible]	Not tried.		[illegible]	[illegible]
[illegible]	Green	[illegible]	[illegible]	[illegible]	[illegible]
—	Good green.	—	—	[illegible]	[illegible]
[illegible]	Ordinary	—	—	[illegible]	[illegible]

LEINSTER—continued.

[illegible]	[illegible]	Temperature		[illegible]	[illegible]
		[illegible]	[illegible]		
[illegible]	—	[illegible]	—	[illegible]	[illegible]
[illegible]	[illegible]	—	[illegible]	[illegible]	[illegible]
[illegible]	[illegible]	[illegible]	[illegible]	[illegible]	[illegible]
[illegible]	[illegible]	[illegible]	[illegible]	[illegible]	[illegible]
[illegible]	[illegible]	[illegible]		[illegible]	[illegible]
[illegible]	[illegible]	[illegible]	[illegible]	[illegible]	[illegible]
[illegible]	[illegible]	[illegible]		[illegible]	[illegible]

[illegible]	[illegible]			[illegible]
	[illegible]	[illegible]	[illegible]	
	—			—
—	—	—	—	—
—	—	—	—	—
—	—	—	—	—
—	—	—	—	—
—	—	—	—	—
—	—	—	—	—
—	—	—	—	—
—	—	—	—	—
—	—	—	—	—

[illegible]		[illegible]	[illegible]	[illegible]
[illegible]	[illegible]	[illegible]	[illegible]	[illegible]
[illegible]	[illegible]	[illegible]	[illegible]	[illegible]
[illegible]		[illegible]	[illegible]	[illegible]
[illegible]		[illegible]	[illegible]	[illegible]
—	—	—	—	[illegible]
[illegible]	[illegible]	—	[illegible]	[illegible]
—	—	—	—	[illegible]
[illegible]	[illegible]	[illegible]	[illegible]	[illegible]
—	—	[illegible]	[illegible]	[illegible]
[illegible]		[illegible]	[illegible]	[illegible]
—	—	—	[illegible]	[illegible]
[illegible]	[illegible]	[illegible]	[illegible]	[illegible]

—	—	—	—	
[illegible]	[illegible]	[illegible]	[illegible]	[illegible]
[illegible]	[illegible]	[illegible]	[illegible]	[illegible]
[illegible]	[illegible]	[illegible]	[illegible]	[illegible]
—	—	—	—	—
—	—	—	—	
—	—	—	—	
[illegible]	Brick,	Cement,	Iron.	[illegible]

LEINSTER—continued.

[illegible]	[illegible]	Temperature.		[illegible]	[illegible]	Remarks.
		[illegible]	[illegible]			
[illegible]	[illegible]	[illegible]	[illegible]	[illegible]	[illegible]	[illegible]
[illegible]	[illegible]	[illegible]	[illegible]	[illegible]	[illegible]	[illegible]
[illegible]	[illegible]	[illegible]	[illegible]	[illegible]	[illegible]	[illegible]
[illegible]	[illegible]	[illegible]	[illegible]	[illegible]	[illegible]	[illegible]
—	Old meadow grass.	—	—	[illegible]	[illegible]	[illegible]
[illegible]	[illegible]	[illegible]	[illegible]	[illegible]	[illegible]	[illegible]
—	[illegible]	[illegible]	[illegible]	[illegible]	[illegible]	—
[illegible]	[illegible]	[illegible]	[illegible]	[illegible]	[illegible]	[illegible]
[illegible]	Old meadow grass.	[illegible]	[illegible]	[illegible]	[illegible]	[illegible]
—	Ordinary meadow grass.	—	—	[illegible]	[illegible]	—
[illegible]	Old meadow grass.	[illegible]	[illegible]	[illegible]	[illegible]	[illegible]

[illegible]	[illegible]	[illegible]	[illegible]	[illegible]	[illegible]	[illegible]
[illegible]	Do.	Do.	Do.	Do.	Do.	
[illegible]	[illegible]	Do.	[illegible]	[illegible]	[illegible]	
—	—	—	—	—	—	[illegible]
[illegible]	[illegible]	[illegible]	[illegible]	[illegible]	[illegible]	[illegible]
[illegible]	Do.	Do.	Do.	Do.	Do.	
[illegible]	[illegible]	Do.	Do.	Do.	Do.	
[illegible]	[illegible]	Do.	[illegible]	Do.	Do.	
—	—	—	—	—	—	[illegible]
—	—	—	—	—	—	—
—	—	—	—	—	—	[illegible]
[illegible]	[illegible]	[illegible]	[illegible]	[illegible]	[illegible]	[illegible]
[illegible]	Do.	Do.	Do.	Do.	Do.	
—	—	—	—	—	—	[illegible]

LEINSTER—continued.

[illegible]	[illegible]	Temperature.		[illegible]	[illegible]	Remarks.
		[illegible]	[illegible]			
—	[illegible]	[illegible]	[illegible]	[illegible]	[illegible]	[illegible]
[illegible]	[illegible]	—	[illegible]	[illegible]	[illegible]	[illegible]
—	[illegible]	—	—	—	—	—
[illegible]	[illegible]	[illegible]	[illegible]	[illegible]	[illegible]	[illegible]
—	—	—	—	—	—	[illegible]
[illegible]	Ordinary [illegible]	[illegible]	[illegible]	[illegible]	[illegible]	[illegible]
[illegible]	[illegible]	[illegible]	[illegible]	[illegible]	[illegible]	[illegible]
[illegible]	[illegible]	—	—	[illegible]	[illegible]	[illegible]
[illegible]	[illegible]	[illegible]	[illegible]	[illegible]	[illegible]	[illegible]

PROVINCE OF

Name and Residence.	No. of [illegible]	No. of [illegible]	Dimensions: Length, Breadth, Depth.	Materials of Silos.			Whether Covered or not.	[illegible]	[illegible]
				Walls.	Floor.	Roof.			
MEATH COUNTY—continued.									
[illegible]	–	1	—	—	—	—	No.	Above [illegible]	[illegible]
[illegible]	–	1	—	—	—	—	—	—	[illegible]
[illegible]	–	1	[illegible]	—	—	—	—	—	[illegible]
QUEEN'S COUNTY.									
[illegible]	1	1	[illegible]	Stone.	Cement.	Iron.	No.	Partly below.	[illegible]
[illegible]	–	1	—	—	—	—	—	Above.	[illegible]
[illegible]	–	1	—	—	—	—	—	—	[illegible]
[illegible]	–	1	—	—	—	—	—	—	[illegible]
[illegible]	1	[illegible]	[illegible]	Stone.	Stone.	[illegible]	—	Partly below and partly above.	[illegible]
[illegible]	1	–	[illegible]	[illegible]	Concrete.	Corrugated iron.	[illegible]	[illegible]	[illegible]
			[illegible]	Stone.	Flagged.	Slate.	Do.	Above.	
[illegible]	–	1	—	—	—	—	—	—	[illegible]
[illegible]	–	1	—	—	—	—	—	—	[illegible]

LEINSTER—continued.

[illegible]	—	[illegible]	[illegible]	[illegible]	[illegible]	[illegible]	[illegible]
[illegible]	—	—	—	—	—	—	[illegible]
[illegible]	—	—	—	—	—	—	[illegible]
[illegible]	—	—	—	—	—	—	[illegible]
[illegible]	—	—	—	—	—	—	[illegible]
[illegible]	[illegible] feet by [illegible] feet [illegible]	[illegible]	[illegible]	[illegible]	—	[illegible]	[illegible]

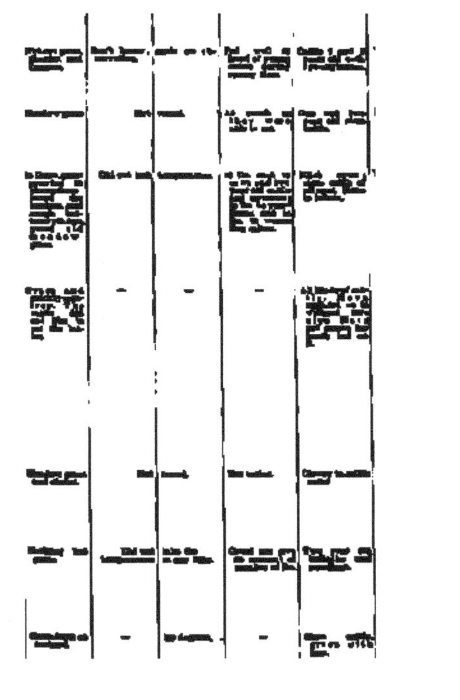

[illegible]	[illegible]	[illegible]	[illegible]	[illegible]		
				[illegible]	[illegible]	[illegible]
[illegible]						
[illegible]	[illegible]	-	[illegible]	[illegible]	[illegible]	[illegible]
			[illegible]	Do.	Do.	Do.
[illegible]						
[illegible]	[illegible]	-	[illegible]	[illegible]	[illegible]	[illegible]
[illegible]	[illegible]	-	—	—	—	—
[illegible]	-	-	—	—	—	—
. . . .	[illegible]	-	[illegible]	[illegible]	[illegible]	[illegible]
			[illegible]	Do.	Do.	[illegible]
[illegible]	-	[illegible]	—	—	—	—
[illegible]	[illegible]	-	[illegible]	[illegible]	[illegible]	[illegible]
[illegible]	-	[illegible]	—	—	—	—
[illegible]						
[illegible]	-	[illegible]	—	—	—	—
[illegible]	-	[illegible]	—	—	—	—

LEINSTER—continued.

[illegible]	[illegible]	[illegible]
		[illegible]
—	[illegible]	[illegible]
[illegible]	[illegible]	[illegible]
—	—	—
—	—	—
[illegible]	[illegible]	[illegible]

ULSTER—continued.

[illegible]	[illegible]	[illegible]
—	[illegible]	—
[illegible]	[illegible]	—
7 days.	[illegible]	[illegible]
[illegible]	[illegible]	[illegible]

[illegible]	[illegible]	[illegible]			[illegible]	[illegible]	[illegible]
		Walls.	Floor.	Roof.			
[illegible]	—	—	—	—	—	—	[illegible]
[illegible]	[illegible]	[illegible]	Clay.	[illegible]	No.	Above.	[illegible]
[illegible]	—	—	—	—	—	—	—
[illegible]	—	—	Clay.	[illegible]	[illegible]	[illegible]	[illegible]
[illegible]	[illegible]	[illegible]	Concrete.	[illegible]	No.	Partly below.	No.
[illegible]	[illegible]	[illegible]	[illegible]	[illegible]	Not drained.	[illegible]	No.
[illegible]	[illegible]	[illegible]	Earth.	[illegible]	Dry.	[illegible]	No.
[illegible]	[illegible]	[illegible]	Flagged.	[illegible]	Yes.	Partly below.	[illegible]
[illegible]	[illegible]	[illegible]	Concrete.	[illegible]	[illegible]	[illegible]	No.
[illegible]	—	[illegible]	[illegible]	[illegible]	[illegible]	Above.	[illegible]
[illegible]	—	—	—	—	—	—	[illegible]

[illegible]	Materials of Silo		
	Walls.	Floor.	Roof.
—	—	—	—
—	—	—	—
—	—	—	—
—	—	—	—
—	—	—	—
—	—	—	—

Materials of Hut.		[illegible]	[illegible]	[illegible]
Floor.	Roof.			
Clay.	[illegible]	Do.	[illegible]	[illegible]
Clay.	Straw.	Mud.	[illegible]	[illegible]
Clay.	[illegible]	Do.	[illegible]	[illegible]
—	—	—	—	[illegible]
—	—	—	—	[illegible]
—	—	—	—	[illegible]
—	—	—	—	[illegible]
Common.	Wood.	Do.	[illegible]	[illegible]
—	—	—	—	[illegible]

ULSTER—*continued.*

[illegible]	[illegible]	Temperature.		[illegible]	[illegible]	[illegible]
		[illegible]	[illegible]			
—	Grass of good quality.	—	—	[illegible]	[illegible]	[illegible]
[illegible]	Grass and [illegible]	[illegible] degrees.	[illegible] degrees.	[illegible]	[illegible]	[illegible]
—	Good grass.	—	—	[illegible]	—	[illegible]

PROVINCE OF [illegible]

Name and Address.	[illegible]	[illegible]	[illegible]	Walls.	Floor.	Roof.	[illegible]	[illegible]	[illegible]
TIPPERARY COUNTY—continued.									
[illegible]	-	[illegible]	—	—	—	—	—	—	
[illegible]	-	[illegible]	[illegible]	[illegible]	[illegible]	[illegible]	—	[illegible]	
[illegible]	-	[illegible]	—	—	—	—	—	—	
WATERFORD COUNTY.									
[illegible]	-	[illegible]	—	—	—	—	—	—	
[illegible]	[illegible]	-	[illegible]	[illegible]	[illegible]	[illegible]	[illegible]	[illegible]	—
			[illegible]	Do.	[illegible]	[illegible]	[illegible]	[illegible]	
[illegible]	[illegible]	-	[illegible]	[illegible]	[illegible]	[illegible]	[illegible]	[illegible]	[illegible]
			[illegible]	Do.	Do.	Do.	Do.	[illegible]	
[illegible]	[illegible]	-	[illegible]	[illegible]	[illegible]	[illegible]	[illegible]	[illegible]	[illegible]
[illegible]	[illegible]	[illegible]	[illegible]	[illegible]	[illegible]	[illegible]	[illegible]	[illegible]	[illegible]

PROVINCE OF [illegible]

Name and Address.	[illegible]	[illegible]	[illegible]	Walls.	Floor.	Roof.	[illegible]	[illegible]	[illegible]
ANTRIM COUNTY.									
[illegible]	[illegible]	-	[illegible]	[illegible]	[illegible]	[illegible]	[illegible]	Above.	—
[illegible]	[illegible]	-	[illegible]	Stone.	Concrete.	[illegible]	[illegible]	[illegible]	—
[illegible]	[illegible]	-	[illegible]	[illegible]	Concrete.	[illegible]	[illegible]	Above.	[illegible]
			[illegible]	Do.	Do.	Do.	Do.	Do.	

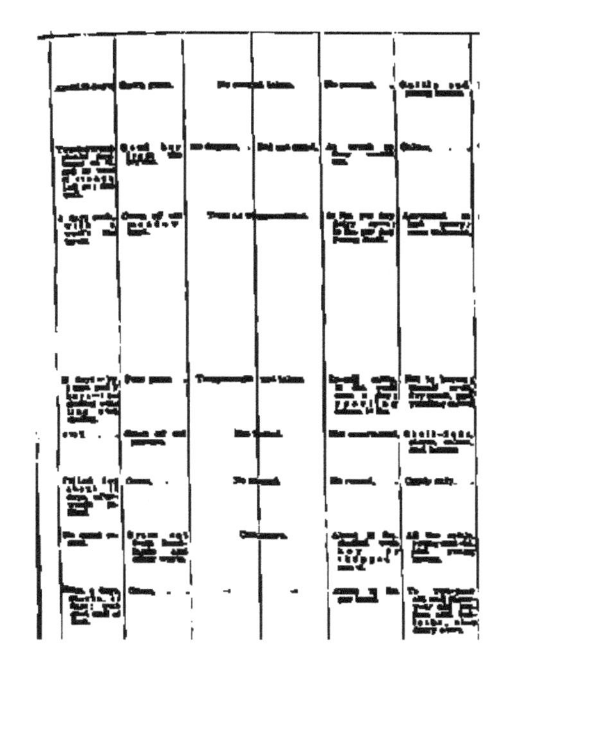

[illegible]	[illegible]	[illegible]	[illegible]	[illegible]	[illegible]
[illegible]	[illegible]	[illegible]	[illegible]	[illegible]	[illegible]
[illegible]	[illegible]	[illegible]	[illegible]	[illegible]	[illegible]
[illegible]	[illegible]	—	—	—	—
[illegible]	[illegible]	—	—	—	—
[illegible]	[illegible]	—	—	—	—
[illegible]	[illegible]	—	—	—	—
[illegible]	[illegible]	—	—	—	—

ULSTER—continued.

[illegible]	[illegible]	Temperature.		[illegible]	[illegible]
		[illegible]	[illegible]		
[illegible]	[illegible]	[illegible]	[illegible]	[illegible] lbs.	[illegible]
[illegible]	[illegible]	—	—	About [illegible] lbs.	[illegible]
[illegible]	[illegible]	See "[illegible]," [illegible]		[illegible]	[illegible]
[illegible]	[illegible]	No account	of heating.	[illegible] lbs.	[illegible]
[illegible]	[illegible]	Cannot say.		[illegible]	[illegible]
[illegible]	[illegible]	Could not	[illegible].	[illegible]	[illegible]
[illegible]	[illegible]	[illegible] degrees.	[illegible] degrees.	About [illegible] lbs. [illegible]	[illegible]
[illegible]	[illegible]	[illegible] degrees, F.	[illegible] degrees, F.	As [illegible] as the	[illegible]

—	—	—	—	—	—	[illegible]
[illegible] feet by [illegible] feet; [illegible] feet deep.	Stone.	Gravel.	Wood.	[illegible]	[illegible]	[illegible]
[illegible] feet by [illegible] feet; [illegible] feet deep.	No walls.	No floor.	No roof.	Dilapidated.	[illegible]	[illegible]
—	—	—	—	—	—	[illegible]
[illegible]	Stone and lime, [illegible]	Cemented earth.	Slate.	[illegible]	[illegible]	[illegible]
—	—	—	—	—	—	[illegible]

ULSTER—continued.

[illegible]	[illegible]	Temperature.		[illegible]	[illegible]	
		[illegible]	[illegible]			
[illegible] days.	[illegible]	[illegible] degrees.	[illegible] degrees.	From [illegible] to [illegible] lbs.	[illegible]	[illegible]
—	Aftermath [illegible]	—	[illegible]	[illegible]	[illegible]	[illegible]
14 days.	Old meadow grass.	[illegible] degrees.	[illegible] degrees.	[illegible] lbs.	[illegible]	[illegible]
[illegible]	[illegible]	[illegible] degrees.	—	[illegible]	To all kinds of [illegible]	[illegible]
[illegible]	[illegible]	[illegible]	[illegible]	[illegible]	[illegible]	
—	—	[illegible]		[illegible]	[illegible]	

[illegible]	[illegible]	Materials of Silo.			[illegible]	[illegible]	[illegible]
		Walls.	Floor.	Roof.			
[illegible]	—	—	—	—	—	[illegible]	—
[illegible]	—	—	—	—		—	[illegible]
[illegible]	[illegible]	Concrete [illegible]	Concrete, with [illegible]	[illegible]	Do.	[illegible]	Do.
[illegible]	[illegible]	[illegible]	Concrete	[illegible]	Level	On level of ground.	Do.
[illegible]	—	—	—	—	[illegible]	Above surface.	[illegible]
[illegible]	—	—	—	—	Not drained	Above surface.	[illegible]
[illegible]	—	—	—	—	—	—	—
[illegible]	[illegible]	[illegible]	[illegible]	[illegible]	[illegible]	[illegible]	Do.
		Do.	Do.	Do.			
[illegible]	—	—	[illegible]	[illegible]	[illegible]	Above surface.	[illegible]
			Do.	[illegible]	[illegible]	Do.	
[illegible]	—	—	—	—	—	—	[illegible]

[illegible]	[illegible]	[illegible]	[illegible]	[illegible]
[illegible]	[illegible]	[illegible]	[illegible]	[illegible]
—	—	—	—	—
—	—	—	—	—
[illegible]	[illegible]	[illegible]	[illegible]	[illegible]
[illegible]	[illegible]	[illegible]	[illegible]	[illegible]
[illegible]	[illegible]	[illegible]	[illegible]	[illegible]
[illegible]	[illegible]	[illegible]	[illegible]	[illegible]
—	—	—	—	—
[illegible]	[illegible]	[illegible]	[illegible]	[illegible]
[illegible]	[illegible]	[illegible]	[illegible]	[illegible]
[illegible]	[illegible]	[illegible]	[illegible]	[illegible]
—	—	—	—	—

[illegible]			
Average Heat [illegible] degrees.	Quantity of Ensilage [illegible] per diem.	To what description of Cattle [illegible]	
[illegible]	[illegible] lbs.	Young stock.	C
[illegible]	[illegible]	Store cattle.	C
—	—	All descriptions of cattle.	C
From [illegible] to [illegible] degrees.	From [illegible] to [illegible] lbs.	—	1
[illegible] degrees.	From [illegible] to [illegible] lbs.	[illegible]	[illegible]
—	[illegible]	[illegible]	[illegible]
[illegible] degrees.	[illegible]	To cattle of all kinds [illegible]	1
From [illegible] to [illegible] degrees.	[illegible] lbs.	[illegible]	1
[illegible] degrees.	[illegible] lbs. per day.	Store cattle.	1

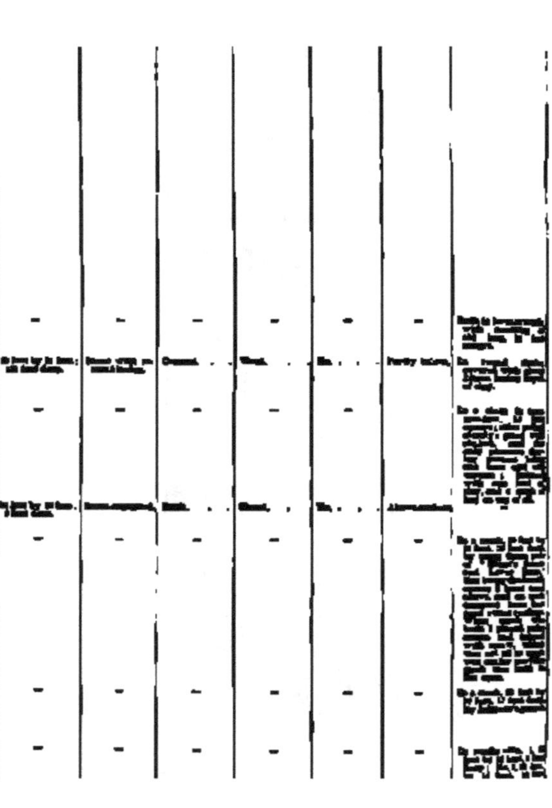

ULSTER—*continued.*

[illegible]	[illegible]			[illegible]	[illegible]	[illegible]
	Walls.	Floor.	Roof.			
—	—	—	—	—	—	[illegible]
[illegible]	[illegible]	Cement, . .	[illegible]	[illegible]	[illegible]	[illegible]
[illegible]	[illegible]	[illegible]	[illegible]	Not drained, .	Above, . .	[illegible]
[illegible]	—	—	—	—	—	[illegible]
—	—	—	—	—	—	[illegible]
[illegible]	[illegible]	[illegible]	[illegible]	[illegible]	[illegible]	[illegible]

CONNAUGHT—continued.

[illegible]	[illegible]	Temperature.		[illegible]	[illegible]
		[illegible]	[illegible]		
—	—	—	—	—	[illegible]

[illegible]	[illegible]	Materials of Silo (?)			[illegible]	[illegible]	[illegible]
		Walls.	Floor.	Roof.			
[illegible]	[illegible]	—	—	—	[illegible]	[illegible]	[illegible]
[illegible]	—	—	—	—	—	—	[illegible]
[illegible]	—	—	—	—	—	—	[illegible]
[illegible]	—	—	—	—	—	—	[illegible]
[illegible]	—	—	—	—	—	[illegible]	[illegible]
[illegible]	—	—	—	—	—	—	[illegible]
[illegible]	[illegible]	Masonry, plastered (?)	Cement (?)	Galvanized iron (?)	Flat (?)	Partly below (?)	—
	[illegible]	Do.	Clay (?)	Do.	Do.	Do.	
	[illegible]	Do.	Do.	Shingled (?)	Do.	Above (?)	
	[illegible]	Do.	Do.	Corrugated iron (?)	Do.	Do.	
[illegible]		Concrete (?)	Concrete (?)	Galvanized iron (?)	Yes (?)	Above (?)	[illegible]
[illegible]	—	—	—	—	—	—	[illegible]

[illegible]	[illegible]	[illegible]	[illegible]	[illegible]			[illegible]
				[illegible]	[illegible]	[illegible]	
[illegible] COUNTY—[illegible]							
[illegible]	–	1	—	–	–	—	—
[illegible]	–	1	—	–	–	—	—
[illegible] COUNTY.							
[illegible]	–	1	—	[illegible]	[illegible]	[illegible]	[illegible]

CONNAUGHT—continued.

THE WEATHER.

Abstract of Meteorological Observations registered at the Ordnance Survey Office (Height above the Sea 163·2 Feet) Phoenix Park, Dublin, during the year 1890:—

The barometer stood highest in 1890, on the 23rd February, at 9 P.M., wind N.E., when it was 30·719 inches; it was lowest at 9 P.M. on 6th November, when it was 28·777 inches. The highest temperature of the air during the year was 74·0 degrees of Fahrenheit on 4th August, and the lowest 16·7 degrees on 31st December. The greatest quantity of rain which fell in a day (24 hours) was 1·40 inch on 22nd August, with wind W. The point from which the wind chiefly prevailed was the W.; it blew from that direction on 118 days, at 9 A.M. The strongest wind was from the S. on the 30th November, when the pressure was 4·20 lbs. per square foot.

1890.	Barometer.							Temperature.											
	[illegible]	[illegible]	[illegible]	[illegible]	[illegible]	[illegible]	[illegible]	[illegible]	[illegible]	[illegible]	[illegible]	[illegible]	[illegible]	[illegible]	[illegible]	[illegible]	[illegible]	[illegible]	[illegible]
[illegible]	[illegible]	[illegible]	[illegible]	[illegible]	[illegible]	[illegible]	[illegible]	[illegible]	[illegible]	[illegible]	[illegible]	[illegible]	[illegible]	[illegible]	[illegible]	[illegible]	[illegible]	[illegible]	[illegible]
[illegible]	[illegible]	[illegible]	[illegible]	[illegible]	[illegible]	[illegible]	[illegible]	[illegible]	[illegible]	[illegible]	[illegible]	[illegible]	[illegible]	[illegible]	[illegible]	[illegible]	[illegible]	[illegible]	[illegible]
[illegible]	[illegible]	[illegible]	[illegible]	[illegible]	[illegible]	[illegible]	[illegible]	[illegible]	[illegible]	[illegible]	[illegible]	[illegible]	[illegible]	[illegible]	[illegible]	[illegible]	[illegible]	[illegible]	[illegible]
[illegible]	[illegible]	[illegible]	[illegible]	[illegible]	[illegible]	[illegible]	[illegible]	[illegible]	[illegible]	[illegible]	[illegible]	[illegible]	[illegible]	[illegible]	[illegible]	[illegible]	[illegible]	[illegible]	[illegible]
[illegible]	[illegible]	[illegible]	[illegible]	[illegible]	[illegible]	[illegible]	[illegible]	[illegible]	[illegible]	[illegible]	[illegible]	[illegible]	[illegible]	[illegible]	[illegible]	[illegible]	[illegible]	[illegible]	[illegible]
[illegible]	[illegible]	[illegible]	[illegible]	[illegible]	[illegible]	[illegible]	[illegible]	[illegible]	[illegible]	[illegible]	[illegible]	[illegible]	[illegible]	[illegible]	[illegible]	[illegible]	[illegible]	[illegible]	[illegible]
[illegible]	[illegible]	[illegible]	[illegible]	[illegible]	[illegible]	[illegible]	[illegible]	[illegible]	[illegible]	[illegible]	[illegible]	[illegible]	[illegible]	[illegible]	[illegible]	[illegible]	[illegible]	[illegible]	[illegible]
[illegible]	[illegible]	[illegible]	[illegible]	[illegible]	[illegible]	[illegible]	[illegible]	[illegible]	[illegible]	[illegible]	[illegible]	[illegible]	[illegible]	[illegible]	[illegible]	[illegible]	[illegible]	[illegible]	[illegible]
[illegible]	[illegible]	[illegible]	[illegible]	[illegible]	[illegible]	[illegible]	[illegible]	[illegible]	[illegible]	[illegible]	[illegible]	[illegible]	[illegible]	[illegible]	[illegible]	[illegible]	[illegible]	[illegible]	[illegible]
[illegible]	[illegible]	[illegible]	[illegible]	[illegible]	[illegible]	[illegible]	[illegible]	[illegible]	[illegible]	[illegible]	[illegible]	[illegible]	[illegible]	[illegible]	[illegible]	[illegible]	[illegible]	[illegible]	[illegible]
[illegible]	[illegible]	[illegible]	[illegible]	[illegible]	[illegible]	[illegible]	[illegible]	[illegible]	[illegible]	[illegible]	[illegible]	[illegible]	[illegible]	[illegible]	[illegible]	[illegible]	[illegible]	[illegible]	[illegible]
[illegible]	[illegible]	[illegible]	[illegible]	[illegible]	[illegible]	[illegible]	[illegible]	[illegible]	[illegible]	[illegible]	[illegible]	[illegible]	[illegible]	[illegible]	[illegible]	[illegible]	[illegible]	[illegible]	[illegible]
Total,	[illegible]	[illegible]	[illegible]	-	-	-	-	-	-	-	[illegible]	[illegible]	[illegible]	-	[illegible]	[illegible]	[illegible]	[illegible]	[illegible]
Mean,	[illegible]	[illegible]	[illegible]	-	-	-	-	-	-	-	[illegible]	[illegible]	[illegible]	-	[illegible]	[illegible]	[illegible]	[illegible]	[illegible]

1890.	Rain.			[illegible]	Cloud.		Wind.																
	[illegible]	[illegible]	[illegible]	[illegible]	[illegible]	[illegible]	N.	[illegible]	N.E.	[illegible]	E.	[illegible]	S.E.	[illegible]	S.	[illegible]	S.W.	[illegible]	W.	[illegible]	N.W.	[illegible]	Calm.
[illegible]	[illegible]	[illegible]	[illegible]	[illegible]	[illegible]	[illegible]	[illegible]	[illegible]	[illegible]	[illegible]	[illegible]	[illegible]	[illegible]	[illegible]	[illegible]	[illegible]	[illegible]	[illegible]	[illegible]	[illegible]	[illegible]	[illegible]	[illegible]
[illegible]	[illegible]	[illegible]	[illegible]	[illegible]	[illegible]	[illegible]	[illegible]	[illegible]	[illegible]	[illegible]	[illegible]	[illegible]	[illegible]	[illegible]	[illegible]	[illegible]	[illegible]	[illegible]	[illegible]	[illegible]	[illegible]	[illegible]	[illegible]
[illegible]	[illegible]	[illegible]	[illegible]	[illegible]	[illegible]	[illegible]	[illegible]	[illegible]	[illegible]	[illegible]	[illegible]	[illegible]	[illegible]	[illegible]	[illegible]	[illegible]	[illegible]	[illegible]	[illegible]	[illegible]	[illegible]	[illegible]	[illegible]
[illegible]	[illegible]	[illegible]	[illegible]	[illegible]	[illegible]	[illegible]	[illegible]	[illegible]	[illegible]	[illegible]	[illegible]	[illegible]	[illegible]	[illegible]	[illegible]	[illegible]	[illegible]	[illegible]	[illegible]	[illegible]	[illegible]	[illegible]	[illegible]
[illegible]	[illegible]	[illegible]	[illegible]	[illegible]	[illegible]	[illegible]	[illegible]	[illegible]	[illegible]	[illegible]	[illegible]	[illegible]	[illegible]	[illegible]	[illegible]	[illegible]	[illegible]	[illegible]	[illegible]	[illegible]	[illegible]	[illegible]	[illegible]
[illegible]	[illegible]	[illegible]	[illegible]	[illegible]	[illegible]	[illegible]	[illegible]	[illegible]	[illegible]	[illegible]	[illegible]	[illegible]	[illegible]	[illegible]	[illegible]	[illegible]	[illegible]	[illegible]	[illegible]	[illegible]	[illegible]	[illegible]	[illegible]
[illegible]	[illegible]	[illegible]	[illegible]	[illegible]	[illegible]	[illegible]	[illegible]	[illegible]	[illegible]	[illegible]	[illegible]	[illegible]	[illegible]	[illegible]	[illegible]	[illegible]	[illegible]	[illegible]	[illegible]	[illegible]	[illegible]	[illegible]	[illegible]
[illegible]	[illegible]	[illegible]	[illegible]	[illegible]	[illegible]	[illegible]	[illegible]	[illegible]	[illegible]	[illegible]	[illegible]	[illegible]	[illegible]	[illegible]	[illegible]	[illegible]	[illegible]	[illegible]	[illegible]	[illegible]	[illegible]	[illegible]	[illegible]
[illegible]	[illegible]	[illegible]	[illegible]	[illegible]	[illegible]	[illegible]	[illegible]	[illegible]	[illegible]	[illegible]	[illegible]	[illegible]	[illegible]	[illegible]	[illegible]	[illegible]	[illegible]	[illegible]	[illegible]	[illegible]	[illegible]	[illegible]	[illegible]
[illegible]	[illegible]	[illegible]	[illegible]	[illegible]	[illegible]	[illegible]	[illegible]	[illegible]	[illegible]	[illegible]	[illegible]	[illegible]	[illegible]	[illegible]	[illegible]	[illegible]	[illegible]	[illegible]	[illegible]	[illegible]	[illegible]	[illegible]	[illegible]
[illegible]	[illegible]	[illegible]	[illegible]	[illegible]	[illegible]	[illegible]	[illegible]	[illegible]	[illegible]	[illegible]	[illegible]	[illegible]	[illegible]	[illegible]	[illegible]	[illegible]	[illegible]	[illegible]	[illegible]	[illegible]	[illegible]	[illegible]	[illegible]
[illegible]	[illegible]	[illegible]	[illegible]	[illegible]	[illegible]	[illegible]	[illegible]	[illegible]	[illegible]	[illegible]	[illegible]	[illegible]	[illegible]	[illegible]	[illegible]	[illegible]	[illegible]	[illegible]	[illegible]	[illegible]	[illegible]	[illegible]	[illegible]
Total,	[illegible]	[illegible]	-	[illegible]	[illegible]	[illegible]	[illegible]	[illegible]	[illegible]	[illegible]	[illegible]	[illegible]	[illegible]	[illegible]	[illegible]	[illegible]	[illegible]	[illegible]	[illegible]	[illegible]	[illegible]	[illegible]	[illegible]
Mean,	[illegible]	[illegible]	-	[illegible]	[illegible]	[illegible]	[illegible]	[illegible]	-	[illegible]	[illegible]	[illegible]	[illegible]	[illegible]	[illegible]	[illegible]	[illegible]	[illegible]	[illegible]	[illegible]	-	[illegible]	-

METEOROLOGICAL OBSERVATIONS

FOR EACH MONTH OF THE YEAR 1890.

By J. W. MOORE, Esq., M.D., F.R.C.P.I., F.R. MET. SOC.

(Extracted from the *Dublin Journal of Medical Science*.)

JANUARY.—January, 1890, proved a tempestuous, mild and rainy month. Rough southerly to westerly winds blew with little intermission, and frequently freshened into strong or violent gales, especially in the west of Ireland. Even in Dublin, eleven gales were recorded, some of them being downright tempests. Almost throughout the month atmospherical pressure was low over the Atlantic Ocean in the W., N.W., and N., high over central and southern Europe. On several occasions thunder and lightning accompanied the storms.

In Dublin the mean temperature (44·5°) was much above the average (41·6°); the mean dry bulb readings at 9 a.m. and 9 p.m. were 44·1°. In the twenty-five years ending with 1889, January was coldest in 1881 (M. T. = 33·5°), and warmest in 1873 (M. T. = 40·6°). In 1867 the M. T. was 35·7°, and in 1885 it was 37·5°. In 1871 and in 1880 the M. T. was 37·0°; in the year 1879 (the "cold year") it was 35·3°. In 1883, the M. T. was 42·1°, and in 1889 it was 42·4°. As a general rule, January in Dublin is not colder, but rather a shade warmer, than December. This is owing to the full development in January of a winter area of low pressure over the Atlantic, to the north-westward of the British Isles, and to a resulting prevalence of S.W. winds in their vicinity. January, 1890, proved no exception to this rule, the M. T. being 0·7° above that of December, 1889 (43·8°).

The mean height of the barometer was 29·740 inches, or 0·141 inch below the average value for January—namely, 29·881 inches, and as much as 0·410 inch below the mean for January, 1889—namely, 30·150 inches. The mercury rose to 30·450 inches at 4 p.m. of the 29th, and fell to 28·693 inches at 7.45 a.m. of the 12th. It had been lower in the early morning hours. The observed range of atmospherical pressure was, therefore, as much as 1·757 inches—that is, a little over one inch and three-quarters. The mean temperature deduced from daily readings of the dry bulb thermometer at 9 a.m. and 9 p.m. was 44·1°, or 0·6° above the value for December, 1889. Using the formula, *Mean Temp.* = min. + (max.—min. × ·56), the value becomes 44·7°, compared with a twenty-five years' average, 41·5°. The arithmetical mean of the maximal and minimal readings was 44·5°, compared with a 25 years' average of 41·4°. On the 16th the thermometer in the screen rose to 55·8°—wind, S.S.W.; on the 29th the temperature fell to 31·1°—wind W.S.W. The minimum on the grass was 24·9° on the same date. The rainfall was 3·373 inches, distributed over 21 days. The average rainfall for January in the twenty-five years, 1865-89, inclusive, was 2·300 inches, and the average number of rainy days was 17·3. The rainfall and the rainy days, therefore, were both considerably above the average. In 1877 the rainfall in January was very large—4·321 inches on 23 days; in 1866, also 4·235 inches fell—on, however, only 18 days. On the other hand, in 1876, only ·406 of an inch was measured on but 9 days; and in 1880, the rainfall was only ·367 of an inch on but 8 days. In January, 1886, 3·244 inches of rain were measured on as many as 26 days. In 1887 ("the dry year"), 1·616 inches fell on 15 days, in 1888 1·237 inches on 9 days, and in 1889, 2·113 inches on 16 days.

A solar halo was seen on the 29th. Lunar halos were seen on the 7th and 27th. The atmosphere was foggy on each of the first two days, as also on the 27th. High winds were noted on 21 days, reaching the force of a gale on eleven days. Hail fell on the 18th, 19th, and 23rd, and snow or sleet on the 19th, 20th, 22nd, 23rd, and 24th. Temperature exceeded 50° in the screen on 17 days, compared with 6 days in January, 1889; while it fell to or below 32° in the screen on only 1 night, compared with 8 nights in January, 1889. The minima on the grass were 25°, or less, on 15 nights, compared with 16 nights in January, 1889.

At the beginning of the month changeable, but for the most part mild, weather held in Ireland and Scotland, while severe cold was experienced in central and eastern England, where also fogs of great density prevailed. These conditions were determined by the persistence of an anticyclone over Germany, France, and England, whereas pressure was relatively low over the Atlantic to the westward and northward of the British Islands. In Dublin the weather was generally fine—calm and fog alternating with clouds and squalls from S.W. Temperature was very unsteady in Dublin, which was on the borderland between the low anticyclonic temperatures of England and the high temperatures of the Atlantic seaboard.

The week ending Saturday, the 11th, was one of stormy, open weather, with frequent falls of rain, which, however, were not heavy on the east coast of Ireland. In Dublin the mean temperature was 5° above the average. All through, an oval anticyclone held over France and Germany—the barometer rising to 30·75 inches at Munich at 8 a.m. of Tuesday, the 7th—while a series of extensive and deep depressions skirted the western and northern coasts of Ireland and Scotland on their passage northeastwards. The week opened with a violent S.W. gale, which was accompanied with severe and fatal thunderstorms in the south-west and west of Ireland. At 8 a.m. of Sunday pressure varied from 28·73 inches at Stornoway, in the Hebrides, to 30·35 inches at Munich. On Tuesday temperature rose to 56° or 57° at many stations in the United Kingdom. In Dublin the mean height of the barometer during the week was 29·870 inches. The mean temperature was 45·4°. Rain was measured on six days, the total quantity being ·282 inch.

Stormy, unsettled weather, and high but variable temperatures prevailed throughout the week ending Saturday, the 18th. The barometer was continuously high over the Peninsula and Central Europe, very low over the Atlantic and Norwegian Sea, and most unsteady in the British Islands and Scandinavia. The result was that strong south-westerly gales raged from time to time on the British coasts. The storms culminated in a tempest on Friday night and Saturday morning. On Saturday afternoon also a violent S.W. gale prevailed, accompanied by driving showers of rain and hail, and by flashes of sheet lightning after dark. On Thursday the air was soft and balmy as in late spring—the maximal temperature being 50·6° and the minimal temperature being 50·2°. In Dublin the mean height of the barometer was 29·767 inches. The mean temperature was as high as 46·5°. The rainfall was distributed over four days and amounted to ·433 inch. Hail fell on Saturday, on the evening of which day also lightning was seen.

The period ending Saturday, the 25th, was most unsettled, stormy, rough and wet. Temperature was much lower than in the two preceding weeks, but it was very constantly. A number of extensive and deep atmospherical depressions passed across north-western Europe during the week, causing violent gales, thunderstorms, and heavy falls of rain and sleet. Of these disturbances, the deepest was that of Sunday, January 19, at 8 a.m., of which day pressure varied from 30·37 inches at Lisbon to 28·62 inches at Stornoway, in the Hebrides. At 9.30 a.m. a violent hailstorm occurred in Dublin, and during the day thunder and lightning prevailed in Ireland, Scotland, and the west of England. Another deep depression came in over Scotland on Tuesday, causing a renewal of bad weather. This system was quickly followed by a cyclone of great intensity, the centre of which passed eastwards south of Dublin, where the wind backed through E. and N.E. to N. and N.W., with a heavy fall of cold rain and sleet. A S.W. to W. gale of exceptional violence blew in the English Channel. A curious effect of the arrival of this depression was to cause a temporary calm in Scotland, accompanied by sharp frost, the thermometer falling to 21° at Aberdeen on Thursday morning and not rising above 19° at that station during the day. A final area of low barometer reached Ireland on Friday night. It brought high temperatures and a strong S.W. gale. In Dublin the mean height of the barometer during the week was only 29·207 inches. The mean temperature was 41·3°. The rainfall amounted to ·932 inch on six days—·304 inch being registered on Wednesday the 22nd.

Although still changeable in many respects, the weather moderated considerably after Sunday, the 26th, on which day a fresh S.W. gale was felt. Both on the 26th and 27th the barometer over the south of France stood about two inches higher than it did off the W. coast of Norway, and consequently westerly winds of great strength prevailed. In Dublin Sunday's gale was accompanied by a very heavy rainfall—more than eight-tenths of an inch being registered in 12 hours. In Dublin the mean height of the barometer in the week ending Saturday, February 1, was 30·123 inches. The mean temperature was 48·3°. Rain fell on four days—the total measurement being 1·204 inches, of which ·843 inch fell on Sunday, the 26th.

FEBRUARY.—This month was remarkable for the contrast it afforded to January. South-easterly and easterly winds, quiet, chiefly fine weather, frequent fogs, and low temperature took the place of the blustering south-westerly gales, heavy and frequent rains, and high, unsteady temperature of the preceding month. The mean atmospherical pressure was nearly half an inch (·464 inch) above that of January, while the mean temperature was 3° below that of January.

In most particulars, February, 1890, may be regarded as a favourable month, but the amount of cloud—71·3 per cent.—was much in excess of the average, 66·0 per cent., and gave rather a gloomy aspect to the season, which was also notable for its foggy character.

In Dublin the mean temperature (41·5°) was 1·2° below the average (42·7°); the mean dry bulb readings at 9 a.m. and 9 p.m. were 40·8°. In the twenty-five years ending with 1889, February was coldest in 1873 (M. T. = 37·9°) and warmest in 1869 (M. T. = 46·7°). In 1886 the M. T. was 39·7°. In the year 1879 (the cold year) it was 40·1°. In 1888 it was as low as 38·6°, and in 1889 it was 40·6°.

The mean height of the barometer was 30·204 inches, or 0·348 inch above the average value for February—namely, 29·856 inches. The mercury rose to 30·744 inches at 11 a.m. of the 23rd, and fell to 29·539 inches at 9 a.m. of the 16th. The observed range of atmospherical pressure was, therefore, 1·205 inches—that is, a little over one inch and two-tenths. The mean temperature deduced from daily readings of the dry bulb thermometer at 9 a.m. and 9 p.m. was 40·8°, or 3·6° below the value for January, 1890. Using the formula *Mean Temp. = min. + (max. — min. × ·50)*, the value becomes 41·6°, compared with a twenty-five years' average of 42·7°. On the 1st the thermometer in the screen rose to 53·5°—wind W.S.W.; on the 16th the temperature fell to 27·9°—wind calm. The minimum on the grass was 25·0° on the 8th and 16th.

The rainfall was only ·608 inch, distributed over 7 days. The average rainfall for February in the twenty-five years, 1865–89, inclusive, was 2·150 inches, and the average number of rainy days was 17·2. The rainfall and the rainy days, therefore, were both considerably below the average. In 1866 the rainfall in February was large—3·762 inches on 17 days; in 1879, also, 3·700 inches fell on 23 days. On the other hand, in 1873, only ·916 of an inch was measured on but 8 days; and in 1887 only ·541 inch of rain fell on 11 days. The rainfall in 1887 was much the smallest recorded in February for very many years.

Snow or sleet fell on the 13th and 25th. Hail fell on the 27th. The atmosphere was foggy on as many as 10 days, namely—the 5th, 6th, 8th, 14th, 15th, 16th, 21st, 22nd, 23rd, and 24th. High winds were noted on 5 days, reaching the force of a gale on only one day—the 18th. The temperature exceeded 50° in the screen on but 2 days, compared with as many as 17 days in January, and with 6 days in February, 1889; while it fell to or below 32°, in the screen on 5 days, compared with only 1 day in January, but with 4 in February, 1889. The minima on the grass were 32°, or less, on 18 nights, compared with 13 nights in January and 21 nights in February, 1889. On 3 days the thermometer did not rise above 40° in the screen.

Fine, quiet, cool weather held almost throughout the first week (1st–8th). The barometer was generally high in central Europe, England and Ireland; low in the extreme north; and relatively low over the Mediterranean and neighbouring countries. Strong S.W. to N.W. winds prevailed to the northward, moderate easterly breezes to the southward, while in the central zone between the northern and southern areas of low pressure, calms and very variable airs were observed, with fogs and frosts at times. Except on the west coast of Norway, the precipitation was small during the week. In Dublin the mean height of the barometer was 30·340 inches. The mean dry bulb temperature at 9 a.m. and 9 p.m. was 40·0°. The corrected mean temperature, deduced from the daily extremes in the shade, was 41·0°. Rain fell in appreciable amount on only one day, the quantity measured being but ·010 inch (on Tuesday). At Christiansund, in Norway, on the contrary, the rainfall for the week up to 8 a.m. of Saturday amounted to 3·82 inches and was distributed over six days. Sharp frosts occurred over central Ireland on Wednesday and Saturday, the 5th and 8th, the lowest readings in the screen at Parsonstown being 21° and 22° respectively, on the mornings of those days.

During the week ended Saturday, the 15th, the weather was throughout cold. Until the 14th it was very dry, with fresh, or strong searching south-easterly winds and much cloud. On that day a considerable fall of cold rain occurred, and Saturday proved bitterly cold, with a westerly wind and a vapour fog. During the greater part of the week an anticyclone, in the centre of which the barometer at one time stood above 30·6 inches, lay over the North Sea, Scandinavia, and the Baltic. It was to this system that the searching S.E. winds of the period owed their origin. On Tuesday the barometer fell decidedly, as a depression approached the S.W. of England from the Atlantic. This disturbance caused very heavy rain in Cork—·85 inch being measured on Wednesday, and 1·22 inches on Thursday, at Roche's Point, near Queenstown. On Saturday the barometer again fell, while the wind became westerly or north-westerly with fog and a low temperature. In parts of England a good deal of snow fell. In Dublin the mean height of the barometer was 29·935 inches. The corrected mean temperature was 36·9°; the mean dry bulb readings at 9 a.m. and 9 p.m. were 35·4°. Rain fell to the amount of ·099 inch on Friday.

Very damp, changeable, dull weather prevailed during the greater part of the third week, which began in Dublin with a dense vapour fog and a very low temperature—27·9° in the screen. Until Saturday, the 22nd, a vast anticyclone lay over the north-east of Europe, while the barometer was low over the Atlantic to the south-westward of the British Islands. Consequently, easterly to southerly winds prevailed, accompanied by frost on the Continent; low temperature, cloudy skies, and gloom or fog in Great Britain; and a mild damp atmosphere, with frequent rain, in Ireland. On Saturday, however, the barometer rose fast in this country, as a new area of high pressure formed over Western Europe, and the week closed with a promise of quiet, cold weather. In Dublin the mean height of the barometer was 30·023 inches. The mean temperature was 43·9°; the mean dry bulb temperature at 9 a.m. and 9 p.m. was 42·5°. Rain was measured on three days, the total down-fall being ·380 inch, of which ·278 inch was caught on Sunday and ·103 inch on Monday. The week began and ended with a dense vapour fog.

In the closing period of the month, from the 23rd to the 28th inclusive, at first mild and cloudy, the weather afterwards became cold and dry, with very keen polar winds, and snow showers in Great Britain and Ireland. The barometer was high throughout in Ireland, while depressions passed in a south-easterly or southerly direction across Scandinavia, the Baltic, and Russia. Hence polar winds prevailed in Western Europe. On Sunday, the 23rd, an anticyclone stretched across England and Ireland, in which countries the barometer stood at 30·70 inches or upward—at 8 a.m. the reading at Belmullet was 30·75 inches, at 11 a.m. that in Dublin was 30·744 inches. Gradients for northerly winds became more and more pronounced until Friday, the 28th, when a great current of polar air was flowing southwards all across Europe, and frost and snow were reported from most British and Continental stations, with a very dry searching air, particularly in Ireland. A solar and a lunar halo were seen on Friday, February 28.

The rainfall in Dublin during the two months ending February 28th has amounted to 3·777 inches on 28 days, compared with 4·683 inches on 35 days in 1889 and 2·344 inches on 28 days during the same period in 1888, and with a 25 years' average of 4·340 inches on 34·3 days.

At Greystones, Co. Wicklow, the rainfall in February, 1890, was 1·083 inches, distributed over 7 days. Of this quantity ·820 inch fell on the 16th. Since January 1st, 5·585 inches of rain have fallen at that station on 19 days.

March.—March, 1890, was a month of contrasts. As in 1889, it opened with very severe weather, a violent snowstorm being felt in the S.E. of England on the 1st and 2nd, the thermometer falling to 6° Fahr. at Hillington, in Norfolk. Warm and cold spells then succeeded each other to the close of the month, and heavy falls of rain occurred at times. On the whole there was a mean temperature above the average, and the rainfall also was in Dublin largely in excess. The mean height of the barometer was ·418 inch below that of February, but ·049 above that of January, 1890.

In Dublin the mean temperature (44·1°) was considerably above the average (42·1°); the mean dry bulb readings at 9 a.m. and 9 p.m. were 44·6°. In the twenty-five years ending with 1889, March was coldest in 1867 and 1883 (M. T. = 39·0°), and warmest in 1868 (M. T. = 47·5°). In 1876 the M. T. was 41·1°, in 1879 (the cold year) it was 45·1°, in 1883 it was as low as 39·0°, and in 1889 it was 41·0°. As a general rule, February in Dublin is only a shade colder than March. This is due to the fact that the Continental anticyclone usually embraces the British Isles and Scandinavia in March, causing easterly winds. In the present year, however, February was 3·6° colder than March.

The mean height of the barometer was 29·769 inches, or 0·154 inch below the average value for March—namely, 29·923 inches. The mercury rose to 30·534 inches at 9 a.m. of the 3rd, and fell to 28·904 inches at 4 p.m. of the 31st. The observed range of atmospherical pressure was, therefore, 1·630 inches—that is, nearly an inch and seven-tenths. The mean temperature deduced from daily readings of the dry bulb thermometer at 9 a.m. and 9 p.m. was 44·6°, or 3·6° above the value for February, 1890. Using the formula, *Mean Temp.* = min. + (max.—min. × ·465), the value becomes

44·9°. The arithmetical mean of the maximal and minimal readings was 45·1°, compared with a twenty-five years' average of 45·1°. On the 15th the thermometer in the screen rose to 58·6°—wind W.S.W.; on the 3rd and 9th the temperature fell to 31·2°—wind, N.E. and W.N.W. respectively. The minimum on the grass was 24·0 on the 3rd. The rainfall was as much as 2·422 inches, distributed over 17 days. The average rainfall for March in the twenty-five years, 1865–89, inclusive, was 2·061 inches, and the average number of rainy days was 16·6. The rainfall, therefore, was much above the average, while the rainy days were slightly above it. In 1867 the rainfall in March was very large—4·073 inches on 22 days; in 1883, 3·749 inches fell on 18 days; in 1840 also 3·423 inches fell on 21 days. On the other hand, in 1871, only ·815 of an inch was measured on 12 days; and in 1874 only ·843 of an inch fell, also on 12 days. In 1887 (the "dry year") 1·426 inches of rain fell on 15 days, and in 1839 1·076 inches fell on, however, as many as 17 days.

The atmosphere was foggy on the 19th, 20th and 27th. High winds were noted on 15 days, reaching the force of a gale on 4 days—the 7th, 8th, 10th, and 24th. Snow or sleet occurred on the 1st, 2nd, 9th, 18th, 19th, and 22nd; and hail fell on the 1st, 2nd, and 8th. The temperature exceeded 50° in the screen on 19 days, compared with only 8 days in February, and 17 days in January; while it fell to or below 32° in the screen on 4 days, compared with 8 in February and only 1 day in January. The minima on the grass were 32°, or less, on 16 nights, compared with 18 nights in February and 15 nights in January. On 2 days the thermometer did not rise to 40° in the screen.

The period ending on Saturday, the 5th, was divided into a very cold and a mild although stormy period—the former lasting until Tuesday the 4th in Ireland, but until Wednesday in England. A small but well-marked depression—which on Saturday, the 1st, had quickly travelled down the east coast of Great Britain as far as Spurn Head, and thence in a south-westerly direction across England—was found over Brittany on the 2nd. It caused heavy falls of snow in the S.E. of England, and showers of hail and snow in most parts of the country. In the wake of this depression an extraordinary fall of temperature took place in the centre and S.E. of England. Early on Tuesday morning the thermometer fell to 15° at Loughborough, 17° at Oxford, 15° in London, 14° at Cambridge, 18° at Dungeness, and 6° at Hillington, Norfolkshire—these were the lowest temperatures experienced in England during the present winter. Milder weather had already set in at the northern stations and spread quickly southwards. A series of deep depressions now travelled eastward across Northern Europe, causing gales, frequent showers, and very unstable temperatures. At 8 a.m. of Friday the barometer varied from 30·14 inches at Rochefort in France to 28·80 inches at Christiansund, in Norway. At 11 a.m. of Saturday a violent squall of hail, rain, thunder and lightning passed over Dublin. The mean height of the barometer during the first week (2nd–8th inclusive) was 30·012 inches. The mean temperature was 46·5°, the mean dry bulb readings at 9 a.m. and 9 p.m. being 47·2°. Rain was measured on four days, the total quantity being ·256 inch, of which ·180 inch fell on Saturday.

During the greater part of the second week (9th–15th, inclusive), strong, squally, westerly and south-westerly winds prevailed, but the weather remained for the most part dry. The general distribution of atmospherical pressure was—low in the north, high in the south. Hence the westerly winds of the period. On Sunday, the 9th, a frost occurred in the rear of a depression, which had passed eastwards across the lowlands of Scotland the previous evening. The wind afterwards backed gradually from N.W. to S.W. and finally to S., from which last point it blew freshly on Friday night. On Tuesday and Wednesday the thermometer rose to 60° or upwards in the shade at several stations in Great Britain—the highest reading of all being 63° at Aberdeen on Wednesday. In Dublin the mean height of the barometer was 29·645 inches. The mean temperature was 47·9°. The mean dry bulb temperature at 9 a.m. and 9 p.m. was 48·1°. The thermometers in the screen fell to 31·2° on Sunday but rose to 59° on Wednesday. Rain was measured on three days—the total quantity being ·857 inch. Of this amount ·190 inch was credited to Sunday, and ·634 inch to Saturday.

At the beginning and close of the third week, changeable, rainy weather prevailed in Dublin—during the intervening period it was chiefly fine and quiet. Between Tuesday, the 18th, and Friday, the 21st, a deep depression travelled northwestwards from the south of Germany to the west of Scotland. It caused very unsettled weather, with heavy falls of rain and sleet, in the S.E., E., and N.E. of Great Britain, while it was very fine in Ireland. The week began with a deep and complex depression lying over this country—the barometer being as low as 29 inches at 8 a.m. of Sunday in Ulster and Leinster. Throughout the week numerous areas of low pressure lay over Western Europe, travelling in anomalous and erratic directions. Hence the changeable weather of the period. In Dublin the mean height of the barometer was 29·495 inches. The mean temperature was 41·7°. The mean of the dry bulb readings at 9 a.m. and 9 p.m. was 41·3°. The rainfall was ·453 inch, distributed over four days. Of this amount, ·188 inch was measured on Monday and ·244 inch on Saturday. Sleet fell on Sunday and Tuesday. There were fogs on Wednesday and Thursday.

The chief characteristic of the weather during the week ended Saturday, the 29th, so far as Dublin is concerned, was a frequent and heavy downpour of rain—the precipitation amounting to 1·003 inches on five days. At the same time a decided increase of temperature was noted generally, so that on Friday the 28th the thermometer rose to [illegible]° in London, 73° in Paris, and 79° at Biarritz. During the week several depressions crossed the British Islands in an easterly direction. Of these, the deepest was observed on Monday, when the barometer sank to 28·904 inches in Dublin, and a fresh S.E. gale and incessant rain prevailed. Two moderately fine days succeeded, but the weather became broken and rainy once more on Thursday, [illegible] and continuous rain occurring on Friday. Bright, dry weather and a fresh westerly breeze followed on Saturday. In Dublin the mean height of the barometer was 29·635 inches, pressure ranging between 28·904 inches at 4 p.m. of Monday (wind, S.S.E.), and 30·058 inches at 9 p.m. of Saturday (wind, W.). The mean temperature was 47·3°; the mean dry bulb temperature at 9 a.m. and 9 p.m. being 47·3°. The rainfall amounted to 2·003 inches on five days. Of this large quantity, ·976 inch was registered on Monday and ·469 inch on Friday.

The last two days were fine, quiet, cool, and dry—the month going out "like a lamb," as it had come in "like a lion."

The rainfall in Dublin during the three months ending March 31st has amounted to 7·470 inches on 51 days, compared with 5·784 inches on 43 days during the same period in 1889, 6·497 inches on 41 days in 1888, and a 25 years' average of 6·411 inches on 51·0 days.

April.—April, 1890, was generally a favourable month. The mean temperature, rainfall, and rainy days were all somewhat below the average. Considered by weeks, the weather was first fine, dry, and quiet; then cold and showery; then dull and cheerless; then unsettled, squally, and showery, and lastly fine.

In Dublin the mean temperature (47·3°) was slightly below the average (47·7°); the mean dry bulb readings at 9 a.m. and 9 p.m. were 46·3°. In the twenty-five years ending with 1889, April was coldest in 1879 (the cold year) (M. T. = 44·5°), and warmest in 1865 and 1874 (M. T. = 50·6°). In 1886, the M. T. was 46·2°; in 1887 it was as low as 45·1°; in 1888 it was only 45·7°, and in 1889 it was 46·1°.

The mean height of the barometer was 29·841 inches, or 0·016 inch below the average value for April—namely, 29·857 inches. The mercury rose to 30·303 inches at 9 a.m. of the 1st, and fell to 29·457 inches at 9 p.m. of the 15th. The observed range of atmospherical pressure was, therefore, only 0·846 inch—that is, a little more than eight-tenths of an inch. The mean temperature deduced from daily readings of the dry bulb thermometer at 9 a.m. and 9 p.m. was 46·3°, or only 1·7° above the value for March, 1890. Using the formula, *Mean Temp. = min. + (max. — min. × ·476)*, the value becomes 47·0°, or 0·4° below the average mean temperature for April, calculated in the same way, in the twenty-five years, 1865–89, inclusive (47·4°). The arithmetical mean of the maximal and minimal readings was 47·3°, compared with a twenty-five years' (1865–1889 inclusive) average of 47·7°. On the 28th, the thermometer in the screen rose to 63·4°—wind S.W.; on the 3rd the temperature fell to 31·3°—wind, calm. The minimum on the grass was 24·6° on the same date. The rainfall was 1·675 inches, distributed over 14 days. The average rainfall for April in the twenty-five years, 1865–89, inclusive, was 2·044 inches, and the average number of rainy days was 15·2. The rainfall, therefore, was considerably below the average, while the rainy days were also deficient. In 1877 the rainfall in April was very large—4·707 inches on 21 days; in 1883 also 3·420 inches fell on 20 days. On the other hand, in 1873, only ·498 of an inch was measured on 5 days; and in 1870 only ·588 of an inch fell, also on 5 days.

No solar halos were seen. There was a lunar halo on the 24th. The atmosphere was more or less foggy on the 1st, 2nd, 3rd, 4th, 11th, 12th, 27th, and 28th. High winds were noted on 11 days, but on only two occasions was the force of a gale attained—namely, on the 7th and 22nd. Snow or sleet occurred on the 10th; and hail fell on the 8th, 10th, 22nd, 23rd, and 25th. The temperature exceeded 50° in the screen on 23 days, compared with 10 days in March, 5 days in February, and 17 days in January. It fell below 32° in the screen on one night only—that of the 3rd. The minima on the grass were 32°, or less, on 13 nights, compared with 16 nights in March, 15 in February, and 15 nights in January. The mean lowest temperature on the grass was 34·1°, compared with 34·4° in 1889, 34·6° in 1888, and 31·6° in 1887. A peal of thunder was heard to the westward at 12·10 p.m. on the 29th.

During the period ending Saturday the 5th anticyclonic conditions, accompanied with fine dry, quiet, cool weather prevailed. The barometer was uniformly rather high and the winds were light and variable. The diurnal range of temperature was large. On the 3rd not a cloud was seen from morning to night. On Saturday the 5th it became evident that areas of low atmospherical pressure were about to encroach on the Irish coasts from the Atlantic—the barometer fell decidedly, clouds increased, and temperature rose. In Dublin the barometer ranged from 30·303 inches at 9 a.m. of Tuesday the 1st (wind N.), to 29·945 inches at 9 p.m. of Saturday the 5th (wind, S.W.). The thermometer rose to 56·2° on Friday, having fallen the previous day to 31·3° in the screen and to 24·6° on the grass. Rain fell only on Saturday night, the resulting measurement being ·016 inch.

Severe weather prevailed during the greater part of the second week—polar winds, cold showers, and frosty nights being experienced after Easter Day, the 6th, which was chiefly fine and mild. On this day a general decrease of atmospherical pressure occurred all over North-Western Europe, and at night an extensive depression travelled eastwards across Scotland, momentarily growing deeper. It caused squally S.W. and afterwards N.W. and N. winds, and rain fell generally. By 8 a.m. of Tuesday, the 8th, the centre of this system had reached the Skager-Rack, the barometer being as low as 28·64 inches at the Skaw—northerly winds, showers of hail, sleet, and cold rain, and low temperatures were prevalent in the British Islands, especially in Great Britain, where also thunder and lightning occurred at many stations. At this station the mean height of the barometer was 29·591 inches. The mean dry bulb temperature at 9 a.m. and 9 p.m. was 43·6°, while the mean calculated from the daily highest and lowest readings in the shade was 45·2°. The rainfall was ·290 inch, on four days; the heaviest fall in 24 hours being ·106 inch on Thursday.

On the east coast of Ireland, as is usual in easterly winds, very dull, cold, cheerless, weather prevailed throughout the third week, and the 14th and 16th were wet in Dublin. In the west and northwest, however, the weather was much finer and brighter, although cold for the time of year. A severe thunderstorm occurred in the counties of Cork and Kerry on Thursday the 17th. During the entire period the weather was determined by a large area of low atmospherical pressure, which advanced slowly northwards and at the same time spread out in an easterly direction across France and Germany, while all through the barometer was high over Lapland and the northern part of Sweden and Norway. Fresh or squally easterly winds, consequently, prevailed, accompanied by low temperature, densely clouded skies, and cold rain at times. Thunder storms were reported daily from France after Sunday. Early on the morning of that day severe frost occurred in Great Britain—the lowest temperature of all being 24° at Nairn. In Dublin the mean height of the barometer was 29·636 inches. The mean dry bulb temperature at 9 a.m. and 9 p.m. was 45·5°; the arithmetical mean of the daily highest and lowest shade temperature was 44·8°. The rainfall was ·602 inch on two days—·439 inch fell on Tuesday and ·081 inch on Wednesday. The mean amount of cloud at 9 a.m. and 9 p.m. was no less than 91 per cent.

At first summerlike, the weather in the week ending Saturday, the 26th, soon became unsettled, squally, showery, and cold; but towards the close of the period a marked improvement was seen. On Sunday gradients for south-westerly winds formed over Ireland, where temperature rose quickly—to 65·6° in Dublin and 63° at Parsonstown. But this change from winter to summer was of no long continuance, for by Monday morning the first of a series of depressions had reached the north coast, bringing with it squalls, showers, and a fall of temperature. A succession of typical showery April days followed—the worst weather of all being experienced in the South of England on Thursday and Friday owing to the formation in that district of a deep secondary barometrical depression. With a veering of the wind to N. on Saturday, the weather improved, becoming bright and bracing. In Dublin the mean height of the barometer was 29·788 inches. The mean temperature was 49·1°; the mean dry bulb temperature at 9 a.m. and 9 p.m. was [illegible]°. Rain fell on five days to the amount of ·352 inch, ·129 inch being measured on Friday and ·118 inch on Wednesday. Hail fell in Dublin on three days and thunder was heard about midday on Saturday.

The weather of the last four days of the month was favourable, a copious but genial rainfall occurring on the 29th.

The rainfall in Dublin during the four months ending April 30th has amounted to 9·043 inches on 80 days, compared with 8·343 inches on 74 days during the same period in 1889, 6·050 inches on 48 days in 1888, and a 25 years' average of 8·406 inches on 65·2 days.

At Knockdolian, Greystones, Co. Wicklow, the rainfall during April, 1890, amounted to 1·463 inches, distributed over 10 days.

May.—Although changeable and generally showery, May, 1890, may be regarded as a favourable month both from a public health point of view and from that of agriculture. Until the 20th rain fell in frequent showers, and conditions were decidedly unsettled. After the date named, however, a succession of bright, spring-like days occurred, giving a wonderful impetus to vegetation.

In Dublin the mean temperature (53·3°) was decidedly above the average (52·0°); the mean dry bulb readings at 9 a.m. and 9 p.m. were 52·6°. In the twenty-five years ending with 1889, May was coldest in 1869 (M. T. = 48·2°), in 1885 (M. T. = 48·7°), and in 1879 (the "cold year") (M. T. = 48·8°). It was warmest in 1868 (the "warm year") (M. T. = 55·5°) and 1875 (M. T. = 54·7°). In 1886, the M. T. was 50·5°, in 1887 it was 51·6°, in 1888 it was 52·5°, and in 1889 it was 54·9°.

The mean height of the barometer was 29·807 inches, or 0·153 inch below the corrected average value for May—namely, 29·960 inches. The mercury rose to 30·253 inches at 9 p.m. of the 22nd, and fell to 29·377 inches at 9 a.m. of the 10th. The observed range of atmospheric pressure was, therefore, 0·876 of an inch—that is, a little less than nine-tenths of an inch. The mean temperature deduced from daily readings of the dry bulb thermometer at 9 a.m. and 9 p.m. was 52·6°, or 6·6° above the value for April, 1890. Using the formula, *Mean Temp.* = min. + (max.—min. × ·47), the value was 52·5°, or 1·5° above the average mean temperature for May, calculated in the same way, in the twenty-five years, 1865–89, inclusive (51·0°). The arithmetical mean of the maximal and minimal readings was 53·3°, compared with a twenty-five years' average of 52·0°. On the 23rd, the thermometer in the screen rose to 65·7°—wind E.; on the 31st the temperature fell to 39·1°—wind, N.N.W. The minimum on the grass was 33·6°, on the 3rd. The rainfall amounted to 2·435 inches, distributed over 17 days. The average rainfall for May in the twenty-five years, 1865–89, inclusive, was 2·036 inches, and the average number of rainy days was 14·6. The rainfall and the rainy days, therefore, were somewhat above the average. In 1886 the rainfall in May was very large—5·472 inches on 21 days; in 1869 also 5·414 inches fell on 19 days. On the other hand, in 1871, only ·378 of an inch was measured on 9 days; in 1876 only ·720 of an inch fell on 6 days; in 1887 only ·628 of an inch fell on 10 days; and in 1888 only ·918 of an inch on 11 days. In 1889, 2·131 inches fell on 17 days.

There were no solar halos, but a lunar halo was seen at 11 p.m. of the 31st. The atmosphere was foggy on the 14th. High winds were noted on as many as 10 days, attaining the force of a gale, however, on not one occasion. Hail occurred on the 14th. The only heavy falls of rain were on the 3rd (·451 inch), on the 16th (·250 inch), and on the 18th (·379 inch). There were no electrical disturbances in Dublin, but lightning was seen on the night of the 24th.

During the month the thermometer in the screen did not fall below 39·1° (on the 31st), and on not a single night was a temperature of 32° or less recorded on the grass. The mean minimal temperature on the grass was 42·2°, compared with 40·7° in May, 1889, 37·5° in 1888, and 37·9° in 1887.

May Day (Thursday), was beautifully fine and bright. A succession of depressions then began to approach Ireland from the westward, causing unsettled weather and falls of rain. On Saturday, the third, an excessively wet day, ·451 of an inch fell.

During the week ended Saturday, the 10th, changeable, somewhat showery weather, and easterly (S.E. backing to N.E.) winds, prevailed. Speaking generally, the barometer stood high over the North of Scandinavia and of Russia, whereas it was low across Central Europe. In the last named district several areas of low pressure were observed from time to time, keeping the weather in an unsettled, showery, thundery state. Tuesday, the 6th, proved fair and bright, but in the afternoon electrical cirri overspread the sky, and a thunderstorm occurred at Holyhead. In Dublin the mean height of the barometer was 29·603 inches, pressure, receding to 29·377 inches at 9 a.m. of Saturday (wind, E.N.E.). The mean temperature was 51·8°. The mean of the dry bulb readings at 9 a.m. and 9 p.m. was 51·4°. Rain fell on the six days to the total amount of ·831 inch.

Very changeable, showery weather prevailed in Ireland throughout the week ended Saturday, the 17th, where the wind generally blew from south-westerly points. In England the beginning and close of the period were unsettled, but from Tuesday to Friday inclusive it was fine, sunny, and warm. On Monday and again on Friday, the thermometer rose to 68° or 70° at the central and southeastern English stations. During the week four distinct areas of low pressure passed across Western Europe from S. to N. Of these the first travelled along the east coast of Great Britain on Sunday, disappearing to the northward of Scotland on Monday, when the second system had already arrived on the Riviera from the Mediterranean. This disturbance reached the Christiania Fjord in Norway by Thursday morning. Lastly two depressions passed northwards across Ireland in rapid succession on Friday and Saturday, causing heavy rains and squalls. In Dublin the mean height of the barometer was 29·844 inches. The mean temperature was 51·0°. The mean dry bulb temperature at 9 a.m. and 9 p.m. was 51·0°. Rain fell to the amount of ·854 inch, on six days. Hail fell on Wednesday, the 14th. Gloom and fog prevailed on Friday.

In the week ended Saturday, the 24th, at first changeable and showery, the weather finally became brilliant and summerlike, with clear skies and a cool easterly breeze. On Sunday morning rain fell in heavy showers and the wind blew freshly from S.S.E. As the day wore on, the weather improved and a depression off the S.W. of Ireland moved away over the Atlantic. On Tuesday morning another depression had advanced to St. George's Channel in an irregular direction from Spain and the Bay of Biscay. It caused heavy rains and great gloom in Ireland and the south of England. As it passed off, an area of high pressure formed over Western Europe, producing a grateful change to bright sunshine and genial warmth—and these lasted to the close of the week. In Dublin, the mean height of the barometer was 29·900 inches, pressure increasing from 29·517 inches at 9 a.m. of Tuesday (wind, S.E.), to 30·233 inches at 9 p.m. of Thursday (wind also S.E.). The mean temperature was 56·1°—the mean dry bulb temperature at 9 a.m. and 9 p.m. being 55·6°. The thermometers in the screen rose to 65·7° on Friday—the maximum of the month. Rain was measured on two days—the total quantity being ·191 inch, of which ·170 inch fell in the 24 hours ending 9 a.m. of Tuesday. Faint sheet lightning was seen on the south-eastern horizon on Saturday night.

Very fine, bright weather held during the greater part of the last week (25th–31st, inclusive), Thursday, the 29th, being an exception owing to the approach of an extensive depression from the northwestward to Scotland, the south of Norway, and the North Sea. At the beginning an anticyclone was found off the North of Scotland, while areas of low pressure were moving eastwards along the southern shores of the British Islands, and a deep depression was forming over the Baltic. Thunderstorms prevailed in the Channel Islands, the S.W. of England, and the S. of Ireland. A succession of beautiful days followed until Thursday, when a depression, with several subsidiaries, approached North-western Europe from N.W. It caused clouds and rain generally and a remarkable fall of temperature, so that on Friday night ground-frost was felt at several British and Irish stations, snow and hail having already fallen in Scotland and the Hebrides. Saturday was again fine and chiefly bright. In Dublin the mean height of the barometer was 30·028 inches. The mean temperature was 53·5°. The mean dry bulb temperature at 9 a.m. and 9 p.m. was 53·4°. The thermometer in the screen rose to 64·6° on Sunday, and fell to 39·1° on Saturday. The rainfall amounted to ·241 inch, all of which fell on Thursday.

The rainfall in Dublin during the five months ending May 31st has amounted to 11·482 inches on 78 days, compared with 10·474 inches on 91 days during the same period in 1889, 9·088 inches on 69 days in 1888, 6·489 inches on 58 days in 1887, and a 25 years' average of 10·494 inches on 81·6 days.

At Knockdolian, Greystones, Co. Wicklow, the rainfall in May, 1890, was 3·050 inches, distributed over 20 days. Of this quantity ·780 inch fell on the 4th, ·450 inch on the 17th, and ·400 inch on the 20th.

June.—A cloudy, showery, windy month of average temperature and atmospherical pressure, and showing a marked preponderance of south-westerly and westerly winds.

In Dublin the mean temperature (58·1°) was slightly above the average (57·8°); the mean dry bulb readings at 9 a.m. and 9 p.m. were 57·4°. In the twenty-five years ending with 1889, June was coldest in 1882 (M. T.=55·5°), and in 1879 (the "cold year") (M. T.=55·6°). It was warmest in 1887 (M. T.=62·3°), in 1868 (M. T.=61·9°), and in 1846 (the "warm year") (M. T.=62·6°). In 1888, the M. T. was 57·5°, in 1889 it was 58·5°, and in 1890 it was 58·1°.

The mean height of the barometer was 29·944 inches, or 0·027 inch above the corrected average value for June—namely, 29·917 inches. The mercury rose to 30·378 inches at 9 a.m. of the 14th, and fell to 29·132 inches at 3 p.m. of the 30th. The observed range of atmospherical pressure was, therefore, 1·246 inches—that is, almost an inch and a quarter. The mean temperature deduced from daily readings of the dry bulb thermometer at 9 a.m. and 9 p.m. was 57·4°, or 4·5° above the value for May, 1890. Using the formula, Mean Temp.=min.+(max.—min.×·465), the value was 57·6°, or 0·6° above the average mean temperature for June, calculated in the same way, in the twenty-five years, 1865–89, inclusive (57·0°). The arithmetical mean of the maximal and minimal readings was 58·1°, compared with a twenty-five years' average of 57·8°. On the 5th, the thermometer in the screen rose to 72·0°—wind S.W.; on the 7th the temperature fell to 43·5°—wind, N. The minimum on the grass was 39·5°, also on the 7th.

The rainfall amounted to 1·930 inches, distributed over 18 days. The average rainfall for June in the twenty-five years, 1865–89, inclusive, was 1·817 inches, and the average number of rainy days was 13·6. The rainfall and the rainy days, therefore, were above the average. In 1878 the rainfall in June was very large—5·058 inches on 19 days; in 1879 also 4·046 inches fell on 24 days. On the other hand, in 1865, only ·100 of an inch was measured on 5 days; in 1887, the rainfall was only ·231 of an inch, distributed over only 6 days; in 1874 only ·406 of an inch was measured on 8 days, and in 1868 only ·677 of an inch fell on but 6 days. In 1886 the rainfall was as much as 4·046 inches, distributed over as many as 18 days.

High winds were noted on 16 days, but attained the force of a gale on only two occasions—the 3rd and 24th. Temperature reached or exceeded 70° in the screen on only 8 days, as compared with 17 days in 1887, only 1 day in 1888, and 10 days in 1889. Thunder was heard on the 11th and 28th, and hail fell on the 29th and 30th.

In the first week the weather was chiefly favourable, although changeable, with squally westerly (W., S.W., and N.W.) winds, much cloud at times, and heavy rain in Scotland and the north, west, and south of Ireland, as well as in the south of England on Wednesday. The barometer was generally low in the extreme N. and N.W., high over the Bay of Biscay and central Europe. In Dublin the mean height of the barometer was 29·931 inches. The corrected mean temperature was 56·7°. The mean dry bulb temperature at 9 a.m. and 9 p.m. was 56·8°. Rain was measured on three days, the total quantity being ·285 inch.

During the greater part of the second week the weather was in an unsettled showery state, and thunder and lightning often accompanied the showers in various parts of the United Kingdom. Areas of low pressure were found in the W. and N.W., but on Thursday, the 12th, an area of high pressure formed over the Atlantic and gradients for northerly winds became established. In Dublin the mean height of the barometer was 29·927 inches, pressure ranging between 29·450 inches at 6 p.m. of Wednesday (wind, calm) and 30·375 inches—the maximum for the month—at 9 a.m. of Saturday (wind, N.W.). The corrected mean temperature was 57·6°, the mean dry bulb temperature at 9 a.m. and 9 p.m. being 56·7°. Rain fell in measurable quantity on four days, the total fall being ·427 inch.

Changeable, cloudy, and at times showery weather prevailed during the third week—particularly in Ireland and Scotland. Some bright intervals were experienced in England. The barometer was relatively high over the Bay of Biscay, France, and Germany; relatively low over Scotland and Scandinavia. Hence the fresh westerly winds, and showers, and clouds of the period. On Tuesday morning, the 17th, a partial eclipse of the sun was well seen through passing clouds—the magnitude of the eclipse was 279 out of 1,000 parts. In Dublin the mean height of the barometer was 30·084 inches. The corrected mean temperature was 58·9°; the mean dry bulb temperature at 9 a.m. and 9 p.m. being 58·2°. Rain fell in measurable quantity on four days, the total amount being ·391 inch.

The weather continued very changeable, squally, and showery during the period ending Saturday, the 28th. The general distribution of pressure was very like that observed in the previous week—that is, a relatively high barometer over the Bay of Biscay, France and Germany, with low pressure to the north-westward and northward of the British Isles and over northern Europe. Hence the prevalence of fresh westerly winds, clouds, and showers. The only serious depression observed was one which advanced rapidly towards the north of Scotland on Tuesday night, the 24th. It caused a dangerous gale in the Solway Firth, and in Scotland north of the Grampians—even in Dublin the wind rose to the force of a moderate gale for a short time. Very heavy showers fell on Friday and Saturday, accompanied by some thunder locally, and hail was also observed about noon on Saturday, when the wind veered to N. In Dublin the mean height of the barometer was 29·981 inches. The mean temperature was 57·5°; the mean dry bulb temperature at 9 a.m. and 9 p.m. was 57·6°. Rain was registered on five days—the total measurement being ·483 inch.

Sunday, the 29th, proved for the most part fine, but a brisk fall of the barometer took place as a depression, which was unusually deep for the time of year, advanced over the kingdom from W.N.W. On the 30th, heavy showers of rain and hail occurred, and the barometer sank to 29·120 inches at 9 p.m.

The rainfall in Dublin during the six months ending June 30th has amounted to 13·418 inches on 86 days, compared with 10·678 inches on 97 days during the same period in 1889, 12·118 inches on 87 days in 1888, 6·711 inches on 67 days in 1887, and a twenty-five years' average of 12·213 inches on 95·4 days.

At Ennisdalina, Greystones, County Wicklow, the rainfall in June, 1890, was 1·780 inches distributed over 18 days. Of this quantity ·410 inch fell on the 11th, ·300 inch on the 4th, and ·340 inch on the 29th.

July.—A very unsettled, squally, showery, cool month, with a great preponderance of south-westerly to north-westerly winds—a very common state of things in an Irish July.

In Dublin the mean temperature (58·1°) was decidedly below the average (60·8°); the mean dry bulb readings at 9 a.m. and 9 p.m. were 57·8°. In the twenty-five years ending with 1889, July was coldest in 1879 (the "cold year") (M. T. = 57·2°). It was warmest in 1887 (M. T. = 63·7°), and in 1868 (the "warm year") (M. T. = 63·5°). In 1886, the M. T. was 61·0°; in 1888 it was as low as 57·3°; in 1889, it was 58·7°. From this, 1887 proves to have been the warmest since the present records commenced, whilst July, 1888, was almost the coldest.

The mean height of the barometer was 29·894 inches, or 0·030 inch below the corrected average value for July—namely, 29·915 inches. The mercury marked 30·238 inches at 9 a.m. of the 30th, and fell to 29·296 inches at 9 p.m. of the 7th. The observed range of atmospherical pressure was, therefore, 0·942 inches—that is, a little less than an inch. The mean temperature deduced from daily readings of the dry bulb thermometer at 9 a.m. and 9 p.m. was 57·6°, or 0·4° above the value for June, 1890. Using the formula, *Mean Temp.* = min. + (max.—min. × ·465), the value was 57·7°, or 2·5° below the average mean temperature for July, calculated in the same way, in the twenty-five years, 1865–89, inclusive (60·2°). The arithmetical mean of the maximal and minimal readings was 58·1°, compared with a twenty-five years' average of 60·6°. On the 18th, the thermometer in the screen rose to 78·6°—wind W.S.W.; on the 5th the temperature fell to 44·4°—wind, N. The minimum on the grass was 41·0° on the latter date, and also on the 10th. The rainfall was 2·171 inches, distributed over 24 days. The average rainfall for July in the twenty-five years, 1865–89, inclusive, was 2·[illegible] inches, and the average number of rainy days was 17·2. The rainfall therefore, was somewhat below the average, while the rainy days were much above it. In 1880 the rainfall in July was very large—6·087 inches on 26 days; in 1877 also 4·391 inches fell on 23 days. On the other hand, in 1870, only ·539 of an inch was measured on 8 days; in 1869, the fall was only ·739 of an inch on 9 days, and in 1868, only ·741 of an inch fell on but 5 days.

High winds were noted on many days, but attained the force of a moderate gale on only two occasions—viz., the 14th and 23rd. Temperature reached or exceeded 70° in the screen on only 4 days. In July, 1887, temperature reached or exceeded 70° in the screen on no fewer than 17 days. In July, 1868, the maximum was 80·7°.

At the beginning of the month the weather was, if possible, more broken, cold and showery than in the previous few weeks. Heavy showers fell almost daily, the wind blew strongly at times and from more northerly and colder points than of late, the amount of cloud continued large by day; while the nights were often clear and very cold for the season. On Friday, the 4th, an area of low pressure advanced to the English Channel and South of England from W.S.W. It caused gales and heavy rain in the S.E. of England at night, when clear cold weather held in Ireland. The week closed with a rising barometer, a northerly wind, and a clearing sky.

During the week ending Saturday, the 12th, the weather showed no improvement, but rather the reverse. Cloudy skies, very low temperatures, raw north-westerly winds, and frequent rains or showers made up the record of a most unseasonable period. Numerous areas of low pressure, or their subsidiaries, travelled across the west and north-west of Europe—for the most part in a north-easterly direction—keeping the weather in a very unsettled, broken state. On Monday, the 7th, a downpour of rain, exceeding an inch, occurred over the greater part of Scotland, and the Grampians and other heights were covered with snow as in October. Even at Parsonstown in Central Ireland the thermometer sank to 33° in the screen on two consecutive nights during the week, and in Dublin the mean temperature for the week was 7° below the average. In this city the mean atmospherical pressure was 29·823 inches. The corrected mean temperature was 54·2°; the mean dry bulb temperature at 9 a.m. and 9 p.m. was 54·3°. Rain was measured on six days, the total quantity being ·443 inch.

The weather of the week ending Saturday, the 19th, was generally warmer and finer, although far from settled, especially in the south of England where severe thunderstorms occurred on Thursday, the 17th, accompanied by torrents of rain. On the whole the barometer remained—as in past weeks—low over the North of Europe, and several subsidiary depressions travelled across France and England, causing the electrical disturbances just mentioned. In Dublin a short spell of summer heat occurred on Sunday, when the thermometer rose to 72·8 in the screen. Early next morning the wind rose to a fresh gale from S.W., and this was followed in turn by heavy showers on the afternoons of both Monday and Tuesday. Temperature was at this time rising fast on the Continent, so that on Thursday readings of 84° were recorded in Paris, Berlin, and Brussels, while 89° was touched at Lyons. In the evening violent thunderstorms raged over the North of France, the South of England, and Belgium—1·78 inches of rain fell during the storm in London, 1·01 inches at Cambridge, and 1·09 inches in Paris. This day was very fine in Dublin. In Dublin the mean barometer was 29·891 inches, the mean temperature was 58·9°, the mean dry bulb readings at 9 a.m. and 9 p.m. being 58·5°. The screened thermometers rose to 72·5° on Sunday—the maximum of the month. Rain was recorded on five days, the total measurement being ·467 inch.

Although far from settled, the weather of the week ended Saturday, the 26th, was finer and warmer than for many weeks past. The barometer was throughout high off the S.W. and S. of Ireland, while several extensive areas of low pressure travelled eastwards across Northern Europe. Hence strong N.W. and W. winds prevailed almost daily. After a moderate rainfall on Sunday evening three blustering, but chiefly dry, days followed. Thursday was very fine, but in the evening dense sprays of cirrus cloud shot up across the sky from W., ushering in a depression, with unsettled weather which lasted to the close of the week. In Dublin the mean height of the barometer was 30·101 inches, pressure ranging from 30·323 inches at 9 a.m. of Sunday (wind, N.W.) to 29·830 inches, at 9 a.m. of Saturday (wind, W.S.W.). The corrected mean temperature was 61·3°; the mean dry bulb temperature at 9 a.m. and 9 p.m. being 60·9°. Rain was registered on four days, the total measurement being ·430 inch, of which ·374 inch was entered to Friday.

The last five days were changeable and showery.

The rainfall in Dublin during the seven months ending July 31st has amounted to 13·587 inches on 118 days, compared with 12·146 inches on 111 days during the same period in 1889, 16·994 inches on 109 days in 1888, 7·636 inches on 80 days in 1887, and a 25 years' average of 11·723 inches on 112·6 days.

At Knockdolian, Greystones, Co. Wicklow, the rainfall in July was 1·489 inches, distributed over 19 days. Of this quantity ·280 inch fell on the 7th, and ·210 inch on the 31st.

August.—Except for a fine warm period extending from the 2nd to the 5th inclusive, and for a few isolated fine, but cool days afterwards, this month proved showery, cold, and squally—the reduction of temperature after the 21st being especially remarkable. The prevailing wind was N.W. and temperature was 2·5° below the average. Happily, near Dublin, there were no torrential rains as in August, 1889, in which month 1·320 inches fell on the 10th and 1·943 inches on the 19th; but the frequency of the showers chilled the atmosphere and delayed the harvest.

In Dublin the mean temperature (57·8°) was decidedly below the average (60·3°); the mean dry bulb readings at 9 a.m. and 9 p.m. were 56·5°. In the twenty-five years ending with 1889, August was coldest in 1881 (M. T.=57·0°), and warmest in 1871 (M. T.=63·0°). In 1883, the M. T. was only 57·1°; in 1879 (the "cold year"), it was 57·7°; in 1887, it was 60·8°; in 1888, it was 58·3°, and in 1889, 58·6°.

The mean height of the barometer was 29·873 inches, or 0·019 inch below the corrected average value for August—namely, 29·897 inches. The mercury marked 30·391 inches at 9 p.m. on the 31st, and fell to 29·359 inches at 4·30 p.m. of the 26th. The observed range of atmospherical pressure was, therefore, 1·032 inches—that is, a little more than an inch. The mean temperature deduced from daily readings of the dry bulb thermometer at 9 a.m. and 9 p.m. was 56·3°, or 1·9° below the value in August, 1888 and 1889, and 1·5° below the value for July, 1890. Using the formula, *Mean Temp. = Min. + (max.—min. × ·47)*, the value was 55·9°, or 2·4° below the average mean temperature for August, calculated in the same way, in the twenty-five years, 1865–89, inclusive (59·3°). The arithmetical mean of the maximal and minimal readings was 57·2°, compared with a twenty-five years' average of 59·7°. On the 4th, the thermometer in the screen rose to 74·8°—wind, S.W.; on the 31st the temperature fell to 41·5°—wind, N. The minimum on the grass was 35·6° on the latter date. The rainfall was 2·790 inches, distributed over 19 days. The average rainfall for August in the twenty-five years, 1865–89, inclusive, was 2·834 inches, and the average number of rainy days was 15·5. The rainfall therefore, was slightly less than the average, while the rainy days were considerably in excess of the average. In 1874, the rainfall in August was very large—4·146 inches on 18 days—and in 1888 also 4·745 inches fell on, however, only 13 days; but the heaviest downpour in August occurred in 1869, when 4·747 inches were registered on 22 days. On the other hand, in 1884, only ·777 inch was measured on 8 days. In 1887, 1·550 inches of rain fell on 15 days, and in 1889, 1·270 inches on 18 days.

High winds were noted on as many as 11 days, and attained the force of a gale on two occasions—namely, the 13th and 22nd. The atmosphere was foggy on the 1st. Lightning was seen on the 15th, and a thunderstorm, with hail, occurred at Greystones, Co. Wicklow, on the 26th. Temperature reached or exceeded 70° in the screen on only 3 days, the 4th and 5th—or 8 fewer than in August, 1887, and one more than in August, 1888. Hail fell on the 23rd.

On Friday, the 1st, the unexpected approach of a shallow depression caused very wet inclement weather.

At the commencement of the week ending Saturday, the 9th, the weather was very warm, temperature having risen to 74·8°, and generally fair. The arrival of a shallow depression on Wednesday caused dull weather with drizzling rain at first, but the evening was beautifully fine. Thursday was clear and fine, with easterly wind. Friday was fine and warm, but a dense haze prevailed during the whole day. Saturday was fine but cloudy, with fresh to strong north-easterly wind. The barometer fell slowly during Thursday and Friday, and quickly on Saturday. The mean height of the barometer in Dublin during this week was 30·185 inches. The corrected mean temperature was 61·6°; the mean of the dry bulb thermometer at 9 a.m. and 9 p.m. daily being 61·5°. The rainfall equalled ·310 inch on two days.

In most respects the weather of the period ending Saturday, the 16th, presented a marked contrast to that of the previous week. Low and varying atmospherical pressure, a reduced temperature, clouds, squally westerly (N.W. to S.W.) winds, and frequent showers took the place of the high and steady pressure, warmth and sunshine, and easterly winds so prevalent in the first week of the month. During the first four days a thunderstorm depression travelled slowly in an east-north-easterly direction across England and the North Sea; while a deep depression passed over Ireland and Scotland from S.W. to N.E. on Thursday night and Friday. This latter disturbance caused fresh S.W. to W. gales and a very general rainfall—the precipitation being greatest in the N.W. of Ireland. In Dublin the mean height of the barometer was 29·694 inches. The corrected mean temperature was 57·4°. The mean dry bulb reading at 9 a.m. and 9 p.m. was 57·0°. Rain fell to the amount of ·459 inch on five days. Sheet lightning was seen on Friday night, the 15th.

The weather of the third week (16th–23rd, inclusive) was in keeping with that of almost the whole season—it was changeable, cool, squally, and showery. A very heavy fall of rain took place on the evening of Friday, the 22nd, and hail fell on Saturday, the 23rd. The general distribution of air-pressure was this—lowest off the N.W. of Norway, secondary depressions crossing the United Kingdom and France from the south-westward, a ridge of comparatively high pressure extending from the Peninsula across Central Europe. On Monday night and Tuesday a thunderstorm depression caused heavy rains in the S. and S.E. of England, but at this time the weather was chiefly fine in Ireland. On Friday, however, a depression advanced rapidly from S.W. across this country, and heavy rains resulted. In Dublin, the mean height of the barometer was 29·869 inches. The corrected mean temperature was 56·6°; the mean dry bulb temperature at 9 a.m. and 9 p.m. was 56·1°. Rain fell on five days, the total measurement being 1·038 inches, of which ·851 inch was referred to Friday. Hail fell on Saturday.

The week ended Saturday, the 30th, was again one of broken weather—cold, squally, and very showery. The barometer was generally low in the N., relatively high in the S., and several well-marked cyclonic systems passed in an easterly or north-easterly direction across North-Western Europe. At 8 a.m. of Thursday, the 28th, the barometer was as low as 28·98 inches at Haparanda, the Gulf of Bothnia. On Friday, the 29th, a decided and general increase of pressure took place, gradients became slight, and the weather improved, although temperature remained low. In Dublin rain fell in greater or less quantity daily. Falls of hail occurred near the city on Sunday and Tuesday—a thunderstorm passing over Greystones, Co. Wicklow, on the afternoon of the latter day. Although conditions were quieter on Friday and Saturday, yet evaporation showers fell locally in Dublin, chiefly owing to the prevalence of variable sea breezes during the daytime. In Dublin the mean height of the barometer was 29·789 inches, pressure ranging from 29·359 inches at 4·30 p.m. of Tuesday (wind, W.N.W.), to 30·150 inches at 9 p.m. of Saturday (wind, N.). The corrected mean temperature was 51·9°—the mean dry bulb temperature at 9 a.m. and 9 p.m. being 51·5°. The rainfall equalled ·640 inch, distributed over six days. On Monday ·238 inch was measured. The week closed with signs of more settled weather, and Sunday, the 31st, was beautifully fine, although very cool.

The rainfall in Dublin during the eight months ending August 31st has amounted to 18·[illegible] inches on 137 days compared with 9·454 inches on 94 days during the same period in 1887, 17·[illegible] inches on 121 days in 1888, 18·923 inches on 134 days in 1889, and a 25 years' average of 17·[illegible] inches on 122·1 days.

At Knockdolian, Greystones, Co. Wicklow, the rainfall in August, 1890, was 2·316 inches, distributed over 16 days. Of this quantity ·460 inch fell on the 10th, and ·[illegible] inch on the [illegible]th.

SEPTEMBER.—As in 1888 and 1889, so in 1890, September proved a fine month, with a high mean barometer. The prevailing winds were from warm quarters—chiefly S.W. There was no excessive rainfall, and temperature was remarkably high. From the 4th to the 15th, inclusive, conditions were anticyclonic, and the weather was summerlike. On the 29th a violent gale occurred, accompanied by very heavy rain. Taken, however, as a whole, the month was very favourable from an agricultural as well as from a health point of view.

In Dublin the mean temperature (59·6°) was much above the average (55·6°); the mean dry bulb readings at 9 a.m. and 9 p.m. were 59·9°. In the twenty-five years ending with 1890, September was coldest in 1886 and in 1883 (M. T.=53·0°), and warmest in 1865 (M. T.=61·[illegible]°). In 1880, the M. T. was as high as 58·6°; in the year 1879 (the "cold year"), it was 54·8°; in 1887, it was 54·9°; in 1888, it was 54·[illegible]°, and in 1889, 55·5°, or exactly the average. So warm a September has not occurred for a quarter of a century.

The mean height of the barometer was 30·081 inches, or 0·161 inch above the average value for September—namely, 29·910 inches. The mercury rose to 30·467 inches at 9 a.m. of the 5th, and fell to 29·237 inches at 9 p.m. of the 30th. The observed range of atmospherical pressure was, therefore, 1·230 inches—that is, a little less than one inch and a quarter. The mean temperature deduced from daily readings of the dry bulb thermometer at 9 a.m. and 9 p.m. was 59·9°; or 6·6° above the value for August, 1890. Using the formula *Mean Temp.=min.+(max.−min.×·476)*, the value was 59·3°, or 3·8° above the average mean temperature for September, calculated in the same way, in the twenty-five years 1865–89, inclusive (55·5°). The arithmetical mean of the maximal and minimal readings was 59·6°, compared with a twenty-five years' average of 55·8°. On the 7th, the thermometer in the screen rose to 71·2°—wind, S.S.E.; on the 23rd the temperature fell to 46·9°—wind, N.W. The minimum on the grass was 42·0° on the 1st and 18th. The rainfall was 2·459 inches distributed over 14 days—the rainfall was somewhat above and the rainy days were somewhat below the average. The average rainfall for September in the twenty-five years, 1865–89, inclusive, was 2·176 inches, and the average number of rainy days was 14·7. In 1871, the rainfall in September was very large—4·048 inches on, however, only 18 days. On the other hand, in 1865, only ·056 inch was measured on but 3 days. In 1888, the rainfall was only ·723 inch on 10 days, and in 1889, 1·018 inches fell on 13 days.

High winds were noted on as many as 15 days, but attained the force of a gale on only three occasions—the 20th, 28th, and 29th. A solar halo appeared on the 10th, and sheet lightning was seen on the night of the 14th.

The first week happily witnessed a marked improvement in the weather, which became much warmer and finer—particularly in the east of Ireland and the S.E. and S. of England. This fortunate change was brought about by the establishment and development of an anticyclone, which had already appeared over Ireland on Saturday, August 30. At the beginning of the period temperature was very low and the wind was northerly. On Monday, September 1, however, a depression to the far N.W. caused a S.W. wind, which brought with it warmth and rain. The downpour was heavy in the N. and N.W. of Ireland, but moderate on the east coast. It blew freshly from S.W. or W. until Thursday, after which day light, variable winds set in. The week closed with beautiful weather. At Munich 7·16 inches of rain fell in the 7 days ending at 8 a.m. of Friday, the 5th. In Dublin the mean height of the barometer was 30·[illegible] inches, pressure ranging from 29·[illegible] inches at 9 a.m. of Tuesday (wind, S.W.), to 30·457 inches at 9 a.m. of Saturday (wind, N.). The corrected mean temperature was 59·5°—the mean dry bulb reading at 9 a.m. and 9 p.m. being 59·7°. The rainfall was ·249 inch on 3 days. Of this quantity ·168 inch was referred to Wednesday, the 3rd, when the fall at Greystones was ·340 inch.

The improvement in the weather observed in the first week developed in, and continued through, the second week. It is true that strong winds were felt at times, while rain fell in the N.W. of Ireland and over the greater part of Scotland on several days; but in the E. and S. of Ireland and almost throughout England the week was practically rainless. At the beginning the centre of a well-formed anticyclone was found over Lincolnshire, where the height of the barometer at this time slightly exceeded 30·50 inches. This system subsequently moved slowly southwards, causing southerly winds and high temperature in Ireland and afterwards less settled conditions in the N.W. of this country. On Wednesday a new, but not so pronounced an area of high pressure began to spread over Ireland from the westward, whence it continued its course in an easterly direction, reaching England on Friday. Under its influence a further spell of fine weather was enjoyed. In Dublin the mean height of the barometer was 30·279 inches. The corrected mean temperature was 60·[illegible]°. The mean dry bulb temperature at 9 a.m. and 9 p.m. was 60·[illegible]°. There was no measurable rainfall at this station, although light showers fell on Tuesday.

The fine weather experienced during the previous two weeks came to end in the course of the third seven-day period, which—having opened fair and warm—closed with a tempest and downpour of rain. This unfortunate change was brought about by the retreat of the anticyclone towards N.E., while barometrical depressions of increasing intensity encroached more and more upon the British Isles as the week advanced. Even on Sunday signs of the untoward change were not wanting in Ireland, where a southerly wind freshened, cloud increased, and sheet lightning was seen after dark. At night also rain fell heavily on the W. coast. It was not until Wednesday morning, however, that the wet weather reached the E. coast, and on this and the following day thunderstorms occurred in England. The most extensive and deepest of the series of depressions arrived on Saturday, which proved a day of storm and rain. In Dublin the mean height of the barometer was 29·776 inches, pressure decreasing intermittently from 30·154 inches at 9 a.m. of Sunday (wind, S.S.E.), to 29·227 inches at 9 p.m. of Saturday (wind blowing a gale from S. by E.). The corrected mean temperature was 57·5°. The mean dry bulb temperature at 9 a.m. and 9 p.m. was 58·0°. Rain fell on five days to the amount of 1·728 inches, ·434 inch being measured on Wednesday, ·310 inch on Friday, and ·878 inch on Saturday. Sheet lightning was seen on Sunday night. The rainfall for the week at Knockdolian, Greystones, was 2·010 inches.

Opening with storm and rain, the fourth week (21st–27th inclusive) closed in sunshine and the warmth of midsummer—the intervening period being one of cloud and sunshine; passing showers and fresh or squally westerly winds. At 8 a.m. of Sunday the centre of a cyclone of great energy was found over Mayo, whence it had advanced from Kerry during the previous night. The barometer read 29·04 inches at Belmullet, but had been down to 28·81 inches at Valentia Island, in Kerry, at 6 p.m. the previous day. Fresh southerly (S.E. to S.W.) gales and heavy rain accompanied the disturbance, while thunderstorms occurred in England and France on its outskirts. The system travelled slowly away to N.N.E., and finally dispersed. On Thursday a large anticyclone advanced from the Atlantic over our southern districts, while depressions skirted our northern coasts. The result was a moderate gale from W. and showers at exposed stations. On Saturday the weather became brilliant and very warm. In Dublin the mean height of the barometer was 30·037 inches. The corrected mean temperature was 55·2°. The mean dry bulb temperature at 9 a.m. and 9 p.m. was 57·5°. The rainfall was ·125 inch on 3 days; of this amount ·058 inch fell on Sunday. A lunar rainbow was seen at Greystones on the evening of Wednesday, the 24th.

The closing days of the month were breezy, and showers fell at times. On the night of the 30th there was a fresh S.W. gale, and rain fell heavily.

The rainfall in Dublin during the nine months ending September 30th has amounted to 20·235 inches on 151 days, compared with 10·968 inches on 118 days during the same period in 1887, 17·092 inches on 131 days in 1888, 19·936 inches on 147 days in 1889, and a twenty-five years' average of 19·731 inches on 142·8 days.

At Knockdolian, Greystones, County Wicklow, the rainfall in September, 1890, was 3·155 inches, distributed over 11 days. Of this quantity ·760 inch fell on the 17th, and ·730 inch on the 29th.

October.—October, 1890, will be remembered as one of the driest, finest, and mildest on record in the east of Ireland. In the west of this country and in Scotland it was much less favourable, the weather being often squally and wet. During the first fortnight temperature was almost always above the average. On the 25th a cold period set in, which culminated in Ireland on the 27th and in England on the 28th—the thermometer in the screen sinking to 20° at Loughborough, 23° at Oxford and Dungeness, and 24° in London. This premature "cold snap" was followed by mild, dull, and damp weather to the end of the month. As regards atmospherical pressure, the general tendency was for an area of high barometer (anticyclone) to stretch across Ireland, England, and Central Europe, while areas of low pressure swept eastwards across Northern Europe.

In Dublin the mean temperature (51·7°) was considerably above the average (49·7°); the mean dry bulb readings at 9 a.m. and 9 p.m. were 50·0°. In the twenty-five years ending with 1889, October was coldest in 1880 (M. T. = 45·4°), and in 1885 (M. T. = 45·5°), and warmest in 1876 (M. T. = 52·1°). In 1886, the M. T. was as high as 52·0°; in the year 1879 (the "cold year"), it was 49·7°. In 1887, it was as low as 47·3°; in 1888, it was 49·1°, and in 1889 it was only 48·1°.

The mean height of the barometer was 30·109 inches, or 0·199 inch above the average value for October—namely, 29·910 inches. The mercury rose to 30·539 inches at 9 p.m. of the 22nd, and fell, to 29·466 inches at nine a.m. of the 28th. The observed range of atmospherical pressure was therefore, 1·073 inches—that is, a little less than an inch and one tenth.

The mean temperature deduced from daily readings of the dry bulb thermometer at 9 a.m. and 9 p.m. was 50·9°, or 8·0° below the value for September, and 5·4° below that for August, 1890. The arithmetical mean of the maximal and minimal readings was 51·7°, compared with a twenty-five years' average of 49·7°. Using the formula, *Mean Temp. = Min.* + (max.—min. × ·465), the value was 51·3°, or 2·0° above the average mean temperature for October, calculated in the same way, in the twenty-five years, 1865–89, inclusive, (49·3°). On the 5th the thermometer in the screen rose to 65·8°—wind, W.S.W.; on the 27th the temperature fell to 34·7°—wind, N.W. The minimum on the grass was 28·9° also on the 27th; on three nights the thermometer sank below 32° on the grass.

The rainfall was only ·829 inch, distributed over 11 days—both rainfall and rainy days were largely below average. The average rainfall for October in the twenty-five years, 1865–89, inclusive, was 3·106 inches, and the average number of rainy days was 17·6. In 1880 the rainfall in October was very large—7·358 inches on 18 days. In 1875, also, 7·049 inches fell on 26 days. On the other hand, in 1884, only ·834 inch was measured on but 14 days, and in 1868 only ·856 inch on 14 days. In 1888, the rainfall was 1·237 inches on 18 days, and in 1889 no less than 4·633 inches fell on 23 days. From these figures, October, 1890, proves to have been the driest on record for more than a quarter of a century at least.

A lunar halo was seen on the 23rd. High winds were noted on 11 days, but attained the force of a gale on only one occasion—the 15th. The atmosphere was more or less foggy in Dublin on the 8th, 9th, 11th, 17th, and 23rd. Lightning was seen on the evening of the 15th. Snow and sleet fell on the morning of this same day, and hail on the 16th.

A great dip in temperature accompanied a ridge of high pressure which travelled from W. to E. across Ireland and England on Wednesday and Thursday, the 1st and 2nd, but the thermometer soon recovered itself as a fresh S.W. wind sprang up.

The general character of the weather during the week ending Saturday, the 11th, was fine in the south, unsettled and rainy in the far north, cold in Scandinavia. The barometer stood high in an anticyclone stretching east and west across Central Europe, and interrupted only for a time on Tuesday, the 7th, by the appearance of a depression over Ireland, which subsequently moved southeastwards and underwent considerable modifications both in size and intensity. This system caused the only bad weather of the period in Ireland and England—a heavy fall of rain occurring on the 7th over the greater part of both countries. In the rear of this disturbance the barometer rose with great rapidity, and the anticyclone became re-established, lasting to the end of the week and causing beautiful weather. Winter seemed to be setting in with considerable severity over Northern Europe as the week passed by. In Dublin the mean height of the barometer was 30·210 inches. The corrected mean temperature was 55·6°. The mean dry bulb temperature at 9 a.m. and 9 p.m. was 51·6°. The thermometers in the screen rose to 64·1° on Sunday and fell to 39·9° on Thursday. Rain fell to the amount of ·[illegible] inch. The prevailing wind was W.S.W.

At first fair and bright, the weather of the week ended Saturday, the 18th, afterwards became unsettled—squally, showery, and cold. Towards the end of the week an improvement took place, so that the period under review proved generally favourable. During the first three days a large anticyclone over Central Europe included in its influence England and the southern half of Ireland, while conditions were cyclonic over the northern portion of the British Islands. Dense fogs occurred at this time in England, where temperature was very low by night and in the mornings. On and after Tuesday, the anticyclone retreated southwards, and an extensive V-shaped depression encroached upon Western Europe. In the rear of its axis, strong N.W. winds sprang up, accompanied by showers of cold rain, hail, and some sleet. At several English stations thunder and lightning occurred on Wednesday and Thursday. On Friday the weather improved and Saturday was fine. In Dublin the mean pressure was 30·064 inches. The corrected mean temperature was 49·4°. The mean dry bulb reading at 9 a.m. and 9 p.m. was 48·6°. Rain fell to the amount of ·161 inch, ·082 inch being measured on Wednesday, the 15th, when hail was also observed. The prevailing winds were W. and N.W.

Dull, but otherwise favourable and mild, weather prevailed during the greater part of the week ended Saturday, the 25th. On Friday conditions became less settled and a considerable rainfall occurred on Saturday morning. At first an anticyclone lay over Ireland, while a very extensive and deep depression had its centre over the Baltic Provinces of Russia. The winds were northwesterly and the weather was fine in Ireland. Four mild, cloudy days followed, with light drizzling showers from time to time in places. On Tuesday night a remarkable "chill" took place on the Continent and over the S.E. of England—at Belfort, in Alsace, the thermometer sank from 61° to 33° in less than twenty-four hours. On Friday the anticyclone moved away southwards, and large depressions began to encroach more and more upon the British coasts—the wind backed to W.S.W. and freshened considerably with rain or passing showers. In Dublin the mean height of the barometer was 30·253 inches, pressure rising to 30·459 inches at 9 p.m. of Wednesday (wind, W.N.W.), the maximum of the month. The corrected mean temperature was 53·3°. The mean dry bulb temperature at 9 a.m. and 9 p.m. was 51·3°. The thermometers in the screen fell to 40·5° on Sunday and rose next day to 59·9°. The rainfall was ·875 inch; there were three rainy days, and the heaviest fall in 24 hours was ·164 inch on Saturday. The prevailing wind was northwesterly.

The weather was in every respect most changeable during the closing period of the month (26th–31st, inclusive). At the beginning, the centre of an extensive and deep depression was found over the South of Sweden, while subsidiaries travelled southwards across the British Islands. Very unsettled weather prevailed, squally northerly winds, with showers of wet snow and hail being reported from many stations. In Dublin sleet and snow fell on the morning of Sunday, the 26th, and the mountains were white with snow. After nightfall lightning was seen, and thunder and lightning occurred in several places. The cold culminated in a severe frost over England on Monday night and Tuesday morning, the 27th and 28th. The lowest temperatures recorded in the screen were 20° at Loughborough, 23° at Dungeness and Oxford, and 24° in London. This premature cold was followed by an extraordinary and rapid rise of temperature, amounting in 24 hours to 33° at Loughborough, 31° at York and Oxford, 27° at Shields, and 32° in London. The remainder of the period was mild, the air being often damp.

The rainfall in Dublin during the ten months ending October 31st has amounted to 21·491 inches on 162 days, compared with 17·368 inches on 153 days during the same period in 1887, 19·219 inches on 157 days in 1888, 24·789 inches on 169 days in 1889, and a twenty-five years' average of 22·840 inches on 160·4 days.

At Knockdolian, Greystones, Co. Wicklow, the rainfall in October, 1890, was only ·600 inch, distributed over 16 days. Of this quantity ·180 inch fell on the 6th, and ·120 inch on the 14th. The rainfall at Greystones in October, 1889, was no less than 6·951 inches on 23 days, or more than eleven times as great as the fall in October, 1890.

November.—A wet, stormy, cheerless month, reminding one of November, 1888, which was the wettest and most stormy November observed in Dublin for more than a quarter of a century. The weather remained open until the 24th, when a spell of snowstorms and bitter cold set in with peculiar suddenness. On the 19th the thermometer rose in Dublin to 63° in the screen; on the 25th it fell to 30·3°. On several evenings bright "afterglows" were seen. A snowstorm on the night of the 26th–27th was the heaviest experienced since the memorable storm of January 17, 1881.

In Dublin the mean temperature (45·3°) was somewhat above the average (44·7°); the mean dry bulb readings at 9 a.m. and 9 p.m. were 44·3°. In the twenty-five years ending with 1889, November was coldest in 1878 (M. T. = 39·5°), and in 1870 (M. T. = 45·8°), and warmest in 1881 (M. T. = 50·3°)

in 1846 and in 1882 the M.T. was as high as 46·4°; in the year 1879 (the "cold year"), it was 43·9°; in 1887, it was as low as 42·6°; and in 1888, it was as high as 47·6°.

The mean height of the barometer was 29·877 inches, or 0·023 inch below the average value for November—namely, 29·900 inches, and 0·257 inch below the mean pressure in November, 1889—viz., 30·134 inches. The mercury rose to 30·404 inches at 9 p.m. of the 19th and fell to 29·787 inches at 6 p.m. of the 6th. The observed range of atmospherical pressure was, therefore, 1·[illegible] inches—that is, nearly an inch and seven-tenths.

The mean temperature deduced from daily readings of the dry bulb thermometer at 9 a.m. and 9 p.m. was 44·7°, or 6·6° below the value for October, and 14·6° below that for September, 1890. The arithmetical mean of the maximal and minimal readings was 44·9°, compared with a twenty-five years' average of 44·7°. On the 19th the thermometer in the screen rose to 62·0°—wind, S.W.; on the 29th the temperature fell to 28·3°—wind, W. The minimum on the grass was 23·[illegible]°, also on the 29th.

The rainfall was as much as 4·219 inches, distributed over 27 days—both rainfall and rainy days were therefore largely in excess of the average values. The average rainfall for November in the twenty-five years, 1865–89, inclusive, was 2·452 inches, and the average number of rainy days was 17·0. In 1876 the rainfall in November was large—3·614 inches on 20 days; in 1872, also, 3·415 inches fell on 24 days; in 1887, 3·019 inches fell on 15 days, and in 1888, 5·549 inches fell on [illegible] days. On the other hand, the rainfall in 1889 was only ·920 inch on 9 days; in 1870, only 1·218 inches were measured on but 11 days, and in 1879 only 1·231 inches on but 10 days. The excess of the rainfall in 1890, and the equally marked deficit in 1889, are evident from these figures.

A solar halo was seen on the 13th. High winds were noted on as many as 12 days, and attained the force of a gale on 5 occasions—the 2nd, 6th, 14th, 23rd and 30th. The atmosphere was more or less foggy in Dublin on the 13th, 17th, 18th, and 20th. Hail fell on the 21th and four following days. Sleet and snow fell on the 20th, 27th, and 29th.

Very rough, unsettled, rainy weather prevailed during the greater part of the week ended Saturday, the 8th. There were, however, some clear intervals, Wednesday and Friday in particular being fine and bright. A succession of cyclonic systems swept across Western Europe, accompanied by gales and rains. Of these the deepest were observed on Sunday and Thursday. At 8 a.m. of the former day the barometer was down to 28·69 inches at Sumburgh Head, in the Shetlands, while it stood at 30·23 inches at Lisbon. Needless to say there were heavy S.W. to N.W. gales over the British Isles. During the next three days a complex low-pressure system travelled south-eastwards across these islands to Germany. But it was on Thursday that the most destructive and fatal disturbance of the week advanced from the Atlantic. Even in Dublin the barometer fell to 29·787 inches at 6 p.m. In front of the centre of this depression southerly gales prevailed, in its rear whole gales from W., N.W., and N. were experienced. A new disturbance caused a heavy rainfall on Saturday. In Dublin the mean height of the barometer was only 29·424 inches—the highest reading was 29·670 inches at 9 p.m. of Wednesday (wind, N.W.); the lowest was 29·787 inches twenty-three hours later (wind, W.). The corrected mean temperature was 45·6°. The mean dry bulb reading at 9 a.m. and 9 p.m. was 44·9°. The rainfall was ·909 inch on seven days. The wind varied between S.W. and N.W.

Very changeable, rainy weather prevailed in Ireland almost throughout the second week, also. Conditions were more favourable in England, especially in the S.E. and E. of that country. The general distribution of atmospherical pressure was: anticyclonic over Northern Europe and also over the Peninsula—cyclonic in the British Islands and their neighbourhood. The centres of low pressure were usually found off the W. and N.W. of Ireland and of Scotland; but on Sunday such a centre lay over the N.E. of England, while very heavy rain fell on the east coast of Scotland, in Cheshire, and in North Wales. On Monday night there was a downpour in and about Dublin. Thursday and Saturday were fine, bright days, and on Friday—with a S.W. wind, clouds and rain—came a great rise of temperature—from 39·2° to 60·6° in a few hours. An anticyclone spread over Ireland on Saturday. In Dublin the mean height of the barometer was 29·678 inches. The corrected mean temperature was 44·2°. The mean dry bulb temperature at 9 a.m. and 9 p.m. was 43·5°. Rain fell on six days to the amount of 1·107 inches, the heaviest fall in 24 hours being ·635 inch on Monday. The wind varied between S. and N.W.

The remarkable mildness of the weather throughout Western Europe was the chief feature of the third week. On Wednesday the thermometer rose above 60° in England and Ireland and to that point in Scotland. All through the week an area of high atmospherical pressure held over France and Germany, while depressions of no great intensity passed northeastwards along the coasts of Ireland, Scotland, and Norway. Hence there was a continued prevalence of S.W. winds, accompanied by high temperature and occasional but not excessive rains. In Russia snow fell heavily, and, as a result, severe frost set in, the thermometer sinking to −11° Fahr., or 43° below freezing point, at Archangel on Tuesday, and at Moscow to −11° on Wednesday and −15° on Friday. In Dublin a very dense vapour fog was observed on Tuesday, but next day the temperature rose to 62° in the screen. This was the highest temperature recorded in Dublin in November since the 6th of this month in the year 1872. In Dublin the mean height of the barometer was 30·203 inches, pressure rising to 30·408 inches at 9 p.m. of Wednesday (wind, S.W., light). The corrected mean temperature was 50·4°, or 6·1° above that of the previous week. The mean dry bulb temperature at 9 a.m. and 9 p.m. was 50·3°. Rain fell on five days to the amount of ·455 inch.

The week ended Saturday, the 29th, witnessed an extraordinary change all over western and central Europe from the abnormally mild weather previously so prevalent to heavy snowstorms and extreme cold. The way in which this change was brought about is noteworthy. On Sunday the centre of a vast and deep depression, in which the barometer was down to 28·70 inches, lay over the Christiania Fjord in Norway; south of the centre warm S.W. and W. gales were blowing, while to the northward of it an inrush of intensely cold E. wind took place. This cold current curved southwards and swept over the British Isles as a keen N. wind on Monday, accompanied with heavy rain at first, and hail and snow afterwards. On Wednesday and Thursday Dublin was visited by the heaviest snowstorm which has been experienced in this city since January 17, 1881. In the suburbs the snow lay to the depth of from 7 to 8 inches. In the S.E. of England the fall was even greater, and a keen frost prevailed, the thermometer falling to 17° in the screen at [illegible] on Friday morning. In Dublin a thaw occurred on this day, but sharp frost prevailed on Saturday morning, when the minimum was 26·3°. The mean height of the barometer was 29·[illegible] inches, pressure ranging between 29·[illegible] inches at 9 p.m. of Sunday (wind, W. by N., strong), and 30·[illegible] inches at 9 a.m. of Wednesday (wind, N.E., moderate). The corrected mean temperature was 33·1°, the mean dry bulb reading at 9 a.m. and 9 p.m. being 33·[illegible]°. The rainfall, which was largely in the form of snow and hail, measured 1·079 inches on seven days—the heaviest fall in 24 hours being ·610 inch on Wednesday, the 26th.

Sunday, the 30th, was a day of storm and rain, and the snow rapidly disappeared under the influence of a S.W. gale and warm rain.

The rainfall in Dublin during the eleven months ending November 30th has amounted to 25·706 inches on 169 days, compared with 15·274 inches on 141 days during the same period in 1887, 25·768 inches on 173 days in 1888, 25·718 inches on 175 days in 1889, and a twenty-five years' average of 25·297 inches on 177·6 days.

At Knockdolian, Greystones, Co. Wicklow, the rainfall in November, 1890, was no less than 5·970 inches, distributed over 18 days. Of this quantity 1·909 inch fell on the 6th, and ·780 of an inch on the 10th.

December.—A very cold, dull, foggy month, with much cloud (76·[illegible] per cent.) and prevalent easterly winds (that is, winds from points between S.E. and N.E.) these conditions were determined by the persistence of an anticyclone to the eastward and north-eastward, while areas of low pressure occasionally skirted the western shores of Ireland, Scotland and Norway in their passage northeastwards across the Atlantic Ocean and the Norwegian Sea. In central and south-eastern England intense frost was felt almost throughout the month, while the weather was at times open in Ireland and Scotland.

In Dublin the arithmetical mean temperature (39·[illegible]°) was decidedly below the average (41·[illegible]°); the mean dry bulb readings at 9 a.m. and 9 p.m. were 36·9°. In the twenty-five years ending with 1889, December was coldest in 1878 (M. T. = 33·8°), and in 1874 (M. T. = 36·[illegible]°) and warmest in 1865 (M. T. = 46·2°). In 1886 the M. T. was as low as 37·9°; in the year 1879 (the "cold year"), it was also 37·[illegible]°. In 1887 the M. T. was 39·[illegible]°; in 1888 it was 43·[illegible]°, and in 1889 it was 40·[illegible]°.

The mean height of the barometer was 30·025 inches, or 0·150 inch above the average value for December—namely, 29·875 inches. The mercury rose to 30·[illegible] inches at 9 a.m. of the [illegible], and fell to 29·[illegible] inches at 9 p.m. of the 18th. The observed range of atmospherical pressure was, therefore, 1·[illegible] inches—that is, a little more than one inch and a quarter.

The mean temperature deduced from daily readings of the dry bulb thermometer at 9 a.m. and 9 p.m. was 35·[illegible]°, or 6·[illegible]° below the value for November, and 1[illegible]·0° below that for October, 1890. Using the formula, *Mean Temp.* = *Min.* + (max.—min. × ·[illegible]), the value was 35·[illegible]°, or [illegible]° below the average mean temperature for December, calculated in the same way, in the twenty-five years, 1865-89, inclusive (41·[illegible]°). The arithmetical mean of the maximal and minimal readings was [illegible]°, compared with a twenty-five years' average of 41·[illegible]°. On the 1st the thermometer in the screen rose to 53·[illegible]°—wind, S.W.; on the 21st the temperature fell to 24·1°—wind, calm. The minimum on the grass was 20·1° also on the 21st. There were 8 days of frost in the screen and 20 days of frost on the grass.

The rainfall was 1·[illegible] inches, distributed over 11 days. The average rainfall for December in the twenty-five years, 1865-89, inclusive, was 2·[illegible] inches, and the average number of rainy days was 18·[illegible]. The rainfall, therefore, was decidedly below the average, while the rainy days were also much below it. In 1876 the rainfall in December was very large—7·[illegible] inches on 22 days. In 1872, 6·[illegible] inches fell on as many as 26 days; and in 1868 (which was otherwise a fine and dry year), 6·[illegible] inches fell on as many as 27 days. On the other hand, in 1867, only ·771 of an inch was measured on 13 days; and in 1871 the December rainfall was only ·777 of an inch on 15 days. In 1883, only ·743 of an inch of rain was measured on but 10 days, but in 1886 the rainfall was 3·[illegible] inches, distributed over as many as 21 days. In 1887 (the "dry year") the rainfall was 1·[illegible] inches on 19 days; in 1888, it was 2·911 inches on 17 days, and in 1889, 1·[illegible] inches fell on 15 days.

A lunar halo appeared on the 21st. High winds were noted on 10 days, but attained the force of a gale on only 2 occasions—the 16th and the 30th. The atmosphere was more or less foggy in Dublin on the 1st, 2nd, [illegible], 9th, 10th, 19th, 20th, 21st, 24th, and 25th. Snow or sleet fell on the 18th, 27th, and 31st. Hail fell on the 7th, 26th, 27th, 29th, 30th, and 31st.

While the weather remained cold on the Continent and in the S.E., E., and centre of England, a spell of damp warmth was felt in Ireland, Scotland, Wales, and the N. of England in the earlier part of the period ending Saturday, the 6th. This was followed by keen easterly winds and lower temperatures generally after Tuesday, the 2nd. On Monday the 1st, a warm S.W. current swept over Ireland, Scotland, and Scandinavia round a depression near Bodö, in Norway, where the barometer was as low as 28·[illegible] inches. On this day, temperature rose to 53·[illegible]° in Dublin and to 57° at Nairn and Leith. The barometer now rose in the N. and fell in the S., a heavy downpour of rain occurred, and an easterly current took the place of the warm S.W. winds. The last three days were dry and bleak. The corrected mean temperature was 45·[illegible]°. The mean of the dry bulb readings at 9 a.m. and 9 p.m. was 45·0°. The screened thermometers rose to 53·9° on Monday. The rainfall was 1·[illegible] inches on four days. Of this amount, ·[illegible] inch was registered on Tuesday. The wind was at first S.W., then calm, and finally N.E. to E.

Throughout the second week (7th–13th) an anticyclone lay over the North Sea, Denmark, and the Southern part of the Scandinavian Peninsula, affecting Germany, France, and England to a less extent. Depressions of no great depth were found over the Iberian Peninsula, and—on Wednesday and Thursday, the 10th and 11th—off the western coasts of Ireland and Scotland also. These barometrical conditions determined the weather of the week. Continuous hard frost held in Germany, Belgium, and the greater part of France. Cold weather and dense fogs prevailed in England; while it was milder—especially on Wednesday and Thursday—in Ireland and Scotland. On these days also considerable quantities of rain fell at most of the Irish stations. In Dublin the fall was only just perceptible—·002 inch on Thursday. The mean height of the barometer was 30·048 inches. The corrected mean temperature was [illegible]°—the mean of the dry bulb readings at 9 a.m. and 9 p.m. being 35·9°. The rainfall was only ·002 inch on Thursday. The prevailing wind was S.E., but from time to time the air was calm, with smoke fog over the city.

Exceptionally severe weather continued to prevail during the week ended Saturday, the 20th, in Germany, France, and the greater part of England. In Ireland and Scotland the cold was less intense, but still considerable, especially towards the close of the period. At 8 a.m. of Sunday the thermometer read 14° at Loughborough, 16° at Oxford, 18° at Cambridge, and 19° in London. It was 28° in Dublin at the same time. At night a shallow depression formed over the British Islands, and the wind shifted from S.W. to N.W. and N.E. in Ireland, with some cold showers on Monday, rain in Scotland, and snow in most parts of England. On Thursday a deep V-shaped depression advanced over Ireland from the Atlantic, and caused a S.E. to S. gale, with heavy rain and sleet or snow at night. The wind shifted to N.W. in the rear of this system on Friday, when the sky cleared and frost set in with haze and fog in Dublin. Meanwhile heavy falls of snow occurred in England, after which the frost stiffened again, and winter seemed fully established as the week drew to a close. In Dublin the mean height of the barometer was 29·771 inches, pressure falling to 29·183 inches at 8 p.m. of Thursday (wind, S.S.E., a gale). The corrected mean temperature was 37·3°; the mean dry bulb temperature at 9 a.m. and 9 p.m. was 36·9°. The rainfall was ·253 inch, on two days—·156 inch falling as rain and sleet on the night of the 18th–19th, when the record at Knockdolian, Greystones, Co. Wicklow, was ·850 inch, and that at Easton Lodge, Monkstown, Co. Dublin, was ·600 inch.

The fourth was another week of inclement weather—interrupted in Ireland and Scotland by a spell of milder conditions on Monday and Tuesday, the 22nd and 23rd. The week opened with severe frost in parts of Great Britain and Ireland, the lowest temperatures at 8 a.m. of Sunday being 14° at Loughborough, 18° at York, 20° at Parsonstown, 23° at Cambridge, and 24° at Aberdeen, Liverpool, and Dublin. In and about the last-named city there was a thick and beautiful rime, and it froze all day. Towards evening a depression, edging in from the west, brought a southerly wind and higher temperature. At 5·30 p.m. a lunar halo was visible. Next day was mild and dull in Ireland—the thermometer marking 40° at Parsonstown at 8 a.m., or [illegible]° higher than 24 hours previously. In England, however, the cold was on this day intense, among the 8 a.m. readings being these—Cambridge, 4°; Oxford, 9°; Loughborough, 10°; London, 14°; and York, 16°. On Tuesday, temperature again gave way in Ireland, but rose in England, although no decided thaw occurred. In Dublin Christmas Eve was frosty, calm, and foggy, but Christmas Day was dull and rainy at first; afterwards there was clear moonlight, followed by slight frost. Hail, graupel, and snow fell in heavy showers on Saturday, when there was a fresh breeze from E.N.E. to S.E. In Dublin the mean height of the barometer was 29·234 inches, pressure rising to 29·454 inches at 9 a.m. of Friday (wind, N.W.). The corrected mean temperature was 37·4°. The mean dry bulb temperature at 9 a.m. and 9 p.m. was 36·9°. The screened thermometers rose to 47·4° on Tuesday, having fallen to 24·1° on Sunday. The precipitation amounted to ·230 inch on four days, ·110 inch being registered on Friday. The wind was variable, and for the most part light.

Very cold, dry, and piercing easterly winds prevailed during the last four days of the month—culminating in a severe gale on the 30th, after which there was a fall of hail, snow, and soft hail (graupel). A thaw set in on the evening of the 31st.

The rainfall in Dublin during the year ending December 31st has amounted to 27·[illegible] inches on 200 days, compared with 27·273 inches on 183 days in 1889, 23·870 inches on 190 days in 1888, 18·601 inches on 160 days in 1887, and a twenty-five years' average of 27·686 inches on 194·8 days.

At Knockdolian, Greystones, Co. Wicklow, the rainfall in December, 1890, was 2·785 inches distributed over 14 days. Of this quantity ·780 of an inch fell on the 2nd, and ·850 of an inch on the 18th.

Rainfall in 1890,

At 40, Fitzwilliam-square, West, Dublin.

Rain Gauge:—Diameter of funnel, 8 in. Height of top—Above ground, 3 ft. 2 in.; above sea level, 50 ft.

Month.	Total Depth.	Greatest Fall in 24 hours.		Number of Days on which ·01 or more fell.	Month.	Total Depth.	Greatest Fall in 24 hours.		Number of Days on which ·01 or more fell.
	Inches.	Depth.	Date.			Inches.	Depth.	Date.	
January,	[illegible]	[illegible]	[illegible]	21	August,	[illegible]	[illegible]	[illegible]	19
February,	[illegible]	[illegible]	[illegible]	7	September,	[illegible]	[illegible]	[illegible]	14
March,	[illegible]	[illegible]	[illegible]	17	October,	[illegible]	[illegible]	[illegible]	[illegible]
April,	[illegible]	[illegible]	[illegible]	14	November,	[illegible]	[illegible]	[illegible]	27
May,	[illegible]	[illegible]	[illegible]	17	December,	[illegible]	[illegible]	[illegible]	11
June,	[illegible]	[illegible]	[illegible]	[illegible]					
July,	[illegible]	[illegible]	[illegible]	[illegible]	Total,	[illegible]	—	—	200

The rainfall was only ·134 of an inch in defect of the average annual measurement of the twenty-five years, 1865–89, inclusive—viz., 27·[illegible] inches.

It will be remembered that the rainfall in 1887 was very exceptionally small—16·601 inches, the only approach to this measurement in Dublin being in 1870, when only 20·859 inches fell, and in 1884, when the measurement was 20·467 inches. In seven of the twenty-five years in question the rainfall was less than 25 inches, and in 1885 it was 20·414 inches.

The scanty rainfall in 1887 was in marked contrast to the abundant downpour in 1886, when 32·954 inches—or as nearly as possible double the fall of 1887—fell on 220 days. Only twice since these records commenced has the rainfall in Dublin exceeded that of 1886—namely, in 1872, when 38·556 inches fell on 238 days, and in 1880, when 34·512 inches were measured on, however, only 188 days.

In 1890 there were 200 rainy days, or days upon which not less than ·01 inch of rain (one hundredth of an inch) was measured. This was in excess of the average number of rainy days, which was 194·3 in the twenty-five years, 1865–89, inclusive. In 1868—the warm dry year of recent times—as well as in 1887, the rainy days were only 160, and in 1870 they were only 145. In 1868, however, the rainfall amounted to 24·935 inches, or more than 8 inches above the measurement in 1887, and even in 1870, 20·859 inches were recorded. Included in the 200 rainy days in 1890, are 21 on which snow or sleet fell, and 28 on which there was hail. In January hail was observed on 8 days, in February once, in March on 3 days, and in April on 5 days. Hail also fell once in May, August, and October, twice in June, 2 times in November, and 6 times in December. Snow or sleet fell on 5 days in January, on 2 days in February, on 6 days in March, on 1 day in April, on 1 day in October, on 3 days in November, and on 3 days in December. Thunder occurred on four occasions during the year—on March 9th, April 24th, and June 11th and 26th. Lightning was also seen on one occasion in each of the following months—viz., May, August, September, and October.

The rainfall was distributed as follows:—7·570 inches fell on 45 days in the first quarter, 5·943 inches on 49 days in the second, 7·442 inches on 67 days in the third, and 6·707 inches on [illegible] days in the fourth and last quarter.

Of the 6·707 inches which fell in the fourth quarter of the year, 4·212 inches were measured in November on as many 27 days.

TABLE showing the Monthly and Yearly Rainfall at Dublin during the Twenty-one Years 1870 to 1890, inclusive; with the Means for the Twenty Years 1870 to 1889.

Year.	January.	February.	March.	April.	May.	June.	July.	August.	September.	October.	November.	December.	Total Amount.
	Inches.	Inches.	Inches.	Inches.	Inches.	Inches.	Inches.	Inches.	Inches.	Inches.	Inches.	Inches.	Inches.
1870,	[illegible]	[illegible]	[illegible]	[illegible]	[illegible]	[illegible]	[illegible]	[illegible]	[illegible]	[illegible]	[illegible]	[illegible]	[illegible]
1871,	[illegible]	[illegible]	[illegible]	[illegible]	[illegible]	[illegible]	[illegible]	[illegible]	[illegible]	[illegible]	[illegible]	[illegible]	[illegible]
1872,	[illegible]	[illegible]	[illegible]	[illegible]	[illegible]	[illegible]	[illegible]	[illegible]	[illegible]	[illegible]	[illegible]	[illegible]	[illegible]
1873,	[illegible]	[illegible]	[illegible]	[illegible]	[illegible]	[illegible]	[illegible]	[illegible]	[illegible]	[illegible]	[illegible]	[illegible]	[illegible]
1874,	[illegible]	[illegible]	[illegible]	[illegible]	[illegible]	[illegible]	[illegible]	[illegible]	[illegible]	[illegible]	[illegible]	[illegible]	[illegible]
1875,	[illegible]	[illegible]	[illegible]	[illegible]	[illegible]	[illegible]	[illegible]	[illegible]	[illegible]	[illegible]	[illegible]	[illegible]	[illegible]
1876,	[illegible]	[illegible]	[illegible]	[illegible]	[illegible]	[illegible]	[illegible]	[illegible]	[illegible]	[illegible]	[illegible]	[illegible]	[illegible]
1877,	[illegible]	[illegible]	[illegible]	[illegible]	[illegible]	[illegible]	[illegible]	[illegible]	[illegible]	[illegible]	[illegible]	[illegible]	[illegible]
1878,	[illegible]	[illegible]	[illegible]	[illegible]	[illegible]	[illegible]	[illegible]	[illegible]	[illegible]	[illegible]	[illegible]	[illegible]	[illegible]
1879,	[illegible]	[illegible]	[illegible]	[illegible]	[illegible]	[illegible]	[illegible]	[illegible]	[illegible]	[illegible]	[illegible]	[illegible]	[illegible]
1880,	[illegible]	[illegible]	[illegible]	[illegible]	[illegible]	[illegible]	[illegible]	[illegible]	[illegible]	[illegible]	[illegible]	[illegible]	[illegible]
1881,	[illegible]	[illegible]	[illegible]	[illegible]	[illegible]	[illegible]	[illegible]	[illegible]	[illegible]	[illegible]	[illegible]	[illegible]	[illegible]
1882,	[illegible]	[illegible]	[illegible]	[illegible]	[illegible]	[illegible]	[illegible]	[illegible]	[illegible]	[illegible]	[illegible]	[illegible]	[illegible]
1883,	[illegible]	[illegible]	[illegible]	[illegible]	[illegible]	[illegible]	[illegible]	[illegible]	[illegible]	[illegible]	[illegible]	[illegible]	[illegible]
1884,	[illegible]	[illegible]	[illegible]	[illegible]	[illegible]	[illegible]	[illegible]	[illegible]	[illegible]	[illegible]	[illegible]	[illegible]	[illegible]
1885,	[illegible]	[illegible]	[illegible]	[illegible]	[illegible]	[illegible]	[illegible]	[illegible]	[illegible]	[illegible]	[illegible]	[illegible]	[illegible]
1886,	[illegible]	[illegible]	[illegible]	[illegible]	[illegible]	[illegible]	[illegible]	[illegible]	[illegible]	[illegible]	[illegible]	[illegible]	[illegible]
1887,	[illegible]	[illegible]	[illegible]	[illegible]	[illegible]	[illegible]	[illegible]	[illegible]	[illegible]	[illegible]	[illegible]	[illegible]	[illegible]
1888,	[illegible]	[illegible]	[illegible]	[illegible]	[illegible]	[illegible]	[illegible]	[illegible]	[illegible]	[illegible]	[illegible]	[illegible]	[illegible]
1889,	[illegible]	[illegible]	[illegible]	[illegible]	[illegible]	[illegible]	[illegible]	[illegible]	[illegible]	[illegible]	[illegible]	[illegible]	[illegible]
Means,	[illegible]	[illegible]	[illegible]	[illegible]	[illegible]	[illegible]	[illegible]	[illegible]	[illegible]	[illegible]	[illegible]	[illegible]	[illegible]
1890,	[illegible]	[illegible]	[illegible]	[illegible]	[illegible]	[illegible]	[illegible]	[illegible]	[illegible]	[illegible]	[illegible]	[illegible]	[illegible]

* [illegible]

† [illegible]

‡ [illegible]

§ [illegible]

TABLE showing the Monthly and Yearly Number of Rainy Days* at Dublin during the Twenty-one Years 1870 to 1890, inclusive; with the Means for the Twenty Years 1870 to 1889.

Year.	January.	February.	March.	April.	May.	June.	July.	August.	September.	October.	November.	December.	Total Rainy Days.
1870,	[illegible]	[illegible]	[illegible]	[illegible]	[illegible]	[illegible]	[illegible]	[illegible]	[illegible]	[illegible]	[illegible]	[illegible]	[illegible]
1871,	[illegible]	[illegible]	[illegible]	[illegible]	[illegible]	[illegible]	[illegible]	[illegible]	[illegible]	[illegible]	[illegible]	[illegible]	[illegible]
1872,	[illegible]	[illegible]	[illegible]	[illegible]	[illegible]	[illegible]	[illegible]	[illegible]	[illegible]	[illegible]	[illegible]	[illegible]	[illegible]
1873,	[illegible]	[illegible]	[illegible]	[illegible]	[illegible]	[illegible]	[illegible]	[illegible]	[illegible]	[illegible]	[illegible]	[illegible]	[illegible]
1874,	[illegible]	[illegible]	[illegible]	[illegible]	[illegible]	[illegible]	[illegible]	[illegible]	[illegible]	[illegible]	[illegible]	[illegible]	[illegible]
1875,	[illegible]	[illegible]	[illegible]	[illegible]	[illegible]	[illegible]	[illegible]	[illegible]	[illegible]	[illegible]	[illegible]	[illegible]	[illegible]
1876,	[illegible]	[illegible]	[illegible]	[illegible]	[illegible]	[illegible]	[illegible]	[illegible]	[illegible]	[illegible]	[illegible]	[illegible]	[illegible]
1877,	[illegible]	[illegible]	[illegible]	[illegible]	[illegible]	[illegible]	[illegible]	[illegible]	[illegible]	[illegible]	[illegible]	[illegible]	[illegible]
1878,	[illegible]	[illegible]	[illegible]	[illegible]	[illegible]	[illegible]	[illegible]	[illegible]	[illegible]	[illegible]	[illegible]	[illegible]	[illegible]
1879,	[illegible]	[illegible]	[illegible]	[illegible]	[illegible]	[illegible]	[illegible]	[illegible]	[illegible]	[illegible]	[illegible]	[illegible]	[illegible]
1880,	[illegible]	[illegible]	[illegible]	[illegible]	[illegible]	[illegible]	[illegible]	[illegible]	[illegible]	[illegible]	[illegible]	[illegible]	[illegible]
1881,	[illegible]	[illegible]	[illegible]	[illegible]	[illegible]	[illegible]	[illegible]	[illegible]	[illegible]	[illegible]	[illegible]	[illegible]	[illegible]
1882,	[illegible]	[illegible]	[illegible]	[illegible]	[illegible]	[illegible]	[illegible]	[illegible]	[illegible]	[illegible]	[illegible]	[illegible]	[illegible]
1883,	[illegible]	[illegible]	[illegible]	[illegible]	[illegible]	[illegible]	[illegible]	[illegible]	[illegible]	[illegible]	[illegible]	[illegible]	[illegible]
1884,	[illegible]	[illegible]	[illegible]	[illegible]	[illegible]	[illegible]	[illegible]	[illegible]	[illegible]	[illegible]	[illegible]	[illegible]	[illegible]
1885,	[illegible]	[illegible]	[illegible]	[illegible]	[illegible]	[illegible]	[illegible]	[illegible]	[illegible]	[illegible]	[illegible]	[illegible]	[illegible]
1886,	[illegible]	[illegible]	[illegible]	[illegible]	[illegible]	[illegible]	[illegible]	[illegible]	[illegible]	[illegible]	[illegible]	[illegible]	[illegible]
1887,	[illegible]	[illegible]	[illegible]	[illegible]	[illegible]	[illegible]	[illegible]	[illegible]	[illegible]	[illegible]	[illegible]	[illegible]	[illegible]
1888,	[illegible]	[illegible]	[illegible]	[illegible]	[illegible]	[illegible]	[illegible]	[illegible]	[illegible]	[illegible]	[illegible]	[illegible]	[illegible]
1889,	[illegible]	[illegible]	[illegible]	[illegible]	[illegible]	[illegible]	[illegible]	[illegible]	[illegible]	[illegible]	[illegible]	[illegible]	[illegible]
Means,	[illegible]	[illegible]	[illegible]	[illegible]	[illegible]	[illegible]	[illegible]	[illegible]	[illegible]	[illegible]	[illegible]	[illegible]	[illegible]
1890,	[illegible]	[illegible]	[illegible]	[illegible]	[illegible]	[illegible]	[illegible]	[illegible]	[illegible]	[illegible]	[illegible]	[illegible]	[illegible]

* [illegible]

† [illegible]

‡ [illegible]

§ [illegible]

TABLE showing the Temperature of the Air in Dublin in 1890, and the Average Temperature for the Twenty Years 1870 to 1889, inclusive, as recorded by Dr. J. W. Moore.

Years.	January.	February.	March.	April.	May.	June.	July.	August.	September.	October.	November.	December.	Year.
1870,	[illegible]	[illegible]	[illegible]	[illegible]	[illegible]	[illegible]	[illegible]	[illegible]	[illegible]	[illegible]	[illegible]	[illegible]	[illegible]
1871,	[illegible]	[illegible]	[illegible]	[illegible]	[illegible]	[illegible]	[illegible]	[illegible]	[illegible]	[illegible]	[illegible]	[illegible]	[illegible]
1872,	[illegible]	[illegible]	[illegible]	[illegible]	[illegible]	[illegible]	[illegible]	[illegible]	[illegible]	[illegible]	[illegible]	[illegible]	[illegible]
1873,	[illegible]	[illegible]	[illegible]	[illegible]	[illegible]	[illegible]	[illegible]	[illegible]	[illegible]	[illegible]	[illegible]	[illegible]	[illegible]
1874,	[illegible]	[illegible]	[illegible]	[illegible]	[illegible]	[illegible]	[illegible]	[illegible]	[illegible]	[illegible]	[illegible]	[illegible]	[illegible]
1875,	[illegible]	[illegible]	[illegible]	[illegible]	[illegible]	[illegible]	[illegible]	[illegible]	[illegible]	[illegible]	[illegible]	[illegible]	[illegible]
1876,	[illegible]	[illegible]	[illegible]	[illegible]	[illegible]	[illegible]	[illegible]	[illegible]	[illegible]	[illegible]	[illegible]	[illegible]	[illegible]
1877,	[illegible]	[illegible]	[illegible]	[illegible]	[illegible]	[illegible]	[illegible]	[illegible]	[illegible]	[illegible]	[illegible]	[illegible]	[illegible]
1878,	[illegible]	[illegible]	[illegible]	[illegible]	[illegible]	[illegible]	[illegible]	[illegible]	[illegible]	[illegible]	[illegible]	[illegible]	[illegible]
1879,	[illegible]	[illegible]	[illegible]	[illegible]	[illegible]	[illegible]	[illegible]	[illegible]	[illegible]	[illegible]	[illegible]	[illegible]	[illegible]
1880,	[illegible]	[illegible]	[illegible]	[illegible]	[illegible]	[illegible]	[illegible]	[illegible]	[illegible]	[illegible]	[illegible]	[illegible]	[illegible]
1881,	[illegible]	[illegible]	[illegible]	[illegible]	[illegible]	[illegible]	[illegible]	[illegible]	[illegible]	[illegible]	[illegible]	[illegible]	[illegible]
1882,	[illegible]	[illegible]	[illegible]	[illegible]	[illegible]	[illegible]	[illegible]	[illegible]	[illegible]	[illegible]	[illegible]	[illegible]	[illegible]
1883,	[illegible]	[illegible]	[illegible]	[illegible]	[illegible]	[illegible]	[illegible]	[illegible]	[illegible]	[illegible]	[illegible]	[illegible]	[illegible]
1884,	[illegible]	[illegible]	[illegible]	[illegible]	[illegible]	[illegible]	[illegible]	[illegible]	[illegible]	[illegible]	[illegible]	[illegible]	[illegible]
1885,	[illegible]	[illegible]	[illegible]	[illegible]	[illegible]	[illegible]	[illegible]	[illegible]	[illegible]	[illegible]	[illegible]	[illegible]	[illegible]
1886,	[illegible]	[illegible]	[illegible]	[illegible]	[illegible]	[illegible]	[illegible]	[illegible]	[illegible]	[illegible]	[illegible]	[illegible]	[illegible]
1887,	[illegible]	[illegible]	[illegible]	[illegible]	[illegible]	[illegible]	[illegible]	[illegible]	[illegible]	[illegible]	[illegible]	[illegible]	[illegible]
1888,	[illegible]	[illegible]	[illegible]	[illegible]	[illegible]	[illegible]	[illegible]	[illegible]	[illegible]	[illegible]	[illegible]	[illegible]	[illegible]
1889,	[illegible]	[illegible]	[illegible]	[illegible]	[illegible]	[illegible]	[illegible]	[illegible]	[illegible]	[illegible]	[illegible]	[illegible]	[illegible]
Average,	[illegible]	[illegible]	[illegible]	[illegible]	[illegible]	[illegible]	[illegible]	[illegible]	[illegible]	[illegible]	[illegible]	[illegible]	[illegible]
1890,	[illegible]	[illegible]	[illegible]	[illegible]	[illegible]	[illegible]	[illegible]	[illegible]	[illegible]	[illegible]	[illegible]	[illegible]	[illegible]